More Skipper Stories

True Tales from Disneyland's Jungle Cruise

David John Marley

Theme Park Press
The Happiest Books on Earth
www.ThemeParkPress.com

Editor: Bob McLain
Layout: Artisanal Text
Cover Art: Trevor Kelly

ISBN 978-1-68390-176-1
Printed in the United States of America

Theme Park Press | www.ThemeParkPress.com
Address queries to bob@themeparkpress.com

This book is dedicated to my wife Deb Marley.

*Anyone who loves books as much as she does deserves
to have at least two of them dedicated to her.*

Contents

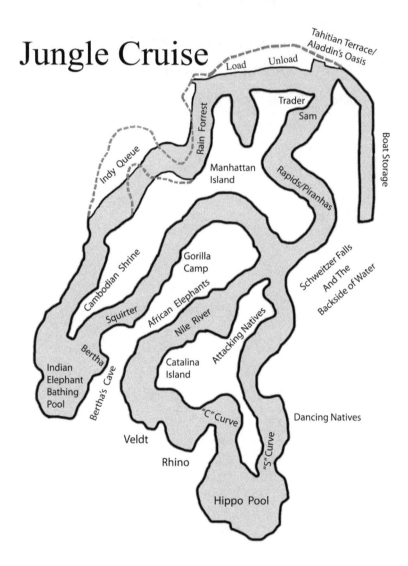

Jungle Cruise

Tahitian Terrace/
Aladdin's Oasis

Load   Unload

Trader
Sam

Rain Forrest

Indy Queue

Manhattan
Island

Rapids/Piranhas

Boat Storage

Cambodian Shrine

Gorilla
Camp

Squirter

African Elephants

Nile River

Attacking Natives

Schweitzer Falls
And The
Backside of Water

Bertha

Bertha's Cave

Indian
Elephant
Bathing
Pool

Catalina
Island

"C" Curve

Dancing Natives

Veldt

Rhino

"S" Curve

Hippo Pool

Introduction

My mom got a copy of the first volume of these stories and was intrigued by the revelations about some of my activities.

—Matt Nerrie

The only thing sure to happen in life are death, taxes, and sequels to popular things. The response to *Skipper Stories*, the first volume in this series, has been fantastic, thanks to everyone who bought a copy or came out to hear me give a talk about my favorite Disneyland attraction. When I was working on *Skipper Stories* I sometimes found it difficult to get people to sit down for an interview. My wife told me not to worry, that once the first book came out I would get flooded with people looking to share their stories.

She was right, as usual.

Calls, texts, emails, Facebook messages all came in fast. I had so many people to interview that I had to finally tell some that their interview would have to wait for another book. If I wanted to wait another year, this book would be the size of a telephone book, if anyone remembers what those are.

More Skipper Stories features interviews with more skippers than the first book. I would say about a third more, but I'm really bad at math, so let's just say "more." Another interesting thing is that most of the people I interviewed wanted to talk on the record. The few anonymous stories here are either from the interviews I did or from skippers I know who only had a story or two to share and wanted to keep their name out.

There is a bond between skippers no matter what era. I talked with skippers from the 1970s and it was like I had worked with them. I was honored to be invited to a reunion of skippers from Walt Disney World, and although their Jungle Cruise is different than the one in Disneyland, we had an instant bond.

Disney likes to focus on the stars, on Walt and the Imagineers who designed these great attractions. In doing so, they neglect the stories of the people who made the attractions run. At a ride like Peter Pan or Space Mountain, it is mostly pushing a button and letting the ride work its magic. However, at the Jungle Cruise it takes a skipper to make Walt's vision of the attraction come to life. This book is part of my on-going effort to tell the stories of the people who literally put their blood, sweat, and tears into Disneyland everyday.

I kept them in their own words and occasionally unique syntax. Some of these chapters titles may sound familiar, but I used stories and told tales you didn't see in the first book. Also, I didn't take out all the swear words like I did in *Skipper Stories*, so you've been warned. It's not bad, but still.

Those of you who work at the Jungle Cruises in Florida, Hong Kong, or Tokyo, you wonder where your book is? It's coming.

Since this is a book of interviews, what historians call oral history, I thought it only fitting that I start off the book with a quote from my friend Matt, and then begin the entire thing by having three skippers explain what the Jungle Cruise is and what makes it so unique. So here they are, three guys who worked in different eras yet have the same basic idea. The last quote, from John Verdone, is, I believe, the single best explanation of what it is like to work the Jungle Cruise that I have ever seen, so read it.

Going on Jungle it taught you to speak to a large group of people that would be varied, and you are trying to hold everybody's interest at the same time. You want the home version of the Jungle Cruise, you take 8 people, you put them in a large SUV, now two of the people have heard your jokes several times, two of those people thought they were in the line for Space Mountain, two don't speak English, and two just want to go home. Now you take those 8 people and you drive them around your neighborhood that you've seen every single day and you tell them a bunch of bad puns, and you do that for 8 hours a day, three trips an hour, and that's the home version of the Jungle Cruise. That is essentially what it is. You have to keep everybody mildly interested, don't entertain everybody, just keep them mildly interested to keep them on the ride and not jump off the boat.

Jeremy Wayland, 2000s

It's like the golden penis on the Little Mermaid cover. That's what the Jungle Cruise is. For the rest of Disney, Jungle Cruise is the golden wiener.

Ritt Meese, 2000s

Picture this. It is August, it is 98 degrees. The park is at capacity. There's a family from Indiana there, a mom and dad and four children. They are pissed off because they've been on so few rides because of the crowds, but now they decide to go on the Jungle Cruise. And the wait for Jungle Cruise is 90 minutes and they wait in the heat. They finally get to the boat and you pull up and this family gets on your boat. The dad looks at you and you can see it in his face that he's thinking, "You had better be good." So what are you going to do? You've got nine minutes to win them back. Not because you love Disney, it's not loyalty to the company. I was never that guy. It's just because that's who we are. That is why we wanted to be on the Jungle Cruise. That is why we were there. So before the boat has left the dock you had to have already created a relationship and bonded with all of the people on the boat. That is the most critical time on the ride. You've got 30 or 40 seconds. So you do a quick check to figure out where people are from. You look to see who you can play off of. I look for one or two people I can play off of. And then off we go. Then you've got this period of time. I've got to be funny in each section, and I have to build a narrative of the funny through the entire ride. Because there're skippers who have great stuff in one place. It is really building the narrative. You've got teenagers, you've got couples on a date and the guys trying to be cool, and you've got the dad, and I've got to say stuff that all of them will like. There have to be a couple of jokes that the teenagers think are for them, usually something snarky and a bit risqué. You gotta have a joke for the dad. There have to be jokes where the kids get one level of it and parents get another level of it. So there is an opening, a middle, and an end, you are building to the crescendo at the unload dock, you do your unload spiel. And then you've got from there at unload to pulling forward to get the next group. You gotta put yourself back to the beginning to take people back out again. I think that is the really hard part, getting yourself ready to start all over again. And you've got to do this 26 times a day. So for people who love this ride, I'm in the category of people who have made their occupation off of it. I think I still do this ride to this day.

John Verdone, 1970s

Now that you've read the introduction, you're ready to enter the crazy world of Disneyland's World-Famous Jungle Cruise!

Glossary

100. Attraction unable to open with the rest of the park.

101. Attraction closed for any reason (medical emergency, fire, mechanical breakdown, etc.).

3 Shot. Used for mechanical failure onboard the boat.

4 Shot. Used for a medical emergency. All boats forward of the sound of four shots are supposed to move full speed to the dock to make way for the boat with the medical emergency on board.

6 Shot. Used when one or both of the Jungle Cruise boat's guide rails came off the underwater track.

Adventure 1. The radio call sign for the most senior manager at Adventureland currently available.

Attraction. All of the rides, shows, and displays at Disneyland are called attractions.

Boat Storage. As the name implies, an area where boats are stored off stage, now behind a huge wall that opens and closes. It is essentially a channel that runs half the length of Main Street. In the 1990s it became a break area for skippers.

Cast Deployment System (CDS). A computerized system implemented in the late 1990s as a way to save expenses by eliminating the need for a lead at each attraction. The CDS system was designed to increase efficiency by having a computer determine the most optimal way for each cast member to use their time. While still used park wide, the CDS system was a total failure at Jungle Cruise.

Cast Member (CM). Any Disneyland employee is called a cast member.

- *Lead.* An hourly CM who runs an attraction as a manager and is always in costume. The lead is almost always a ride operator and not a salaried member of management. A lead can also work at their attraction as a ride operator. Every attraction usually has four main leads, ranked A to D, with a number of other leads not regularly in rotation.

- *Manager.* A salaried CM who oversees all the attractions of a land and usually dresses in business casual attire. At Disneyland, Adventureland/Frontierland is run as one business unit. Most managers will have worked as hourly CMs at some point and each attractions manager gets trained on all the attractions in their area.
- *Ride Operator (RO).* Self explanatory.

Cat Walk. The narrow dock that lies between the main dock and the jungle. The cat walk can only be reached via boat.

City Hall. This Main Street building is the headquarters of Guest Relations, where guests can get a birthday sticker, a note to use the handicapped entrances to rides, and most importantly for skippers, to make an official compliment or complaint.

Deadhead. Taking a boat around the jungle without guests. This is done when something in the jungle needs to be inspected by a lead or later in the day when the dock becomes overcrowded and it is faster to send an empty boat out than to have guests sitting on a boat waiting to reach the exit dock.

De-Rail. The technical term for when one or both of a boat's guide rails comes off the track.

ER (Early Release). This is a request that a CM will make to leave work early. At Jungle Cruise there was an ER List which was first come, first served. So, if you were ER1, there was a good chance you could leave work early. ER 5? Slim chance.

Foreman. an earlier term for Lead.

Front Load. The front door of the Jungle Cruise boat. The front-load skipper stands with his back to the skipper driving the boat and faces the skipper at rear load. The front position loads guest into the right side and center section of the boat. It is also their responsibility to make sure that boats are not getting backed up at the dock.

GC Shift. Guest Control Shift usually means working crowd control for parades, Fantasmic, or a special event.

Inn Between. The cast member-only restaurant located backstage behind the Plaza Inn restaurant.

JUBA. Jungle Upstairs Break Area. A small office space above the Adventureland Traders, directly accros from the Jungle Cruise that was used as a break area for skippers in the 1960s thru the 1980s.

Jungle Central. The radio call sign of the lead cast member at Jungle Cruise, or whoever happens to be in the shipping office.

KA (Knowledge Assessment). A test, usually multiple choice, that cast members are given at the end of various parts of their training process.

K Lot. The CM parking lot on Katella Avenue. Since 1998 most CMs park there and take a tram to the employee entrance to the park.

Land Locking. A policy begun in 2003 that restricts CMs to one particular land. Prior to this, a CM could work at any attraction anywhere in the park.

LOG. See OG.

Max/Maxing. To "max" is to take a longer break than allowed.

OG (aka LOG or SOP). OG stands for Operation Guidelines and is the rulebook concerning a particular attraction. For a Jungle Cruise skipper, to be non-OG means you're not doing jokes from the script.

PA (Performance Assessment). A final test given by a lead or manager to make sure the newly trained CM knows how to do every aspect of their job, including all safety and emergency procedures. At the Jungle Cruise, the PA usually lasts more than an hour.

Plaid. A plaid is a person from City Hall/Guest Relations. They are called plaids due to the plaid shirts or vests that they wear. They usually accompany celebrities around the park.

Points. The attendance system of the Disneyland Resort is based on points. If you receive too many points in a year you may be suspended or fired. It is normally 3 points to call in sick and 1.5 points if you're late to work.

Presenteeism. A policy of strict enforcement of the points system. Begun in 2004, this policy led to hundreds of Disneyland cast members being fired, resulting in manpower shortages. But it lowered the park's operating costs since the replacement cast members made less than the people they were replacing.

Princess Rotation. A rotation without a boat or dock position. This is rare and only used on very busy days. The "princess" is in charge of strollers, working at greeter, and occasionally getting into a boat to relieve a tired skipper.

Rear Load. The back door of the Jungle Cruise boat. The loading skipper faces both the front load and driving skipper. They load the left side of the boat. At the beginning and ending of each day, rear load is the only load position open, since the entire boat can be loaded from that rear door.

Rotation. Every attraction has its own rotation system, and the Jungle Cruise has perhaps the most unique. While many attractions have one single rotation (greeter, load, unload, etc.), the Jungle Cruise has as many as five rotations running at a time, each with up to four people. Each rotation is focused on a particular boat.

- *2-man.* One person on a dock position, one on the boat. This is usually only done the first and last hour of the day, since neither can take a break. Technically, this isn't even a real rotation, it's just a 3-man waiting for the third skipper to arrive.

- *3-man.* One person on dock, one in the boat, one on break. This is a skipper's favorite rotation because they get a 20-minute break every hour instead of a 15 minute break.

- *4-man.* The most common rotation when the park is busy during the day. It has one dock position, two boats, and one person on break. A skipper shares their boat with one other skipper and they take turns on break or at the dock position in cooperation with the other boat.

Set Up. As in "grab a set up." A set up includes an ammo box with a microphone, gun, ammo, and occasionally an air horn.

Shipping Office. The office for the Jungle Cruise, located on the dock. This is where the lead can normally be found.

Shuttle, The. The name of the vehicle that transports CMs from the K Lot, or other parking area, to the CM entrance to Disneyland.

Skiff. A small boat used by the lead or maintenance to quickly access the jungle. Until the early 2000s, the skiff was located near the dock and had a small outboard engine. Later it was moved to a hidden spot in the Indian elephant bathing pool and its engine was removed.

The Skip Phrases. These are simple phrases, used mostly at the dock.

- *"Move it up, Skip."* Used when a skipper is wasting time at unload or is in the way.

- *"Hit it, Skip."* Used at the loading dock when the boat is clear to leave.

- *"Hold it up, Skip."* Used when asking a skipper to stop their boat to load a special guest.

- *"Kill it, Skip."* Used in an emergencies when a guest or CM falls into the water near a boat.

- *"Back it up, Skip."* Used when a boat is coming off the catwalk or moving from the dock back to storage.

SOP. See OG.

TDA. The Team Disney Anaheim building is the center of park operations, casting, and Disneyland University. The beautiful building was designed by Frank Gehry and opened in 1995.

Theme Park 1. The radio call sign for the manager who in charge of operations at the park.

Track Switch. There are three track switches at the Jungle Cruise, all of them between Trader Sam and the exit dock. The forth track switch, the "Dominguez Switch," was removed with the Indiana Jones renovation in the mid 1990s. Before 1995, these switches were manual and each in their own location. After 1995, a central console was put in to control all the switches.

Trader Sam. The infamous "head salesman" of the jungle is also the attraction's mascot. Leads and managers will leave notes for the CMs signed "TS". He is also the place with a lighted warning to skippers about track switches. Often boats will stop at Trader Sam while track switches are being moved.

WDI. Walt Disney Imagineering, the company started by Walt Disney that creates all of the attractions and shows for the Disney parks.

Westside/Eastside. Disneyland is split into two halves which has created a decades long rivalry. The Eastside includes Fantasyland, Toontown, and Tomorrowland while the Westside is considered to be Main Street, U.S.A., Adventureland, Frontierland, New Orleans Square, and Critter Country.

Westside Diner/The Deck. Once a CM-only restaurant located underneath New Orleans Square, and the site of a large underground kitchen serving all the restaurants above it. This restaurant was primarily used by westside CMs and was shut down in the early 2000s.

CHAPTER ONE

High Hopes and Low Standards

The Jungle Cruise is a dream job for many. Some people's obsession with the Disneyland attraction begins during childhood while others realize it's their dream job in their teens. Some of my favorite stories are from those that walked in unsure and quickly realized that they had found their forever home. One of the great things about Jungle Cruise is that I have yet to find a person who worked there and hated it. They may have eventually gotten burned out, but they never hated the attraction. This is why so many normal, rational people could become obsessed with working at a theme park.

I had quite a reverence for this attraction. Walt loved this attraction and I got paid to play there.

Brian Vestal, 2000s

When I was 6 or 7 I had my first trip to the park and my favorite thing was the Jungle Cruise. When we got home, I re-created the Jungle Cruise in a pool at my grandma's house. I placed my stuffed animals and dolls around the edge of the pool and I cut things out of paper for decoration. I put the hose over the diving board to make bubbles in the water and I would pull my sister on this floaty and I would describe things to her. I was obsessed. So when the guy asked me about Disneyland I told him that story and he said, "Would you like to work the Jungle Cruise?" and I told him that it was my dream to work it. Then he said, "I'm not supposed to tell you this, but you are totally working the Jungle Cruise. Don't tell anybody. We don't want people to know that we are assigning positions today or giving people what they ask for, but I can't think of anything better for you." I went home and told all my friends and family about it.

Andrea Freeman, 2000s

Jungle Cruise is where I wanted to go. I grew up in El Monte and as a kid we came here once a year and I loved Jungle, I loved the corny jokes. There is a magic, Disney magic, at Jungle where you have a boatload of people and you are cracking jokes for them. I really wanted to do that. I made it clear in my interview that that's what I wanted to be doing. The person that interviewed me even teased me about it, asking me questions like, "Are you okay with walking on a path near tropical foliage?" and "Are you worried about being outside near water?" They made it sound like maybe I was going to Jungle Cruise, but I got the Opera House.

Javi Gonzalez, 2000s

I can remember as kid being there and liking it, I thought it was cool, I thought standing in front of people you get to talk to the whole way was a big deal. The other thing I thought was cool when I was a kid was the guys who robbed the stage coach at Knott's Berry farm. I think it was a ham actor thing, I dug it, didn't buy into the pixie dust, didn't buy into the whole Disney history, it was just I wanted to work the Jungle Cruise. I didn't have this motivation to work at Disneyland for 15 years; I just thought being on Jungle Cruise was cool. My end goal was to work in broadcast radio, and I was a part-time radio jockey in 29 Palms called Q96. I thought that being on the Jungle Cruise would help with local pronunciations, and that's why I wanted to work there.

Jerry Whitfield, 1980s

I specifically hired in wanting Jungle Cruise. When you do a group interview with 2 or 3 other people, they are just trying to figure you out, and I knew if I made an effort, I knew it wasn't the time, but I made an effort to say, I really want to be in attractions and I specifically want to be at Jungle Cruise. And they seemed to not care about it, it didn't really have that much to do with them. From the very beginning I told them that's what I want. I knew it was Disney, it's a huge workforce, and it is almost like going into the military blind, undeclared, and they could just stick you somewhere. I'm sitting there thru all of this and at the end you have that smaller orientation where they give you your placement, and my piece of paper had a room with 10 people in it, and mine said "undeclared." I really want Jungle Cruise, and the people said, we'll place you and there were two people running the orientation, and it's a small class, and the guy next to me (had been next to me) didn't show up, probably said this isn't for me, there was an empty seat next to me and everyone else had been placed and his little piece of paper said "Jungle Cruise" on it. I started scheming right away. Can I just switch when nobody is looking? So I went up to them and asked, "Hey, is this guy not into it?" They said we don't know, and I said, because for the whole time I was here that was what I wanted and for a dozen reasons this guy is placed there and doesn't show up. Because if that was what he wanted he would have shown up, so he didn't want it. So I asked, can I have that, and they said sure, whatever you want. They were in the middle of a conversation and I had to interrupt them. I got it and it was pure dumb luck and I feel super lucky because if they had put me in a store or sweeping something up, I wouldn't have worked there. I didn't even need a job.

Ritt Mesee, 2000s

I went down to Casting with a friend of mine; at the time I was living in Camarillo. So we went into Casting, filled out the paperwork, and we each got called in to talk with the casting guy, and I said, "I really want to work Jungle Cruise, and if I can't work Jungle Cruise, I don't want to work here, I don't need a job. I'm an hour and a half away." I didn't want to drive that far every morning to push a button for "it's a small world" or sell churros. I wanted to do something that I could actually bring to the table. And they were kind of like, "Well, young man, that's not how it works, you work where we need you, you can't just come in here and request where you want to go." And I said, "Sure, I get that, that's fair, but I'm just telling you if you don't have Jungle Cruise, I'm not interested right now." So they send me out, and about 5 minutes later they call me back in and he tells me to have a seat. He sits at his computer screen, and he turns the monitor and he has my IMDB page up. He goes, "Why do you want to work at Disneyland." I said, "I don't want to work at Disneyland, I want to work at Jungle Cruise, you are missing the point. That page you are looking at is exactly why. I can bring something to that. I am a performer and I want to work at Jungle." He goes okay, fine, and he called over and talked to Gerry asking if they needed people, and a couple days later I had Jungle and Randy was training me and off we went. Then I had to drive every day for an hour and a half to get to work. It was not smart, looking back at it.

Brandon Kleyla, 2000s

For some people working at Disneyland is a family legacy.

Disneyland was always very special place for me. Everybody in my family except my mother had worked at the park. My dad was a manager in merchandising. My sister worked foods and my other sister working attractions on Big Thunder. So we have a long family history being there. It's a really cool place to be and I wanted to make the most of it. I worked really hard to get to attractions, I spent a year and a half in purgatory working outdoor vending, trying to get that inside track myself by getting to know a manager who would be able to hook me up with the manager in Adventureland. I didn't push the idea of being attractions, I made it very clear I wanted to be at the Jungle Cruise. I didn't want to go work at Star Tours or Space Mountain; Jungle Cruise is what I really wanted to do. It is very special to me. There is no other place like it in the world. People try to replicate it, nobody can do it. You see it everywhere. I hear flight attendants trying to crack Jungle Cruise jokes. To me it's never the same without that old lousy PA and a random group of tourists. So I really appreciated it because I didn't get to do it every day. It wasn't a job that I needed, it was a job that I wanted. When I left to go to grad school it was really sad for me to leave because I knew I was probably never going to come back, and that is probably still the case.

Matt Nerrie, 2000s

My sister was mad at me. She said I got her dream job, and I said well it sucks to be you, you're not 18. Then she realized she had two family members at Disney, and decided she didn't want to work for Disney.

Siobhan Armstrong, 2000s

One skipper worked at the park for two years before finally making it to the Jungle Cruise.

At the time I was hired they were not hiring in Adventureland. So I quickly learned that I was going to Disney California Adventure and I remember getting the slip of paper telling me where I was going and I was so sad because I wanted to be a skipper so bad. I ended up loving Seaside, but all I wanted to do is tell bad jokes on a boat. That's what I kept telling people, "I just wanna tell bad jokes on a boat."

I had wanted to be a skipper since I was a kid. I was an annual passholder for 13 years before I worked there. Since I was five the Jungle Cruise was my favorite attraction. From the moment that I could conceptualize working at Disneyland I wanted to be a skipper.

J'amy Pacheco, 2010s

Skipper J'amy has the same unique name as her mom, who also worked at Disneyland. This caused both confusion and comedy.

My mom works in guest relations so she is all over the park. When I was being trained at Fantasyland people would randomly say to me, "I know your mom!" I didn't know quite how to respond to that. It happens still all the time, people will say, "I love your mom!" It's funny because she was as determined to get me on the Jungle Cruise as I was determined to get on the Jungle Cruise. So anytime she met anybody from Adventureland she would tell them, "My daughter wants to be a skipper." And I would see random cast members and they would say, "Oh, you're J'amy, I hope you make it to the Jungle Cruise." I know these people now, but at the time it was odd because I had no idea who they were. So when I got to Jungle I was already famous or infamous as the girl whose mom really wanted her to go to Jungle. It was a lot of fun. People get us confused. It's funny when guests from my mom's tour come to Jungle and ask for my boat.

J'amy Pacheco, 2010s

I hired in without any preconceived ideas. A buddy of mine ended up being my roommate that summer after I hired in; Phil also worked on Jungle Cruise and told me, "You're a drama major, you're going to end up on Jungle Cruise."

Larry Kaml, 1980s

I grew up in Sacramento and I visited Disneyland with my mom when I was 10 and loved the Jungle Cruise. Then in high school I dated this girl who was really into Disney and I went to the park a bunch of times with her. That's when I fell in love with the Jungle Cruise. I thought it was the best job where you got paid to act like Jim Carrey, who was a huge inspiration for my physical comedy. Then in college Disneyland people came to Sacramento State and told us about the college program, so I came down and then relocated to Cal State Fullerton.

They told me that I had three options: one was janitorial, and something else, and the third was attractions. This was during my phone interview while I was still home in Sacramento. I told them attractions because I wanted the Jungle Cruise, but when I got to orientation they said, "All we have for you is Storybook Canal Boats." I had this friend in Sacramento who kept telling me that they were going to give me Storybook. So I told them politely that I didn't want that, I wanted the Jungle Cruise, and they said they didn't have any openings there, but if I didn't mind working Grad Nites and stuff for three weeks, then another training session will open up. So I did Grad Nite Guest Control for three weeks, directing traffic, and finally got Jungle Cruise.

Brian Vestal, 2000s

I was graduating high school and had been accepted to Cal State Fullerton, and right before Easter they were hiring, that is the traditional hiring time around Easter break. So I go in and I have my interview with this woman from the personnel department and we have this great conversation just going back and forth and back and forth and she asked me, "Gosh, if you could work anywhere in the park, where would you want to work?" And I told her, "I've always wanted to work the Jungle Cruise, it seemed like a really nice place to work." And so she says, "Well, I'm not going to hire you. All I have open now are jobs in the foods department, some jobs in merchandising, I don't have anything open in attractions." And so I leave. It's coming up as my senior year after high school before college. I think I can hang out and go to the beach every day. I had the whole thing planned out. Then the first week of June I get a phone call from somebody at Disneyland and they say, "Hey, we'd like to offer you a job." At that point I was still more interested in hanging out at the beach and taking it easy. Then the guy on the phone tells me, "Well, it's a job at Jungle Cruise," and I immediately said, "I'll take it."

John Verdone, 1970s

Some people don't want to work at the Jungle Cruise but end up loving it.

In our orientation class all but two of us went to Autopia, me and this other guy. At the time I hated Jungle Cruise, I thought the jokes were just awful and demeaning to the intelligence and everyone is going, "Why, you are so lucky, you want to trade?" and I said no. It wasn't until I got to know the people that I wanted to stay, but I don't want to tell jokes, it's not who I am, but it had changed who I had become. I don't like talking out loud to people. I've changed a lot around that. I don't like being the center of attention, I don't like commanding a crowd, and all of that was such a challenge, but after a year or so, I was good. Then I was like, "No, you can't make me leave."

Kat Thrailkill, 2000s

CHAPTER TWO

Training Days

Disneyland is world famous for its rigorous training programs and over the decades the training at the Jungle Cruise has only gotten longer and more involved. Currently, training to become a skipper can take as long as four days, but back in the 1960s training rarely lasted more than a couple of hours.

Tom Nabbe was hired by Walt Disney himself. After spending years playing Tom Sawyer, he graduated into attractions and eventually to the Jungle Cruise.

I wasn't one of those "get a round of applause every time the boat came in" types of person. Jungle Cruise wasn't really high on my list of attractions. In September 1961, when we went into winter hours, the supervisor of the area gave me a script and said, "Tom, memorize this, you start working at Jungle on Wednesday morning." So I memorized it over Monday and Tuesday and showed up at Jungle on Wednesday morning and made about three trips. After that, I was a qualified Jungle Cruise skipper. I worked all that winter at Jungle. What used to fascinate me was that one skipper got a standing ovation after every trip and another guy, Earl, used to get one just about every other time. It was always the goal, but my love was the rafts and the keel boats.

Tom Nabbe, 1960s

Skipper Ken Snow began his Disneyland career in foods where he was trained by Oscar Martinez. "We called him the Old Man even back then," recalled Snow.

I was working at Hills Brothers on Main Street and you are interacting with everybody. I was the sandwich maker. It was my first family, I was an only child, so at 19 I felt like I had a family. And you understand a little bit more about yourself, how you interact with people and with each other. Going over to attractions, you are very excited, handed a script. I'm afraid of public speaking, and I was all, "Wait, I have to talk to people and run the boat?" It was scary, and I was really frightened, but after I realized they don't shoot you while you're talking, I never shut up.

Ken Snow, 1970s

Since I grew up in the area I have been on the Jungle Cruise so many times I felt like I knew all the jokes on my first day working there.

Andrew Green, 1980s

I remember being trained, and the first time you took the boat out around the jungle solo and you just really hope you remember the spiel. During training I hit the boat in front of me at the dock, and one of the old leads, Don, he didn't scold me, but he made me drive him around the jungle on a deadhead. Don was the guy! He was intimidating, he didn't talk much.

Vince Fragasso, 1980s

At times the park has had worker shortages that required them to train lots of people at once. This usually happened right before the summer rush began.

Honestly, when I found out where I was gonna work, I freaked out a little bit. Me and the public speaking were not the best friends. I had to get over that real quick, didn't I? It was very nerve-wracking, of course. Going from hating public speaking to now I'm on a boat with 15 other skippers all going through training and they all knew exactly what they had to say at every point and you had to deliver. It was very stressful and you have the lead evaluating you to make sure that you are ready to go on it. We had 15 guys on the boat when I was training. It was fun, by passing the line basically it was a whole boatload of skippers, all the guest were like, "What's going on here?" So we just did a couple rounds and everybody got a turn to do different bits of the jungle. We didn't each do our own whole jungle, but basically random bits.

Keith Hart, 1990s

While many didn't care for public speaking before coming to Jungle, many didn't realize how the ride operated.

I thought I would just be working the dock. I didn't realize that it was a full rotation. I didn't realize that skippers in the boat were the same as the skippers on the dock. As an annual passholder, you don't notice that as much as you don't notice that there is a rotation. I just thought I'd start out on the dock and after a couple months I'd get to be in a boat. I thought there was an audition. I was just excited to work at Disneyland because I had a lifelong dream of working there. I was excited. I was also intimidated because I didn't realize that I was going to be in a boat.

Maureen McLandrich, 2010s

However, not everyone wanted to work at the Jungle Cruise and devised ways to get out of it.

I worked at the Haunted Mansion in 1975 with a guy named Mark, one of the smartest guys I've ever met, incredibly funny. He was told that he would be trained for Jungle Cruise. He went to the training and tanked it on purpose, he just messed up, and they said, "Mark, I don't think the Jungle Cruise for you." And he never had to work it and now he's a corporate lawyer. He hated the idea of having to spiel to 24 groups a day so much that he acted stupidly and made it seem like he was incapable of dealing with the spiel. So management wouldn't let him work the Jungle Cruise.

Dave Lewis, 1970s

Some people show up less than fully prepared to work Jungle.

I went to orientation and I did all of that stuff at the Disney University and I came back a couple of weeks later. I reported to the Jungle Cruise in my costume. And I was there with another new fellow so there were two of us. The trainer, whose name was John McCoy, asked us if we knew our spiel. So I said, "What is the spiel?" And so he asked me, "You didn't get a spiel at the orientation?" And I asked him again, "What is a spiel?" And he said, "It is the script. They should've given you the script at orientation. It's what you were supposed to have learned and have memorized by now so we could train you on how to drive the boat." But I never got one, so he grabbed one and said, "Now go sit on that rock over there by the Tahitian Terrace and read it and memorize it while I take this other guy on the boat." The other guy had the script for three weeks. So time passes and eventually they come back around. The guy in the other boat and my trainer say just bring the script with you, and you can read it as you need to. I had recently read a book on memory and how to improve it, so I actually did okay memorizing parts of the script. He took me around a bunch of times. By the end of the day I was taking boats out by myself. Funny enough, the other guy could not get the hang of it and he had the script for three weeks. It turns out the guy was a college baseball player and he only got hired so that the manager, Glen Hicks, could have him on the Adventureland baseball team. So it didn't matter that he couldn't figure out how to drive the boat and do the spiel.

Dave Lewis, 1970s

I grew up stuttering, really badly. It started when I just in the 3rd grade and I had to go to speech class, which was traumatizing for me to get pulled out of class and now I'm some kind of weirdo. Then I lost my speech impediment, but I started to stutter because I was aware of my speech. I went all the way through high school, through college, as a stutterer, and if I couldn't say a word, like all stutterers, I would use another word. In fact, in high school, I would go to the teachers and ask them not to call on me because I'm such a stutterer and asked them to give me a break, and most of them would. So then I got hired at Disneyland, and I could do the spiels, and if I worked by myself, and the guests don't know what you're supposed to say, so there would be days where I couldn't say words with a "w" or an "m," I would stutter on that, so I would just substitute. So I get on the Jungle Cruise and I've got a spiel now, and they are going to find out I stutter and I'm out of here, I can't do it. I brought the spiel home and I practice and practice, got on the boat and the guy training me is a guy that I also worked with on the subs, so he knew I knew how to operate rides, and we went around a couple times, and he could see that I was struggling with the spiel and stuttering, and he said, "Look, I can see that you know how to run the boats so go by yourself." He knew enough to let me go by myself, and as soon as he wasn't there, and the guests didn't know what I was supposed to say, I was able to use my old tactic of word substitution. After getting used to that on the Jungle Cruise, it cured my stuttering. I still stutter sometimes, everybody kind of stutters, but not near as bad as before. So, Jungle Cruise saved my life. That's one of the really big things about Jungle Cruise that helped me. Because after that, I was working for the phone company and I had to get up and do presentations and public speaking and I wasn't afraid, I'd just get up and use that command voice, and just do it. That's one of the best things I got out of Disneyland, other than my wife.

David Schwab, 1970s

Part of the fun of training was when you had an interesting trainer.

My trainer was a debouched dirty old man that told dirty jokes the whole time. I know we go through the training with the lawyers and that we aren't supposed to be training this way, but I felt pretty debouched myself, not as far gone as I am now, but you know getting a sense of who I'm working with, and mostly we hung out back stage. The second day, the culottes, he handed me my costume, at costuming, I put on my pants, the zipper usually goes in front, and I had my hands in my pockets, so turn them around, and of course I walk out and he goes, "Hey, good on you, most people put them on backwards the first time." Putting on culottes and zipping up zippers in the back is not as easy as you think it is. When we started to take empty boats and it's getting awkward, he goes, "Joke slayer," because I'm screwing up the beginning and screwing up the end, then we pass other boats, and I'd get real quiet. My first few weeks were like that. Eventually, I'd get the ones that started giving the end of the jokes, I started to get a pattern and a rhythm, and it started falling into place. It took repetition and repetition and going on other people's boats and listening to how they were delivering before it finally felt right, before I started dreaming in spiel.

Kat Thrailkill, 2000s

My trainer at Jungle Cruise mostly worked Main Street vehicles and also worked Opera House. He was small with thinning hair, very skinny guy, very dry, I remember he had a double derail, right underneath Schweitzer, and I remember going, "Um, this is 6 shots," and in the background you hear the guests screaming because the boat is filling up with water, and he's all calm under everything, he fit perfectly on Main Street vehicles and Opera House. I mean he was a skipper and a trainer, but after I trained I never saw him again after that.

Jeremy Wayland, 2000s

It was fun getting the script and practicing driving the boat. I remember we would be at the dock and I would be practicing as we drove to the rain forest. As soon as the boat was out of sight of the dock, my trainer would grab one of the seat cushions and lean it up against the engine. He would watch me give my notes, and after another trip or two he would just sit there and read the newspaper and smoke a cigarette. I asked if everything was okay and he told me, "Oh yeah, you're doing great, we just have to do a certain number of trips around the jungle during training." I felt comfortable right away. I was going to major in speech at Cal State Fullerton.

John Verdone, 1970s

I don't remember doing much work, I remember being told what to do, I remember practicing all the time and the trainers making fun of us. Mocking us in a skipper way. Probably the whole time I worked there I would say the "mighty bangle tiger" and that bugged my trainer.

Helen Medina, 2000s

My trainer Jeremy would put me on other people's boats and he put me on the most controversial boats, like Skipper John's, and I'm sure

Jeremy told him to give me the full monty. So, within my second day of training, that's what they told me, this is what you are going to be doing and that's okay, so to me it was like, oh wow, there are not many rules here. Where Jeremy was the exact opposite, he was going as quick as possible, I hate this, and he was like a very surly teamster about it but in a good way. He hated it but loved it. He made me love the ride. The whole hiring process is so much more than hiring into any other company. Am I buying a house? It was a four-day process, and I was just adamant the entire time that I want Jungle Cruise. To each of them it was, "I don't know you're going to get thrown into a...spin the wheel and see where you end up." For that to happen, for me to get that piece a paper, that was a crazy lucky thing and then to get that trainer on Jungle Cruise—I expected him to be some kind of mentor that would judge me harshly and I would have to live up to a certain level. If you got signed up for SNL, and Chris Farley had to sign you off, you'd be, oh man, I need to impress this guy. I ended up with the trainer whose attitude was, "I hate this shit, good luck it's your funeral."

Ritt Mesee, 2000s

My trainer Benny was the best. It's hard to remember specifics, but I do remember that it was a lot of me trying to find out from Benny what I could get away with once I got signed off on the spiel.

Brian Vestal, 2000s

All trainees are not created equal. It's easy to get intimidated when your fellow trainee was a skipper before.

I remember being on the boat and my training partner Leo going first. I'm sitting there and Leo's telling these jokes, and he says, "Yeah I'm a re-hire." So then it's my turn and I'm trying to memorize the jokes, but they aren't funny, it's how you deliver it. I'm telling these jokes and I'm totally ruining them. I remember coming back and people saying, "You're such a joke slayer." I was like, oh, god, I got to get better at this. I had to work hard. I remember my first boat, and I was fumbling the throttle, pretending I'm turning it the wrong way, I've got the mic too close to my mouth and you can't hear anything, I'm just mumbling the whole time. I finally get through and we pass it, and I look at them at the guests at the very end and they are getting out of the boat, and it's just silence. So, I finally get signed off. I struggled to park the boat; luckily nobody got injured. I remember watching other people. I saw all these guys and how they delivered it and carried themselves. They were really good models to go off of. At that time, it was like the golden era of the Jungle Cruise.

Tameem Sabry, 2000s

I didn't want to stop training, that's how fun it was. My trainer Kelly is one of the core cast members of that time, and she was able to introduce us to everyone. If your trainer vouches for you, you are golden. We were very fortunate. Kelly was really chill, and she let us figure it out.

I think the great thing about being a trainee, especially when the trainer has a great sense of what they are doing, we had every break, we had some of the older skippers who just listened to our spiel and gave us great feedback, and it was great training environment. I remember then I kind of knew this is why companies respected hiring people from Disney because the go through a rigorous process and make sure people have the tools and the feedback they need.

Jeff Bautista, 2000s

Kaz was the best. I can't imagine anybody being a better trainer than her. During training I was super nervous because you got this impression that Jungle was a huge honor and so there was a lot of pressure that came with getting trained there. I remember feeling very nervous that I wasn't going to be good enough and I thought I'd be okay, but once training started I was afraid I wasn't cut out for it. All the safety stuff was hard. The script stuff was easy, but the safety stuff really freaks me out. Kaz made a journal for each of her trainees and she put your favorite jungle animal on it and the little steering wheel and I was reading it the other day in preparation for this interview. And I was reading through some of my entries. The idea that Kaz had was that not every day at Disneyland was going to be great. You would take the journal and you would write down the great thing about each day that you work there. So that when you look back you will have all of these positive memories.

Tiffany Davis, 2000s

Training was exciting and scary. I was so eager to work Jungle Cruise after I got it, and Jeremy was a trainer there, he didn't ever campaign to work there, he didn't like being there, he was more person to person. He would say I like working monorail, I sit in a cocoon by myself and I don't have to cheese it up with people. So when he trained me, I went in there thinking I was going to be the best skipper on the planet, I'm going to take 20-minute trips, and Jeremy trained me on how to do a 5-minute trip. Right off the bat he was tailgating every skipper, almost shaming them about being so slow. You can be in it and yet resentful of Jungle itself. So it was funny to me that he would just run through and somehow still get applause because people thought it was an act. But that was really...he didn't want to be there. He's a daytime guy, so he was quick

Ritt Mesee, 2000s

I was super excited. I was always bad about controlling the boat. I had two bumps during my time there. I was struggling to control the boat and my trainer was laughing at me. I had so much fun. It was just exciting to be there in the first place.

Andrea Freeman, 2000s

One brave skipper had to deal with training for her first job during final exam week of her first year in college.

I spent four days of training with a guy name Julio. I was so nervous that the whole thing is kind of a blur. I remember walking in, and I remember opening procedures. It was my first job, so I was trying to be good, trying to be by the book. Training was very hard for me because my training at Jungle Cruise was the same week as six of my finals. This was my freshman year of college. So I would go to Jungle and I would leave training and take a final. I had to reschedule a couple of my finals, it was so stressful. Probably the most stressful week of my life which is why it was all a blur. All my finals turned out fine and my grades were great. I would be studying for my calculus final and then I would take a break to study my Jungle Cruise spiel. I took notes during my training. I treated it like a college class.

Maureen McLandrich, 2010s

The best compliment I ever got, or the one that had the most meaning to me, came from my trainer, Kaz. After I had been a skipper for a few months she rode my boat and told me that my delivery was so energetic and I seemed so positive that I could say anything. Then she said, "With your delivery, you could get away with saying the F word...but don't you dare!" (For the record, I never, ever swore while I worked at Disneyland.)

David John Marley, 2000s

One skipper was lucky enough to have a dad who had been a stand-up comic who helped her with the script.

On the first day of training at Jungle Cruise they send you home with the script. I went home and called my dad because I was so excited and I literally read the entire script to him and he and I went through it and figured out which jokes I should do. We just laughed and laughed and he gave me some one-liners to add. I used to do a part of his routine when I was working at the Jungle Cruise. I would say, "There's something that a lot of people don't know about me is that I'm a twin. And when I was born I remember this very clearly, the nurse came in and laid me and my twin down by my mom, and my dad looked at us and said, "Honey, those are two of the ugliest babies I've ever seen, pick which one you want because I'm going to drown the other one, and that was the day I learned how to swim." It had nothing to do with the Jungle Cruise, but it was one of his old bits and people would laugh.

Tiffany Davis, 2000s

At the end of your training you have to take a test called a "performance assessment," or PA for short. This is a 45-minute test where you have to show competency on every aspect of working at Jungle Cruise. The final part is doing a trip with guests. By that point the new skipper is usually exhausted after days of training.

The first thing I did on my PA was to make a non-LOG joke. I said, "Wave goodbye to all the pretty people on the dock, now wave goodbye to all the ugly ones." And I thought, *Oh shit!* From then on, I kept it as OG as I could. I didn't worry about being funny, just following the script.

Javi Gonzalez, 2000s

During my PA we come up to the tiger and I said, "Over on the left is a Bengal tiger; feel free to take pictures, he's wearing his trunks."And then I realized I was a little premature in my joke. I don't really remember anything past that, but Kaz said I just kept going and I made it into a running joke.

Tiffany Davis, 2000s

If a trainee passes all the tests, they get to become a skipper and take their first solo boat and the world is theirs.

The first boat with actual guests was so much less stressful. I think it was because all the guys knew exactly what I was going to say and they were going to say the same thing. But once I got real people on the boat it somehow became mine and not just a clone copy of everything.

Keith Hart, 1990s

It was all a blur, we went through it, I don't think they told me I was getting guests, they loaded the boat, I don't think it was great, people were generally polite, which is unusual at the Jungle Cruise, usually they would just stare at you like they want you dead.

Helen Medina, 2000s

I remember doing my first spiels and in hindsight you are a deer that just got born. You can kind of walk and it's impressive that you can do it, but at the same time it's like, you are walking funny, dude. You're all wet. When I saw a new skipper, that's a B-, but that's an A+ in regular life. It's crazy that you are driving a boat around telling jokes about plastic animals at Disneyland, that's kind of weird. I remember trying some stuff out even during training because I was so excited. My own jokes, and at first Jeremy was like, oh, that's cool, but you're still new so ease into it, just wait or you will look too anxious. But for me, I had been such a fan. It's like going to Comic Con and then suddenly being cast in an Avengers movie and you're like, ohhh, this is really happening. So I was okay to wait and double dutch and see how I can make it fit. That was a good training note, just feel it out first and see what you can double dutch in as far as jokes cause there is always a temperature or a climate and you can't put your finger on what you can or can't get away with, and of course who the lead is, and if it's day or night.

Ritt Mesee, 2000s

In my era when you got trained, the trainers would say, "Yeah, we are gonna practice going around, don't worry about anybody in your boat until you're ready, just get a feel for controlling the boat." And then what they would do, when they knew you were ready, they would just pick up the seat cushions and put them in the frame of the doorway and that was the cue for the loaders to go ahead and put people on. So it was always you are there for the practice trip and then there were people on the boat. It was kind of like a sink-or-swim thing. So I remember that part of it, and I remember the joke about, "Hey, any first-timers? Hey, me too! You think I'm joking, don't you."

Larry Kaml, 1980s

My first boat was one of the most rewarding feelings I've ever had. That first trip there were no more trainers, no more fellow trainees, no leads. It was my boat, my inaugural trip. It was just me and the people. And I hate to use the word magical, but it was just this magical feeling. It was just great. I had no nerves and it was like I had been doing it my whole life. I remember the time we got done and I circled back to the dock, they were clapping, and I felt like it meant something because when you start out it takes a while to get that kind of reaction from your guests in the boat. Now that I think about it, wonder if my trainer told them to be nice to me because it was my first trip. Kaz took a picture of me as I pulled up to the dock for my first trip. It was the best feeling in the world and I remember thinking I'm going to do this for a long time.

Tiffany Davis, 2000s

My first boat was actually a lot of fun because it was at night, it was my first solo trip, and my trainer, John, sat in the first boat. The guests were always better at night; they all clapped at the end and they all went "whoo!", but that was it and I was Jungle Cruise for life.

Jerry Whitfield, 1980s

I was super nervous about my first boat and I didn't think I was going to be because I've done theatre for years. I just thought, *This is going to be so amazing, it will be the best thing ever,* and I remember the trainer sitting there and looking at me and nobody laughed at anything and I felt ridiculous. So that was my first boat.

Andrea Freeman, 2000s

It was nerve-wracking. I screwed up every joke, I couldn't remember punch lines. I got mixed up, I made some African veldt jokes at the gorilla camp. I didn't realize that my mic wasn't working really well because I was so excited. So I got a lot of no laughs, but I learned the timing and things got much better.

Javi Gonzalez, 2000s

My trainer didn't tell me that I was going to have guests on my boat, so I gave the loaders the deadhead sign as I pulled up. When I turned around and saw people getting on the boat I thought I had messed up and they hadn't seen my signal and I looked at my trainer and she was smiling. I don't really remember the boat, I just remember thinking, *This is it. Now I have to be funny.* It wasn't a disaster or I would have remembered it. I remember that people laughed. It was at night and I vividly recall the sight of people getting on the boat and panicking for a second, then realizing that I was going to be fine.

J'Amy Pacheco, 2010s

I've always been one of those drama kids that did the theater thing. Enough to know that I craved it, I'd be excited, put me up there. It's funny, because when I finally got in a boat of my own, you just look at these people, and you realize they are five feet away from you or just inches away, and they are looking at you intently and expect that the ride will be fun. I heard I did alright. It was clock work like that, it wasn't a problem of delivering the lines, it was feeling connected to your audience. They are there, and they expect something from you and you better deliver—at least that's how I took it. That's what I remember most about my first boat.

Jeff Bautista, 2000s

Back then my dream was to become a radio disc jockey. So I emulated a lot of the sounds of classic rock DJs as part of my spiel. The trainer thought it was cool and said, "Well, you clearly have some experience of this." But I thought that I sounded like an idiot because I'm not on the radio, I'm talking to human beings, so I toned it down.

Dave Lewis, 1970s

My mom had some anxiety, so she had a prescription filled to calm her down. I stole some and took them. I don't know if it really helped or not, but it was a great placebo. I just needed to calm myself down. It was really tough. The first weekend was tough, but that's when I took the pills, so maybe I was doing much better than I thought. After that, I just got into the groove. And you listen to everybody else and some people had tremendous gifts of gab and banter. You learn the timing of the squirter and the other animation.

Ken Snow, 1970s

I can remember coming home when I was brand new, I was still living with my folks and I was maybe a month into my first summer at Disneyland. I remember telling them, "Mom, I could do this for the rest of my life and be happy." It was just a natural fit.

John Verdone, 1970s

Becoming a trainer is like getting Disneyland's seal of approval, but it is also a lot of work. It is sort of like being an elementary school teacher. You are not just teaching the mechanics of the attraction, you are teaching the social skills they will need to survive working at the Jungle Cruise. The first step to becoming a trainer is being interviewed by a manager and the leads.

The final step in the interview process for becoming a trainer is being interviewed by a lead and a manager. I figured that since I was already teaching at the college level I would at least make it to the interview stage. I also figured that once I got to the interview they're going to have all kinds of questions for me that would quickly reveal me to be a less-than-ideal skipper. So my hopes weren't super high that I would become a trainer. I went into the interview, all nervous because I'm sure they had already found out that I didn't follow the script at all. Thankfully, that question never came up. I got a lot of softball questions and they quickly told me that I was going to be one of the new trainers.

David John Marley, 2000s

Skipper Jerry Whitfield explains the complexity of training.

I would usually do my training in the storage area. You know if you're coming in the door, so I just kept the doors open and I would stay on that one pole and I would say, "OK, you need to line up that pole with this pole." I would kick the boat around and let the guy play with the motor and I can do that until I felt that they had it down enough so by the time they got out there they were fine and the other thing I would do is I would set up in the conference room and have them rehearse their spiel over and over and over again. So, by the time I got them on the ride they were all pretty confident because when people make mistakes in the Jungle Cruise it tends to be when they were trying to remember their spiel and then control the boat at the same time, so I spent a lot of time early on getting them to feel comfortable with their spiel. That way, they don't have two things going on in their head by the time they got out there, and it was easy for them to control the boat.

There's a lot to do. By the time they got to do their solos it was at night, so they had a control both the mics and the spotlight and now the other stuff, like the guns. The idea was to get them comfortable as much as possible before they got in the boat and that seemed to help. I had one guy named Dave who on his second trip had a mechanical breakdown. He did 3 shots and I was like, "Yeah, dude, you're on this, so I guess I can sign you off."

Jerry Whitfield, 1980s

During the summer of 2004, was my last summer at the park, I was doing a ton of training. It seemed like I could just count on having to be at the park at 5am on Friday. On the one hand it was a lot of fun, but on the other hand, I was a college professor so I was already teaching all the time and I worked at Jungle Cruise to get away from having to teach. And yet management believed in me enough that they had me do a lot of training, which was a big compliment. I got tired of training people, but I never complained because I knew there were lots of people that wanted to be trainers and never got the opportunity. But there'll be days we'd be doing deadheads by trainees, and I just couldn't take it anymore, so I'd pull up to the dock, grab the mic, and take out a boatload of guests.

David John Marley, 2000s

I like it a lot, we had a lot of fun. Those guys remembered me and my training after the fact—you don't think they do but they did, and it was kind of cool, they were really great guys. Since Jungle Cruise was the first ride you go to, I trained a whole summer so then later when I became a lead it was an easier transition because all these guys already knew me from the trainer thing. It made it kind of cool and nice and I didn't have a lot of drama when I became a lead.

Jerry Whitfield, 1980s

I remember having this trainee who had clearly spent years performing. On his very first trip without guests, it was just me and my two trainees, and this guy was amazing. He had the script memorized and his timing was perfect. I thought, *Man, people are going to think I'm an amazing trainer and I didn't even do anything!*

David John Marley, 2000s

There can be an ego rush for a skipper at times. Hearing a crew laugh and seeing them enjoying something you have said is very fulfilling, but that can change the focus from them to you. One of the tough parts about being a trainer is helping the skippers understand the show is for the guests. You've got to get them to focus on the guests rather than themselves. That can be tough to do with self-confident males fresh out of high school and just finding their way in life. When done correctly, the Jungle Cruise let me work selflessly while allowing me to get that selfish gratification of guest appreciation. It can be a nice work-life balance. It's not many jobs where your customer walks up to you and says, "You are the best." Whoa. That's nice.

David Schoenwetter, 2000s

I had a few trainees that thought this was their night at the Improv and I had to slap them down during the training. No, this is not your stand-up comedy hour, you are here to give a tour around the jungle, sprinkle in some jokes. I was told that these are really lame jokes, and I said this is how it goes, if you say something on the script and they go to City Hall, you are backed up, but you tell something that's not on it, and they complain, you are up shit creek. Once you are out of my training and I sign you off of this thing, that's it. You had to keep your boat steady while loading people and talking to them. You had to multi-task and you can identify those that can't do it. You have to say, okay, this person is going to be a danger, they are going to break somebody's back if they are front load or rear load. Unloading is no problem, the boat can move a little bit with people stepping off of it, but it's different when you are trying to dock it and you've got people stepping down into a moving vehicle. Tell the joke at the same time docking it, I just couldn't do it.

I thought of them as my kids, even after I signed them off. You are still watching over them, making sure they do their job right.

Jeremy Wayland, 2000s

Even after you are a skipper, the training continues. There are updates to the attraction, the script, and in this case, a refresher course on safety procedures.

When reopening with the new dock, the Jungle Cruise skippers were given a unique opportunity. Since the Jungle Cruise was already closed, the dock was complete, and there were a few days until official opening with necessary tests already conducted. They gave us full shifts to go over downtime situations so that we as cast members would know what to do in any situation in any position. In this particular instance, we were going over 3-shot situations. They needed a "skipper in distress" and I volunteered. Half the skips stayed on the dock by the radio; Jungle Central and the other half were piled on my boat. Next to me were two trainers. One I had known and one I had just met because she was always at Big Thunder Mountain. We proceeded to the Indian elephant bathing pool and I did my 3 shot there. I radioed in and as I did the trainer began to ask the crew of skips, "Okay, we need a reason why we 3 shot. Anybody?" I don't know who, but somebody yelled out, "Bees!" Then somebody else shouted, "Bees!" I looked around and all of a sudden the whole boat was chanting. "BEES! BEES! BEES! BEES!" I looked at the trainer I had just met, she looked up gleefully and said, "Say, Bertha's head fell off!" I turned to the trainer I did know. "Don't say bees. Don't say Bertha's head fell off." I radioed in, "Bees and Bertha's head fell off." Silence. Radio silence and silence in the boat. Then the radio came back in, "So...you can still proceed forward." The entire crew thought about it and then the realization happened that we still could have moved. Thinking quick, I radioed, "Oh! And there goes our engine! That's convenient." However, between when I said, "there goes our engine" and "that's convenient," they radioed, "We're sending a rescue boat." So the trainer I knew began berating me: "Don't say 'that's convenient' when they're sending a rescue boat!"

Eddie Agin, 2010s

It was called spiel training, but the ones I taught were for Jungle Cruise. It was at Disneyland University, it was something that they had the skippers come to as a supplement and I suspected it was because they were worried about skippers getting too far off-script. This would be in 1982 or 1983. We all knew to follow SOP at the time, but once we went we got on the ride at least the old school guys were there. The thing we learned very quickly was that you kept out of trouble by engaging your crew. You got a good sense for looking at your crew in figuring out who's gonna complain, who's not gonna complain, and it big advantage we had in those days in that people did not have phones with video cameras in them. If they did have a camera, it was one of those huge things with a big VHS tape in it. It was about an hour class, and it was offered by cast activities.

Jerry Whitfield, 1980s

Sometimes casting would send you random people who didn't want to work the Jungle Cruise or were totally unsuited to it.

You are responsible for the new people. You would have the most different people and you're like, "Why would you want…" They didn't have casting then, so it was throw them over here, we have some holes and we need to fill these holes. I'd get some of the weirdest people, not good at all for Jungle Cruise.

Jeremy Wayland, 2000s

I had an informal arraignment with a manager when I had a bad trainee. Some trainers wanted to sign everyone off, and management wanted as many bodies as they could. I, however, wanted the right people to be working there, and if I thought you couldn't cut it, I'd call Bill and say, "I got someone here for Toontown." A while later Bill would come down, talk to the trainee about an exciting new opportunity that just opened up in a different area of the park, and off they would go. I once had this guy that was really cocky and a know-it-all and as he walked away with Bill he said, "Bye, losers, I just got a better job." The poor idiot.

David John Marley, 2000s

One day this guy shows up… My sleeves were always rolled up, I never wore shorts on Jungle, these are not legs for shorts. I wore the pants every damn day, I wore the coat, but my sleeves were still rolled up underneath it. So I get this one guy and his sleeves are all the way down. Then his top button is all prim and proper, and in the break room I asked him what he likes to do, and he says, "Well I have my knives and we do this with my knives." And it was the creepiest freaking person in my life, and I had this girl with us and she's going, okay, and he'd get out there, and he would say, "Why aren't they laughing at this?" He'd literally start questioning everything, and it was something about this guy that freaked me the hell out. This was right after Columbine and I'm thinking this is one of those kids, this is a crazy one, this is going to be a problem, he is not going to fit in with Jungle. As he got more comfortable, he kept talking about his damn knives. I finally took him aside after day two and said, "Listen, you know what, you are having problems with the dock thing, and you don't have this, I'm sorry I'm going to save you your day three and just tell you I'm not going to sign you off, please go talk to the scheduling and see if there is another thing, I'm just going to save you time, you are not going to get signed off on this ride." And he goes, "Okay". He didn't show up for day three and the girl we were training when she showed up for day three said, "Oh, thank god." She was so happy, she said he was so creepy. And he was the most creepy guy. It turns out he never went to scheduling, he never came back to the park, they mailed his check, he never showed up, he just disappeared. That was one I will never forget. He had light blond hair and an Aryan youth thing going for him. If I put that guy on Jungle Cruise, the ride might not be there today.

Jeremy Wayland, 2000s

I had this trainee who said he wanted to be an animator for the Walt Disney Studios so he moved to California and this was the only place in the Disney company that was hiring. He didn't want to work Jungle, hated speaking in front of people, and messed up driving the boat, but he thought this was the way to get a job in Burbank. He worked one shift after he got signed off and then vanished.

David John Marley, 2000s

Every week I'd have three days of training, a guest shift, then three more days of training. Literally I had an entire summer where I trained non-stop, it was like every other trainer got lead or another position, and it was like I was out there turning out more bodies to tell jokes. At times I felt I was doing a disservice and at times I felt guilty, full disclosure. I'm not funny, I'm humorous at times, I fully acknowledge I'm not funny, but I don't try to go over the edge. I will make sure they will show up for their shifts, I will make sure they are responsible for docking the boat, will make sure they go by an SOP spiel, make sure they maintain the material. If they go beyond that, I'm happy that they made it on their own, that's their own credit, their own personality and talent. They did that in spite of me, not because of me.

Jeremy Wayland, 2000s

Despite all of that training, trainees and new skippers can still make mistakes.

Training those people was so fun, they ran the damn squirter so many damn times I remember soaking the boat, oops, gotta do it again, oops, gotta do it again. They never adjust for the weight of the people in the boat. They do it right for the training spiel, but they never figured out when you have 40 people in the boat it is not going to stop on a damn dime. It's going to go right by and you are going to hose the first 3–4 people. I remember my trainer, just like everybody else, did it. I ran through and he is trying to shield people and here I am sitting on the side of the boat going, no, let them soak.

We just had a skipper that signed off that thought it would be funny to shoot everything in the god-damn jungle. I kid you not, this guy's out there, just got signed off on the ride, it wasn't my trainee, and he thought it would be funny to shoot everything in the jungle, so we are at the dock and we hear 30–40 shots, the guy is reloading, and we call security, we get the manager on the dock, and the skipper says that he needs more ammo, and we say that you had enough for 7 trips. He was literally shooting everything because he thought it was funny.

Jeremy Wayland, 2000s

Skippers that wanted to improve their spiel never stopped learning.

Every time I got breaks, I didn't know anybody, and I didn't smoke, so I didn't want to sit back there in the boat house or in storage. I would just ride other people's boats. I'm in a three man, so I would sit in everyone's boat and I would learn from everyone. I remember the one guy whose boat I couldn't get on was Gerry York. He wouldn't let anyone on his boat.

Ritt Mesee, 2000s

CHAPTER THREE

Jokes

Skippers tell a lot of jokes, but what do they think is funny? It all depends on the skipper's personality and on the era they worked at Disney. Comedy styles change with the times and famous comics and popular movies shape the popular culture and skippers. Add to that a script that is either treated like holy scripture or a list of suggestions depending on the person and the era.

Skippers live to entertain people and for most that means at times going outside the script. Disneyland gets complaints when skippers say something offensive, but they also get complaints when they all appear to be robots.

I asked skippers for their favorite jokes and got a wide variety of responses.

I got in trouble for this one. I can't claim originality for it. At load I'd say, "How many of you are ready for a really exciting ride!?" (Cheering from the boat passengers). Then I'd say, "Indiana Jones is next door."

Lawrence Janiec, 2010s

My favorite joke was about the hornbill. I'd drive by and say, "There, folks, is the African hornbill. It gets its name from the white stripes on its wings." Nobody would get it and I would laugh and laugh. When I worked there the hornbill was right at the beginning of the ride so if somebody got that joke and laughed, you knew you had a good crew and knew that person will be watching the whole trip to try to catch more of those kinds of jokes.

Andrew Green, 1980s

My favorite joke is traveling past bamboo and saying, "Over here we have some native bamboo. Now, bamboo can grow up to five stories tall out here. Some people will tell you six, but that's another story." It's such a quick, gut-churning joke that those who get it will instantly cringe and I love that reaction.

Eddie Agin, 2010s

Ritt always had the best and most abstract jokes and we all tried to top him and we failed. He wrote the joke on the Nile with the two elephants where you point out the first one and talk about how rare it was and then you look at the second one and say, "That's a polar bear."

Andrea Freeman, 2000s

I had a couple favorite jokes. One of them is, "Forward ladies, forward ladies, I love forward ladies." I love that joke. Especially when they were attractive because you could just flirt with them the whole time. So, I was notorious for that. The second joke I heard others do when the dad would come on the boat, but his family was still on the dock, "Oh, sir, you forgot your bags." People would laugh. I like to get down on it with the light and the squirter, I like squirting the guests especially if it was hot, I wouldn't warn them ahead of time. Especially if I had a heckler.

I like looking at the gorilla. I'd look at him and say, "Something you don't see every day, but I do, over and over and over again." I liked the *deja vu* jokes: "On the right-hand side here we have the African bull elephant, they are known for their long ears and elongated tusk." Then we move on and I'd say the same joke again and people would say, you just said that, and I'd say, oh sorry, *deja vu*. It worked for the people that were paying attention. I love saying at the lost safari, "Oh wow, look at that, that's something we don't see every day, look at all those rocks, some people take it for granite."

Tameem Sabry, 2000s

I like the jokes where I'm the idiot and I would do the joke where I would enter the jungle from the load dock and I would say, "As we enter the jungle, you will notice the climate changes immediately, it's amazing, right?" I would stop the boat and tell everyone to take a deep breath of air. "Smells lively, right?" Everyone is nodding, because it's where the misters are going off. "Yeah there are a couple dozen bacteria and viruses going on here that the doctors have no idea about, it's amazing." Then I would just motor on. Or I would go to the dancing natives and they would be dancing and chanting and I would stop and say that I would translate for them. "Hehehe." I would just nod my head and say, "Yeah, okay, ahahahah." I would nod and chew on that, and my wheels are turning and everyone is watching me for about half a minute and then I'd say, "Yeah, no, I can't translate, they are speaking some other language, I can't tell you what they are saying." You are just an idiot and cocky the whole time. Sometimes I would have Steven Segal in my mind and then be real cool and self confident and cocky and say just the dumbest things on top of that. I think that was fun, because honestly half the people weren't expecting jokes.

Ritt Mesee, 2000s

A lot of people did this joke, but I fully committed to it. When we didn't have lots of boats on the river and we got to the attacking natives, I would do this big one-woman show about how I was going to save everyone and I would completely stop the boat and tell everyone that I had this under control. I would jump onto the side of the boat and pull myself onto the bow and yell at the natives and make them all bow down. Then the natives would bow and people would laugh. I would do it if I had a hip crew who was really into it. I would go totally overboard.

Andrea Freeman, 2000s

I used to joke where we would sing with the dancing natives. There is a part in their song where you can hear this horn blowing in the background— "da da da da." They would repeat it back to you. I told the guests we were asking permission from the natives to continue on our journey. So you did this call and response and then I would say, "Okay, we're clear to go." That was a joke we wrote and we never got in trouble for it. I think their attitude was that as long as your joke was in good show, they didn't care. They were very strict about it; you just couldn't make stuff up that was inappropriate. They were pretty lax about having you follow the script, so especially at load and unload, we could do a lot.

Andrew Green, 1980s

Some jokes are taken from popular movies.

My favorite hippo pool joke was by a skipper named Rick. Right after he fired the gun, he said, "Hippos are easily startled, but they'll be back, and in greater numbers."

Lawrence Janiec, 2010s

I would pass Schweitzer Falls and as we turned I would tell everyone, "You know, only the Jungle Cruise mixes its water in a real waterfall, that's the only way to get it just right." No one ever got that joke, but it made me happy. Some of the jokes I did were just to keep me entertained after doing those trips over and over and over again. You have to do something to keep it fresh for yourself, you're out there for five or six trips, you get tired and things start to go haywire.

Javi Gonzalez, 2000s

Here's another Willy Wonka reference.

A skipper entered the hippo pool at night and began to sing like Gene Wilder in *Willy Wonka*: "There is no earthly way of knowing, which direction we are going." He did a big chunk of the song and the boat loved it. Turns out he was fired two weeks later for going off the script.

David John Marley, 2000s

Some skippers liked the old standards.

My favorite jokes were, sadly, all of the ones that were the tried and true. There are certain jokes that I didn't even like, but guests expect them: "The Elephants with their trunks on," or if you did a trip without saying the backside of water, you were going to die. Don't even go there. So for me it was a trick to see how I could make it work. "Yes, the elephants with their trunks on."

I loved doing trips at night because you could do tricks with the light. The fastest bull elephant in the jungle—and you flash your light over to the right and look, there he is again, that was a good one. I'd pull up to the attacking natives, and that is such a tough sell to me, they are not throwing spears, everyone could see that. So I would go, "How many times do I have to go through this, you know me, I bring you food every night, you know me, now just stop!" And they would back up and then I would say, "Go back down into the plants right now, I don't want to see your faces again." Then you turn around to the guests and apologize for the behavior. Then point out other stuff. "No, wait, Marley's coming in the next boat, wait for him, okay, drop down and wait, don't ruin the surprise for him. We're going to get out of here now." When you can master the timing of those guys you got the boat eating out of your hand, because most guys do the (sound effects of spears flying toward you). Everybody does that, but if you can master the time, guests are amazed. Everybody can see they are not throwing stuff, they are not a threat, it's a silly scene, so it's like do something completely different, and you can't do that during a lot of day trips because it's too busy.

Brandon Kleyla, 2000s

Truly gifted skippers knew that you had to test each boat to see what jokes you could get away with. The trick was to subtly build your set as you went along so guests would hear something truly unique.

I think you have to know what you can get away with and when. The water buffalo is at the end of the tour, so by then you know what you can get away with. Usually, I felt like I could read my boat by the time I pulled off the dock. I would even look at them at the unload, I would look at the queue and figure out which ones would be on my boat, minus the other two boats in front of me, and even as I was loading it was like a science thing—as I was loading I was tailoring my jokes to them. It was kind of like Steve Irwin the Crocodile Hunter saying animals are so beautiful and majestic, just look at this hind quarter, look at this musculature, and I'm like, he was really close to being creepy, and I thought, why not. Joey Hurley would do a crocodile hunter, he was amazing at it, he had the accent down, but I would just use my own voice and say, "Wow, just look at that with its powerful hind quarters and its anatomical musculature," and I would slowly get lost in its eyes, and slowly throttle back and slow down, like somebody should have lit a candle, pull out some roses kind of thing. Then you are just like, "Yeah, its big brown eyes and its soft pouty lips," then you kind of catch up with yourself and you realize there are a bunch of kids and adults on your boat, and you are like, "Oh," and you clear your throat, but that was the last joke before Trader Sam, so if it's bad you are done in a minute. Sorry about that. I wouldn't have started with that joke, you have to build a rapport with each boat.

Ritt Mesee, 2000s

One guy I worked with had memorized the script to the letter, including every directive. It would go something like this: "Welcome aboard the insert boat name here. My name is state your name and I'll be your skipper and guide down the rivers of adventure. Face guests while pulling away from dock. Point to dock. Everyone turn around and take a last look at the dock. Pause. We may never see them again. Turn toward the bow of the boat." He did this the entire trip.

Dave Lewis, 1970s

A good skipper knows where all of the laugh lines are before he even leaves the dock. The longer I worked there, the more I became a minimalist. There were some guys who tried to see how few words they could say on a trip, but that is not what I did. Instead of doing joke after joke after joke, I wanted to see what was the best spiel you could deliver with the least amount of jokes, but it still had to be a great spiel.

John Verdone, 1970s

There were times that we would have contests to see who could go through the jungle and say the fewest words. One year a guy won because he only said 14 words. He would just drive and drive and then say, "Bathing elephants." Then drive and drive and then say, "Look out," and then drive and drive.

John Verdone, 1970s

I always got a good response from "There's something, you don't see that every day" that I do that is not SOP. There was one joke that I only told once, my very last trip ever, August 21, 1996, native village: "And here you can see natives celebrating the sacred dance to celebrate the kill of that lion. Now, I'm not sure where the women of the village are because the last time we came through here, we took pictures of the native girls, but they haven't developed yet." This was my last trip and half the people on my boat were other skippers.

Larry Kaml, 1980s

My favorite was the Dr. Albert Falls joke. It went over so many people's heads—that is why I loved it. The best joke I ever heard was from a guest. I did the old, "See those limestone formations over there? Most people take them for granite." And this guy in the front of the boat looks at me and says, "No schist!" and I cracked up. I loved the jokes that were a dig on Disney. At the rapids I would say, "We have to be careful going through these rapids; any one of those jagged rocks could tear a hole in this boat and it's just a watery grave 3 feet below."

Andrew Green, 1980s

Certain times I will just say things that are not questionable, but then afterwards I'll wonder. Like once I was coming back to the dock and I said, "This trip was brought to you by buoyancy and regret." It was really funny, but I had no idea where it came from.

My favorite joke is one that I came up with. I do the OG joke where you are at the dancing natives and you ask for a vote to see if everyone wants to go forward. When no one votes or says anything I say, "Oh, it's just like being with my family. You sit in silence and pretend I'm not here." My niche of humor is that I'm dead inside and my family hates me, I'm going to die alone. I have played with how I tell it and people really like it.

Sometimes as I leave the dock I'll say, "Who's ready for adventure?" and the boat will yell "Yeah!" and then I'll point to Indy and say, "Well, there it is, the Indiana Jones Adventure, but you are stuck on the Jungle Cruise where we have hippos, hippos, and you guessed it, malaria!" and that always gets a good laugh.

J'Amy Pacheco, 2010s

A skipper named Joey came up with this joke, and I became very passionate about it. When we were in the hippo pool and didn't have our guns, I'd say, "Oh, look at these hippos, looking all cute and friendly, blowing bubbles, wiggling their ears, but they are really just a bunch of killers, they are filthy hippo-crites." The people would never get it or didn't want to laugh. I liked it when one person was really enjoying it.

Helen Medina, 2000s

I did a joke at night where I was looking for a snake that was somewhere on the boat and then I would open up the skipper's crate and that's it, there it is, and I would grab the chain of what looked like a snake at night. Then I would slam shut, then open it back up and say, "It's gone," and then pretend it was behind a little kid. That was fun.

Brian Vestal, 2000s

Since I was a trainer at the time, I remembered every joke and every deviation of the joke. I used to challenge myself, when the annual pass-holders would come on they would finish the jokes, and so I'd stop the scene and tell another joke and if they got that one I'd tell another joke, and I would tell it until they didn't get the punchline on something. I kind of used the boat to amuse myself. I did the blindfold tour where you put the blindfold on and you purposely misname the animals and everyone is laughing. But I knew exactly where I was; I'd done that tour backwards and forwards. Everyone had the jungle nightmares where they go around and there's no dock and they can't stop the boat, you go to Trader Sam and you are back in the damn rain forest. I would wake up from those dreams. The blindfold tour was fun because you purposely say the wrong joke at the wrong scene and people would laugh, and I could still see where the squirter was so nobody got wet, but it was fun. I did the Sean Connery tour, I did the jittery card tour, where you pretend to drop the cards and pick them back up again.

Jeremy Wayland, 2000s

I guess my favorite jokes were the ones that connect to the guests. Jungle Cruise was a relief from the rest of the park. I would say jokes at the unload spiel "OK, that was a fun time, we had some silly laughs, but I want to remind you guys that Walt Disney said..." Then I say some sentimental stuff like, "When you really believe your dreams really do come true for just $100 plus parking." I think everyone got that because you didn't have to point it out, it was that whole Disney magic if you could afford it, and everyone got it whether they were rich or poor or this is just their one time they will come in five years because they live in Chicago. Everyone got that. I really like the jokes that connect with the guests. I feel a lot of the jokes were the skipper-to-skipper jokes that you only get on the inside. They were just inside jokes that would happen in your own off-time that would bleed into your work and, hey, we are in costumes and nobody is going to get this. It was really about a relief from the rest of the magic, a relief from the magical park. The jungle is meant to be a bit deprecating; we are not at Knott's Berry Farm making fun of Disneyland. We are in Disney and Imagineering has approved some of these jokes. Oh, yeah, the most feared creature, the mother-in-law, or that's the person under the monorail, or the difference between the African and the Indian elephants is the tusks, the ears, and these are newer fiberglass as opposed to the latex polyester of the previous generation,

Ritt Mesee, 2000s

There was one joke no one could escape, the infamous "backside of water" joke.

The backside of water was the one joke you had to do. That was like the touchstone for the world. If you didn't do that joke, the world would go spinning off into space. Plus, for guests who've been on the boat, it was like a moment in a Steve Martin comedy show where everybody could yell the same thing together. Even though the guests know that joke and it's not funny anymore, they still wait for it and they cheer.

John Verdone, 1970s

Sometimes, if the boat was into it, I would set up the backside of water joke for the entire trip. I kept telling them that they were going to see the most incredible sight. I kept talking about it for the entire trip. I would kind of blow the spiel. I'd say things like, "If you think that elephant in the shower is amazing, just wait until you see what fantastic thing is waiting for us." Then I would really sell the backside of water as best I could, then just coast the rest of the way to Trader Sam.

Brian Vestal, 2000s

Some people went the opposite direction with the joke.

I would flip the lights around from the interior to exteriors and dance around and let it peter out and fail. I think dying sadly was the joke: "You've got Star Tours over here, you got big Thunder, here is a rock with water."

Ritt Mesee, 2000s

I like the hippo pool for jokes, and I always hated the backside of water. I wouldn't do the joke. I would comment on the toucans, I would talk about rocks "taken for granite." Sometimes I would just freak people out and tell them to duck and I would stay down until we were out of the backside of water.

Helen Medina, 2000s

The single most important skill a skipper has is the ability to adapt their spiel to each different boat.

There were different crowds on different days, so could I make the three-year-olds laugh? It was kind of a fun exercise and I think it made me better. Skippers have what they think is funny, but in a deeper philosophical sense, you would wonder why didn't the audience laugh, maybe they were a bad audience? Maybe partly true or they weren't set up right or they wandered in and didn't know what they were getting into. I think one of the rules is because you were funny, and it's not up to you to want it funny, it is up to te audience. Or it's how you play it. Who's the bad dancer, the guy in the lead, or the girl? Somebody has to—you have to read each other. One of the things I learned at Jungle was that as soon as they leave the boat, my eye is on the queue, who am I getting in my next boat. The script has a whole bunch of staff, there's night stuff and day stuff, there's 200% more stuff on script than off script. So you read it as you go and it is almost improvy. A lot of skippers would give their monologue and when it was day on Saturday or night on Wednesday, it was the exact same. You have to tailor it a little. You had an arsenal of jokes, the script itself has several per spot, so you can choose, and I would have all of that in my head. Depending on the group, I would know which joke was best. That kept it from being monotonous, surfing, not autopilot. Sometimes you would work a crack, everybody is cold and they don't know you are joking and there are two teenagers in the back, and they are getting it because they are annual passholders and they like those PG jokes. And when they start laughing it becomes contagious and the rest of the boat is, "Oh, I see, the guy up front is not crazy."

Ritt Mesee, 2000s

I like to hang upside down in the boat. Not when we were in motion, but I would put my feet up on the bar and hang upside down for a couple seconds, just to see if anybody noticed. Sometimes people were so busy looking around at the jungle that they didn't notice and I kept talking. Every shift I would try to make up something new. I was always looking for something out there that I could talk about. It made every day an adventure. I used to mess with the mic a lot. At night I would make it sound like a radio transmission was interfering with my spiel. It would come from Indy and I would talk back and forth with them. I would do accents on trips. I would use the trips as a way to practice. The Crocodile Hunter was really popular then, so I would often do that or an English accent.

Brian Vestal, 2000s

CHAPTER FOUR

Joke Slayers

Disneyland policy regarding the script at Jungle Cruise seemed to change year to year. Generally speaking, the rule was that you could ad lib as long as it was in the spirit of the attraction. Other times the rule was, "You can't get in trouble for saying something once." Then at other times, usually when a brand-new manager arrived in Adventureland, the rule became, "Stick to the script or you will be fired." Most if not all of the people making these rules had never worked a single shift at Jungle so they didn't understand that there were times, out of boredom or necessity, that you had to deviate from the script. Skippers handled this delicate balance with varying degrees of success over the years.

It went through many cycles. There were times where the ad libs were actually taking over the spiel and people from WED would come down and ride the boats and check everybody's spiel. Then later an edict came down that said you had to stick to the script verbatim, and they got a lot of complaints at City Hall so they loosened that back up. And then it just went back and forth; tighten it up, loosen it up, tighten it up, loosen it up. So it went through several scenarios.

Tom Nabbe, 1960s

I stayed true to the original script. I still have a copy of the original spiel from 1990. I tried to stay fairly true. We had one skipper who did stuff like, "Let's make like a hockey goalie and get the puck outta here," and there happened to be a suit in the bushes who sent him home. And so I didn't want that experience. I tried to interact with the guests directly and make it as much fun as possible using stale old recycled jokes that everyone has heard.

Keith Hart, 1990s

Back then I didn't have the gift of gab like I do now. I was very much a rule-oriented person, so I followed the rules. I had perfect attendance and that kind of thing.

Tom Nabbe, 1960s

I generally follow the script. They gave you like two pages per scene, so there was a lot of jokes. I always tried to keep it themed to the ride and the era it was set in. That was the magic. Tomorrowland is the future, Adventureland is the past.

Brian Vestal, 2000s

I think the jokes worked. They seemed to work. I was there in 1985 during a big celebration, so there were lots of VIPs and Disney people and there was a pressure to stay on script. I guess it was a conservative time.

Vince Fragasso, 1980s

Meanwhile there were skippers who didn't care for the script and wanted to do their own thing.

That's the crime against Jungle Cruise, they make you stick to the script 100%, because the best jokes didn't start off in the script. Some impromptu thing that just popped into someone's head. Any time you are too regimented is a bad thing and I think Jungle Cruise especially, because who knows what hilarious things we are missing out on. I think a better attitude would be if you go off script and somebody complains there will be consequences; to me that's how to go about it.

Rev Vandervort, 1990s

I think the script joke was a good skeleton, and you could just build and add on it. Everyone is going to come up with their own way of delivering it. I think that was kind of a cool thing because you could hear a script joke that was done mechanically and there are reasons that are funny, but there are other ways to be funny. Some are deprecating where you are the idiot. I like the jokes where I'm the idiot.

Ritt Mesee, 2000s

One of the best things about working there was how the skippers kept trying to one-up each other or mess with each other or see something on the river and yell to them. It was so fun to do that stuff.

Andrea Freeman, 2000s

I went to the San Diego Zoo once and wrote down all the Latin names of the animals that are also at the Jungle Cruise. Then if I had a boat full of guests that were not very responsive, I would just start reading off the Latin names. I gave them what I call the "Mutual of Omaha" tour (later called the National Geographic Tour).

Terry Eaton, 1970s

I did a lot of my own stuff, but I did follow the script when needed, if it was a day shift or a Sunday morning. I would pick out when I would do the regular stuff, and when to do the illegal stuff, jokes like Walt Disney's first attempt at the monorail, don't leave your kids in the Small World, those jokes were always a staple for me, but then a lot of it was randomness, whatever seemed funny to me and fortunately it was funny to the people in the boat. I talked about the Bengal tiger mating with the animal cookie because the guy had a thing for sweet stuff. Just dumb things, funny but not crass, just play it up with the actions you do.

Jeff Bautista, 2000s

It was always the bitter ones they cut out. "You may not see this every day, but I do, every single day." The riff on the anaconda: "He just wants to give you a hug and be your main squeeze." The Bertha jokes I tried to get it back in, because it was themed so you just had to reword it, you couldn't say she's been in there for "many years." But you could say, "She showered, look at all the wrinkles." It was some of those that really did it for me. Some of the new ones for the piranha scene I liked as well.

Kat Thrailkill, 2000s

There was kind of an unwritten rule that you don't steal someone else's joke, you can pay homage to it, you weren't shunned if you copied a joke, but skippers didn't like it.

Jeremy Wayland, 2000s

Regarding the freedom that we have, it depends on the person and what lines they want to try to push or cross. But I was taught was that if it's in the OG, it's fair game. I will also do the unofficial jokes that are still part of the jungle since they're in the spirit of the OG and they're not offensive. Also at the jungle the freedom in your spiel depends on who you are. It has a lot to do with favoritism and the respect that you've earned from the leadership team. For example, Kipp's spiel isn't as OG as most. He does a joke about Mrs. Knott's Chicken as he leaves the dock. If Kipp says that he's not going to be corrected, but if a new skipper said that they would get corrected. I think the freedom you have with your OG depends on who you are at Jungle. I don't think that's right, but it's the unsaid rule.

Anonymous, 2000s

Skippers periodically get to have input on the script.

I knew that the summer of 2004 was going to be my last at Disneyland. I had juggled my work at Disneyland with my full-time job as a history professor, but now my wife and I were expecting our first baby, so something had to give, and I knew it had to be Disneyland. On the very day I was going to tell management that I was leaving, the new schedule came out and instead of having a "J" for Jungle on the schedule, or even a "T" for Tiki Room, it said something like SP. I had no idea what that was, but it was every weekday, 9 to 5, for the next two weeks.

I walked into the manager's office and asked him what SP meant and he said, "Oh yeah, I forgot to ask you. We are doing an update to the Jungle Cruise script and I wanted to know if you would like to be a part of the team. It will be six skippers, me, and an Imagineer working in TDA. You can wear business casual clothes and write jokes all summer." I immediately called my wife and said, "Honey, God wants me to stay at Disneyland all summer!"

And that is how I spent the summer of 2004. I got to hang out with some super-funny people and write jokes all day. They showed us schematics of the changes that were coming to Jungle (explosion in the river at the gorilla camp, the piranha attack) and we got to write jokes for that. We would take turns doing our spiel for the leads and the Imagineer. They told us, "Just do your regular spiel, you won't get in trouble." So I did my best regular spiel, which didn't have a single joke from the script on it. After we were done, a lead said, "You are totally non-LOG, why have I never heard a single complaint about you?" I guess it was because my jokes still fit the theme of the Jungle Cruise.

So we wrote jokes, laughed a ton, randomly put on our Jungle Cruise costumes to test out new material. It was the best summer ever. I could leave the park happy—well, as happy as I could be about leaving Disneyland.

David John Marley, 2000s

A skipper who used to work at Jungle Cruise years ago came back to work there and told us that he had written most of the material on the script. Everybody knew he was lying.

Anonymous, 2010s

Since every skipper was given the same jokes, their delivery, their comedy style, is what made them unique. The style changed based on personality and who the popular stand-up comics were at the time. Over the decades, Steve Martin (who was never a skipper), David Letterman, and even, surprisingly, Sam Kinison.

The beauty of it, it's not a robot, you can't ever get a robot to do that, everyone brings their own flare.

Ritt Mesee, 2000s

I just developed my own style and back then, we had a canned spiel, but I don't think anybody used it, you just developed the kind of taste that fit you. You would ride with other people and pick up jokes and that kind of stuff.

Gordon Lemke, 1980s

You also had to learn to adapt your spiel to every type of audience imaginable.

We learned a lot of stuff in the Jungle Cruise, the jokes, we didn't realize early on, that a lot of it is regional. You have a boat load of Chinese tourists, so jokes about the Republican party means nothing to them, they didn't get the joke. So, you figured that out after a while and came up with other things.

Jerry Whitfield, 1980s

A skipper's spiel is an ever-changing thing. The danger is that, over time, a skipper will lose the spark and lose the guests. Sometimes it's the guests, sometimes it's the skipper.

At first everybody loves my trips. I was getting big laughs, and I was enjoying myself even though I hadn't written these jokes. Then there were times that I would say the same jokes with the same style and people would not respond at all. And that really used to eat at me. I would think, *Man, I must be awful.* I talked to a guy who was a veteran and I told him my problem and that it was really bothering me. I said, "I must really stink." And he said, "Listen, look at the time today, it's after lunchtime. People have eaten their full. It's hot out here. They don't care about what you're saying. They're sitting on a boat because it's relaxing and they're getting off their feet. If they're not laughing at you, it's not your fault. Don't think that it's your fault." That was one of the best pieces of advice I've ever gotten on the Jungle Cruise. I was only 19 years old at the time. I didn't understand any of the ins and outs of stand-up comedy. I didn't understand that not all audiences are going to be the same. I thought they would always love everything that came out of my mouth.

Dave Lewis, 1970s

Skipper Ray was a really funny guy; he had a lot of attitude. He got so burnt out at the Jungle Cruise that he created this killer spiel as the boat was being loaded and as he left the dock. Everyone would be laughing and he would get around the corner and just stop talking. He sat on the stool with his back to the guests, mic in hand, and just let the boat drive. He didn't say a word about anything to anyone until he got to Trader Sam, then he would stand up and start hitting them with one-liners and get the entire boat all fired up. People were laughing again. Nobody knew that he didn't do a damn thing out there. I was on a boat and saw him on the other side of the falls just sitting on the stool and doing nothing. We didn't know until he told us about it.

Dave Lewis, 1970s

When you reload your guns I would play that they were very serious. You had all the little kids up on the railings watching this guy loading a gun. So I played it very seriously for them. Your life depends on me loading this gun. It was always that type of thing.

Once we got going I would always do my stuff, but I always played it very serious. Most skippers would turn around and face the guests, but most of the time I wouldn't, I'd tell them, "I have to drive the boat, I have to see where I'm going, this is not on a track, this is real." It was fun for the parents watching their young kids and the skipper taking it so seriously. You'd get your steering just right; you'd turn left, and you'd go right, and you do your stuff. I never just hit it and let it spin, we'd go into that tree.

Brandon Kleyla, 2000s

What the jungle taught you is how to work off of people. I tried a few jokes to see what they like, and depending on what they laughed at I could figure out what kind of crowd they were. And if they just stared at you blankly, you knew they didn't speak English so it didn't matter what you said. There were times when I would just sit on the stool and face forward leaning over the dashboard and I would have the microphone in my hand and I would just spin the wheel of the boat and I would just talk and then sometimes I wouldn't say anything. Sometimes the guests laughed hysterically and other times you could hear a pin drop. So you learned about the nature of comedy and humor, but you also learned how to present yourself. You learned how to sell yourself, but you also learned how to sell all of that crappy animation. Let's face it, a lot of the animation is pretty cheesy, especially back then. Compared to Pirates of the Caribbean, it's just embarrassing. But you learn how to sell it.

Jeff Rhoads, 1970s

Sarcasm was picking up in those days. There were certain skippers that really stood out because of their personality types; they just had very good spiels. There were dead-pan type of guys and guys way over the top and then those kind of the middle and they adjusted based on who was on their boat. I tended to pick on people on the boat.

Jerry Whitfield, 1980s

So what stand-up comics inspired Jungle Cruise skippers?

I do remember another thing when I was there. David Letterman was very popular, so many of the skippers took on a Letterman-style sarcasm. That tended to be off SOP. I think my last two years is when the Letterman-style sarcasm came in strong. I would make fun of the jokes for being so dry. I'd say things like, "My oh my, we're having some fun now, huh, folks?"

Vince Fragasso, 1980s

I loved the elephant squirter, I really tried to sell it. I liked the physical humor. Steve Martin was a huge influence on my comedy life. He was absurd in a non-absurd environment. I would set up jokes and do them at the end. I used to tell guests that I had rubber feet and then at the end of the trip I would go to move and just collapse on the floor and say, "Ah, my rubber feet!" I just wanted to have fun on the boat.

Brian Vestal, 2000s

There was one skipper name Rob who fancied himself a stand-up comic. Besides working at Disneyland, it was very popular to go see stand-up comedians. This is the era of Sam Kinison, who was this angry yelling comic, and I think we saw ourselves as an extension of that world.

Fred Martin, 1980s

I do remember people coming up to me and saying, "You were the best skipper I've ever had." That happened to me twice. I think I was probably a pretty lousy skipper.

Rev Vandervort, 1990s

Adaptive is the the key word for my style. From the very first boat, I immediately engaged with the audience. That carried all the way through. It kind of became a thing. I would look at my crew around me and who my boat was and tailor to what I think I would need, and if I couldn't get a good read, my default style would be random, a mix of whatever came to my mind. And if I got a certain response, I had a whole book of other jokes and went along that line. So, every tour it felt like it was crafted for them. The worst boats are straight-faced, people not paying attention, because the people weren't giving me any feedback other than, "I don't want to be here." So, then it would either become National Geographic or how few words can I say to get through this cruise.

Jeff Bautista, 2000s

Working on the Jungle Cruise, if you got a reputation of having high energy, people would expect that of you all the time, so I would start off mellow, slow and subtle, and it helped me get through the 8 hours. One thing I liked to do was to find someone clearly uncomfortable being on the boat, or who didn't like me, or thought the ride was stupid, so I would make excessive eye contact. That was fun. They would start to look away.

Helen Medina, 2000s

My comedy style was dry. During the load process, it was "So where you from?" and they would answer, and you'd say, "Oh, I'm sorry." Then we would go into state jokes. "Oh, you're from Ohio, me too, what street?" If they are from Minnesota, "Oh, did you drive here, was that your tractor I saw in the parking lot?" If they are from Idaho, "Hey, have you been to our sister park's Budland? It's got these great rides, Potatoes of the Caribbean, Country Bear Yamboree, Great Moments with Mr. Potato Head." If you ever got Alaska or Hawaii, "Is this your first trip to the United States?" You just develop rapport and you can see who is responding, who speaks English, and what's going on. Once you got out on the river: "The rain forest where it rains 365 days a year, giving the plants kind of a waxy, almost plastic like appearance." It was that kind of dry humor. "Oh, you got giraffe, gazelles, kazoos, kazebras." If it got real slow, you would sing "You Light Up My Life."

Gordon Lemke, 1980s

When I started I could not do the dry jokes, I went for the super upbeat jokes, I was the dopey skipper, but now I can pull off the dry jokes in a way that works for me. Going on other skippers' boats really helps. I have two versions. I'm either kind of dry in the sense of "I'm dead inside" like I'm jaded and have seen everything. And the one I do the most is the dopey skipper who thinks they know how to do everything but keeps messing things up. I like to come to Jungle Cruise with a lot of energy, so I usually only do the dry spiel at the end of the night when I'm tired or if it's really hot and people are not really listening.

J'Amy Pacheco, 2010s

It was kind of dry, more sarcastic, where things came off mean but not too mean. By the time I got to Jungle Cruise I thought of myself as a veteran. I'd been at the park for 6 months. I learned that being chatty at Opera House is very different from having to be funny. I'm a chatty person, but doing comedy is different.

Javi Gonzalez, 2000s

Every day I would do one spiel that was totally SOP, so I wouldn't forget it, and in case a supervisor or some VIPs got on my boat, I would have it down. The rest of the time I did whatever I wanted to do, based on what I knew worked. I had ridden somebody else's boat and picked up some jokes from them. I would try those out, I tried to make them fit my personality. I'd try different things. We had a guy that was super animated, I think he was Filipino and had just a hint of an accent. He was very hyper and jumpy. His name is Jim. So I did a couple of trips where I tried to imitate him. I would do one where it seemed like I was almost asleep. I tried to do one with an Australian accent, but I lost the accent about halfway through. It didn't impress anybody. I did anything you can do just so I wouldn't get bored. I did stuff I knew I wouldn't get in trouble for him in case something weird happened.

Dave Lewis, 1970s

Being a woman at the Jungle Cruise brings with it special challenges when it comes to comedic style.

I don't do the airhead Barbie tour. Why make myself a target? That's not my personality either. Very dry sense of humor and I'm very sarcastic and sassy. I have a very OG spiel with a very sarcastic delivery. I always alter my spiel based on the people in the boat. If there's a lot of children, I keep it very OG, I mostly point out the things that I'm seeing. If it's more of an adult boat, I will poke fun at the guests and make it more interactive. If a boatload of guests is just not into it, will ease up on the spiel. If the guests are into it, I give a much more involved spiel. I like to make fun of myself during the trip. I think when you make fun of yourself guests relate to you more. I think when women come off as sarcastic sometimes it's not accepted as well as when a man does it. It's our societal norms. Like if it was a man being assertive he's assertive, but if a woman is assertive she's being bitchy. I think that carries over to the jungle. Your guests say, "You're my favorite female skipper," or they will say, "You're very funny for a girl." What I find frustrating is those comments come from adults that have young girls with them. What kind of example are you setting for them?

Maureen McLandrich, 2010s

There are some jokes that female Jungle Cruise skippers cannot quite get away with because I think audiences will give more leeway to men. There is a joke that I will never tell, because it's not my style, but also because I could never get away with it. Telling a slow-moving guest that the are the strongest man in the world because they're holding up the entire boat. Or another one that is iffy is when you tell the guests to look under their seats to try to find their sense of humor. For a female skipper, any joke when you're making fun of the guests has to come from this place of being silly, not from trying to insult them. There is one male skipper who gets away with all kinds of jokes that I never could do, I would be gone, and I know it's because of that leeway that audiences will give you in the things that you say, but with the crew it is different.

J'Amy Pacheco, 2010s

CHAPTER FIVE

Jungle After Dark

The overwhelming majority of skippers prefer to work at night. In fact, I only met one that liked to work days and that was only because he had an active social life at night. The Jungle Cruise is actually two different rides. During the day, it is bright and funny, but also quick, crowded, and often hot. In the evening, the pace slows. There are few boats, few guests, and skippers have time to do jokes that they can't do during the day. The next time you are at the park, ride the Jungle Cruise once during the day and once at night and experience this amazing metamorphosis.

During the day, guests just aren't focused on what you're saying. That's why I think skippers like to work the night shift better because during the night shift you could direct where guests were looking and with the spotlight. It kind of forced them to listen to you. The whole thing about Jungle Cruise was the search for the good crew. You know the Jungle Cruise was a lot of fun if you had a good crew; if you didn't have a good crew, it was boring and monotonous, and that's why people don't like working it. Because after the summer, you are all done.

Jerry Whitfield, 1980s

The Jungle Cruise at night was really amazing. It had an entirely different aura about it. It is a totally different animal the night. I think it seemed a little riskier at night. I could mess around more. I could do jokes that you couldn't normally do during the day, since the kids were asleep and it's mostly adults.

Javi Gonzalez, 2000s

I mostly worked nights which is fine with me because during the day it was so hot. I knew they would have code 90 or code 100 when you can pull up the sleeves of your shirts, but that didn't matter to us because we were already wearing shorts and we rolled up our sleeves if we wanted to. During the day it was too busy, they'd be running ten boats, at night you'd have maybe three.

Andrew Green, 1980s

Often times little kids, who loved Jungle Cruise during the day, would lose it there at night. At nighttime the jungle looks so dark and menacing, boats leave the dock and disappear into the nothingness. I saw it first-hand years later when I brought my girls to the park. They loved Jungle during the day, but were terrified at night. I had to keep reminding them that it was the exact same ride that we had already been on.

David John Marley, 2000s

It kind of worked out that during the day you didn't have time to goof off with your fellow skippers; it was just work, and you got through it quickly which is great if you don't like the days, but time moved by slow at night which is great if you like the night. So the times I was there in the day were cool and I would just end up hanging out at the park after work because all my friends were on at night, so I would ride their boats as a guest and I would enter through the back door so I wouldn't have to wait in line. The great thing was seeing everyone do their spiel and I'm not even on the clock, I'm not wasting time or goofing off, and I was already there. What am I going to do? Everyone that I would go out with at night were the people that were currently working there until midnight.

Ritt Mesee, 2000s

One of the great joys of working the Jungle Cruise is the deadhead. For whatever reason, usually because the dock is getting backed up, a skipper will take a deadhead, a drive around the jungle without guests. The jungle is beautiful at night.

I loved taking deadheads, it was something about being in that place, and not anyone around you. It was at night and you are just there and it's quiet and you can only hear the sound track going—the birds. It's relaxing. I loved just sitting there and having a cigarette. I'd just sit there and smoke. Sit there in the elephant pool. Wait for the next boat to come. I'd floor it to the hippo pool and then sit there. It's slow enough that they didn't have to take an eight-minute trip, so I would just chill. I remember one time there was a full boat, and they knew I was taking a deadhead, and they came on me real quiet, and they were going into the hippo pool, and they put on their flood lights and had everyone in the boat go "AAAAAAHHHHHHHHHHH." I got so shocked. That was a good time. I loved the camaraderie we had with each other.

Tameem Sabry, 2000s

There were also jokes and attitudes that you could get away with at night that would never work during the day.

I tried to make it more of a party boat at night time. Whatever I could do to make the boat a party, that's what I'd do. If Fantasmic was going on, I'd do the whole Fantasmic spiel on the boat. It was so loud you could hear it. When you are in the jungle you can hear the echo, so there's no theme at that point on the cruise. It just overtakes it. The guests would laugh. The thing for me while Fantasmic is playing, you have those flares that pop up and I feel like I'm in Vietnam.

Tameem Sabry, 2000s

My nighttime joke at the backside of water was to do my version of Fantasmic. I'd say something like, "I know you couldn't get to see the show because of the crowds, so allow me to present you with Jungle Cruise Fantasmic!" Then I would flash the lights on and off as I sang the show's theme song. At the end I would turn off the lights, put the spotlight on me, and say in a nearly perfect Micky Mouse voice, "Some imagination, huh?" People loved it, it was my regular bit. One night a guest said, "I recognize your voice, you do the Mickey Mouse cartoons! So you work at the studio during the day and here at night?" I said that I didn't, but she just laughed and said "sure!" and exited the boat.

David John Marley, 2000s

One of the things that Skipper Danny and I loved to do was have this joke with a long set-up that had a wacky punchline. We would take turns doing this. Let's say I was in the jungle, so I'd go back around behind Main Street and climb up into the hippo pool and Danny would enter (driving the boat) giving the most National Geographic serene voice beautiful explanation of the hippos in the jungle and saying, "Quite often, if you listen carefully, you can hear a baby hippo calling out to its mother," and then I would yell, "Hey, mom!" We would do stuff like that. I don't know if we started that joke, but we did it when nobody else was doing it.

Brian Vestal, 2000s

I do them differently mostly because I do jokes that you can't do during the day. The "Hey Mom" joke in the hippo pool only works during the night. I mostly work nights, I've had very few day shifts. It also depends on the weather. On hot days people just want to sit down for 8 minutes. Which is ok, I get it. It's nice when you hit that time of night when the guests are just punchy and will laugh at anything. Or when you have groups of people that have never been on the Jungle Cruise before. I like nights better, the sunsets are beautiful. Although I had a morning shift and the jungle is so beautiful in the early morning, too. I think there is this sense that the jungle itself has a different feel at night. The place is more jungly at night. It feels more like a real jungle at night.

J'Amy Pacheco, 2010s

Unlike most attractions at Disneyland, the Jungle Cruise shuts down quickly after closing time. Indy can remain open for an hour or more after the park closes due to the line and then the closing procedures. At Jungle, the ride is all but shut down as the last boat is in the jungle. That way when the boat returns all that needs to happen is to shut down that last boat, shut off the jungle, and the skippers are free. For example, if the park closes at 10pm, the Jungle Cruise is closed for the night by 10:15pm. Some skippers made sure it might even be faster than that.

My last summer on the Jungle Cruise was at night, the summer of 1976. That summer the foremen called me "Last Trip Lewis" and they always made sure I took the last trip. You'd sit at the dock and maybe have five or six people sometimes and then they'd send you. I created this spiel that made it seem like it was a nine-minute trip, but it was only five so that we could get the hell out of there. I would floor it whereever I could floor it without the risk of taking it off the rails. I skipped every other animation, stuff was on fire, and animals were roaring, and I was already talking about what was up ahead. I got around quick and the foreman liked that, so he made sure I was always the last boat.

Dave Lewis, 1970s

Just because the Jungle Cruise closed quickly didn't mean that skippers went right home. Many were clever enough to take advantage of having this huge living jungle all to themselves.

We had skiff races. At night we would close up the ride, turn off the work lights, get the skiff to the middle of the dock, set a watch to keep time, then haul ass backwards around the jungle to see who had the fastest time. Not backwards, but just the opposite direction. This one guy named Keith won every time. You could hear him, he never backed off the throttle the entire time. I wasn't that fast, I would coast, I hit a couple of hippos once. I knocked off an ear and maintenance would be all pissed off.

Dave Lewis, 1970s

One time Danny was out there with Bertha, taking a shower. It was so funny because you get so used to seeing things a certain way and suddenly there is a guy in the shower. He had a towel over his face because even though it was after hours we didn't want a picture of it floating around. We did this at night when a lot of the animation was turned off, that's another thing, with all the lights and animation off, it also became kind of a "Where's Waldo" thing. So often they would take a spotlight and try to find us in the Jungle. I remember that skiff they had by the elephant pool that was floating there so I stood on it and struck a pose like I was looking for something in the jungle. It was like the movie ET when ET is in among the stuffed animals, so that's what we did, and people would scream when they found out. Once at the dancing natives I tied a shirt around my head and we had this green monkey that had velcro on his hands and I wore that as a belt. The natives were wearing nothing but a loincloth, so I tried to fit in with that, but I had this bright neon green monkey instead. It was fun. The after hours ones were lots of fun.

Brian Vestal, 2000s

The Jungle Cruise gets done really quickly at night. The process to shutdown is very easy. So if the park closed at eight that last boat went at eight and by 8:10 we were done. But because of the walk time we all had to wait before we could clock out. So there was this window of time when people were just standing around doing nothing. I thought this is a great chance to create team bonding and to have this cool wrap-up party. One of the first story times I ever did was about after the tsunami in Thailand and this zoo had a baby hippo and a turtle that created this friendship and people really liked that. So I said, "Well, stay tuned, I'll have on the next night."The next night I told a story about how Walt and Lillian wanted to have a picnic while Disneyland was being built. First they went to Tom Sawyer Island, but there weren't a lot of trees on the island and it was too hot so they decided to leave. Walt said, "Let's go over to the Jungle Cruise" and somehow they got over to the back island which we now call Catalina Island and they had a picnic there. As they were sitting down to have their picnic, they smelled something and Walt realized they were standing on the island that had just been covered in fresh fertilizer, but they stayed and had their picnic there. I told that story to them because I wanted to emphasize that Walt had been a part of this attraction. It's one of the few places at the park where he actually walked around. The hand of Walt was heavily involved in the creation of the Jungle Cruise. I wanted them to realize how special this place was.

Tiffany Davis, 2000s

One of the most recent myths of the Jungle Cruise is the Jungle Monster. In the past few years, when shutting off the ride, skippers will wish the Jungle Monster a good night, so that the attraction will open safely the next morning. Two years ago a skipper asked me how old the myth was, and I had to confess that I'd never heard of it before. It turns out, it's not old at all. Here is the story of the birth of the Jungle Monster.

I knew there was a methane pipe over by the track switch, and that's where the Jungle Monster story comes from. I hate it so much. I was there when skippers said, "You have to say it's the Jungle Monster." The Jungle Monster is a combination of a methane bubble at the gas switch and a faulty PA system. A lead named Steve invented it. When you are closing down the attraction you have to give the closing spiel. The PA was terrible and gave back horrible feedback. So Steve thought it was funny after he gave his closing spiel to say, "Goodnight, Jungle Monster." The methane bubble would be happening by the track switch and everybody would be like, "Oh, it's coming up, I can see it." And we thought it was funny and we would ask Steve to say goodnight to the Jungle Monster. Steve would say no. He had an interesting sense of humor.

Siobhan Armstrong, 2000s

CHAPTER SIX

Fun on the Dock

The Jungle Cruise dock is where most of the wild antics consistently occur. Skippers are having their first interactions with guests on the dock and testing out which jokes will work on their new boatload of passengers. Most importantly, the dock is where skippers try to impress each other, and that's the problem.

Someone told us how to say "eat my shorts" in Swahili. Phonetically, it is pronounced "JAY-pah-TAH!" We'd work that into load and unload spiels just to crack each other up. This was decades before Bart Simpson made "eat my shorts" an internationally known phrase. Someone came up with this call where one guy would yell, "Shorts!" and we'd all respond with "Eat 'em!" Stupid stuff, but it unified us as a group of like-minded idiots.

Dave Lewis, 1970s

Just stupid things like if a skipper would ask for a glass of water, someone would bring out a cup with the word "acid" written on it and show it to everyone, like it was a secret, and you would drink it and pretend to die.

Helen Medina, 2000s

A skipper named Jake was always funny, and I don't know how he got hold of a big chain link, he strings it up and hammers it over the dock as people are coming in. We would say, "We don't know what he's doing, but he works for free." Then Jake would goof off, and he had the chain around him. He would just have the chain wrapped about his neck and feet, it was about 10' long. I don't know where in the hell he got that.

Ken Snow, 1970s

A Skipper named Paul and I would sneak underneath the stairs in the queue area. There's a chess board in there and we would just freeze like our hand was over a chess piece, we would just hold as still as we possibly could. The guests would come by: "I think I saw him breathe."

We are trying to not blink, and our eyes are watering. I found a copy of *National Geographic* from the 30s and it had this story in it about some jungle outpost somewhere, the guests would be there in no man's land to load and Paul would be there, and I would run up and say, "Paul, Paul, we got our article published in *National Geographic*, look, look." And in the magazine there is the picture of this guy and he has his back to the camera so you can't see his face, and he has this big hat on, and he has this donkey and they are standing in the middle of this river. Paul says, "Is there a picture of me with the donkey?" And I'd say, "Yeah, here it is right here," and I'm showing the picture to the guests. Paul says, "What was it you told me that day?" "Get your ass out of the river."

Larry Kaml, 1980s

Loading jokes I always had a lot of fun with because that is your first meet and greet. People are going to judge you and think that this skip's okay. Being a female, sadly you have to win them very quickly.

Jen Chavez, 2010s

As we left that dock I would try to tip my hat to my guests that this was going to be a wacky trip. So as I approached the loading dock, even at no-mans, because a lot of times the people in line were watching, trying to figure out who they were going to get as their skipper. So I would sit on the captain's crate and pretend to peddle the boat forward to the loading dock.

As people loaded on my boat, I would say, "Come on down, come on down, let the the kids come on down. Not too far, you gotta leave room for my ego." And I would ask them super silly questions and do things to set up the idea that I really didn't know what I was doing driving the boat.

Brian Vestal, 2000s

Shipping office jokes:

I would do stuff on the PA in the shipping office. I liked to call out bingo numbers and sometimes a guest would yell out "BINGO!"

Brian Vestal, 2000s

My favorite thing to say over the PA was sports scores. I'd say, "Ladies and gentlemen, while you wait in line for the World-Famous Jungle Cruise, I'd like to update you on the latest baseball scores. 3 to 7, 0 to 5, 8 to 12, and finally a tie at 4 to 4 in the 8th inning."

David John Marley, 2000s

We did a lot of boat house spiels. You would pick on one of the guests and say, "When you get off, one of the lines is on the left, one of the lines is on the right, one of the lines has a lot of people, and one of the lines has about four people, I don't want to tell you how to live your life and how to spend your evening, but one of those lines will get you on a boat a lot quicker, and one of the lines will make you miss the fireworks. Make smart choices." A manager would come over and say you know everyone in Adventureland can hear that, and I'm all, "Yeah, I know."

Brandon Kleyla, 2000s

I remember watching the girls walk in. That one joke, where you are looking right at the person and you announce a missing person, you describe her while you are looking right at her cause there's that mesh right there. "She's got brown hair, blue eyes, white shirt, blue shorts, about 5' 9", if you see her, send her my way. I've been looking for her all my life." I love the rubber-band joke, but they used it in *Spiderman*. I loved doing Kermit the Frog now that the Muppets are owned by Disney. "Today Jungle Cruise is brought to you by the letter 2 and the number 1." "Ladies and gentlemen, we have two lines, one on the left and one on the right, please use both lines." People would get so confused. "When you get to the front of the line, hand your elbow to the skipper, be careful of fetishes." Use his announcement voice and say something outlandish about the skipper loading the boat, just to get a rise out of the person. At night they had the music from 1920s; I would just sit there and sing into the mic to confuse people.

Tameem Sabry, 2000s

There is a shipping office joke in the OG where you put out a missing person's report and you describe a guest you see in line. One day a friend of mine described a guy she saw in line and his girlfriend came running into the shipping office, yelling, "Girl, I would like to see you try to steal him, I will beat you up." So as a woman I feel like I have to toe the line because I don't know how some people are going to react.

J'Amy Pacheco, 2010s

Exit dock jokes

Danny and I would do elaborate mini-shows at unload. Sometimes I would sit in the tree by unload and scare them as they left. I'd yell out, "Thanks for coming." We did a lot of exit dock pranks. We would do a dance. Sometimes we'd grab a paddle and pretend that we were rowing toward the boat.

You had to know who was in the boat. Some skippers just wanted to unload and move on, but others who knew that Danny and I were on the exit dock knew we would be up to something. One time we made a cheerleader pyramid of skippers. There were so many props there to use. We would be characters, do Australian accents or something. Some of the dry skippers would look at us and say into the mic, "Stay in school, kids," and I loved to play the fool for that because I was there to entertain.

There was a barrel and sometimes we would pretend to roll it or stand on it. Or we could take ropes and pretend that we were pulling things that the guests couldn't see. You could do this at night when you were only running four boats. You couldn't do that during the day when it was all about quickly unloading guests.

Brian Vestal, 2000s

Some skippers developed elaborate exit spiels.

The standard unload spiel was, "Watch your step, watch your head." One skipper, John, would say, "If you miss your step and bump your head, please watch your language, there are kids around." And he would just continue with that and go into a deep, dark, shadowy Vietnam memory, "Watch your language, there are kids around, watching, waiting, listening, writing down information, storing this information in secret government bases deep underground in the mesas of Arizona, stockpiling information, waiting for the day they arise above the earth's surface and revolt upon the capital marching with their tiny torches and their tiny hands, you will rue the day." Just this craziness and by then everyone was off his boat, which is the funniest part because he went off on this Oscar-winning rampage and by then, the last person is at the bazaar looking back and John is still talking, no boats in front of him at load or no-man's land. And the boats behind him are going, okay, John's finishing his end of days spiel.

Ritt Mesee, 2000s

There was one skipper that always bragged about all the applause they would get. When she pulled up to the dock she'd say, "Let's give a round of applause to the Jungle Cruise!" Then she'd start to clap. A bunch of skippers told her that she couldn't force people to clap and then brag about all the clapping." I've seen other skippers do it, and I think it's a cheap way to get applause.

Anonymous, 2000s

The hardest part is the ad libs at the dock. Out in the jungle you have visual cues to help you remember what to say. Learning how to ad lib was an important part. I remember there was a really long list of cannibal jokes, just one after another. But you had to go on somebody else's boat to learn them. I would ride other boats and pick stuff up.

Fred Martin, 1980s

When Disneyland took away the guns, they gave us air horns that we were to use for distress signals. One fun thing we liked to do was to remove the plastic horn from the can and push the tip of the can against an unsuspecting skippers back or leg. Instead of a noise, it would shoot freezing CO_2 on them and make them scream. Good times.

David John Marley, 2000s

This skipper named Alex and I had a fun banter. She would be on the little bridge by the oasis, and I'd be coming around and say, "Hey, is everybody having a good time?" And she would just be waving me down and yelling, "Hey!" and I would say, "Hey, Skipper Alex, what's happening?" She would ask, "Hey, what are you doing on Thursday night?" and I'd say, "I don't think I'm doing anything." She goes, "I got a new lawn mower and it says it needs a big jerk to start it." She'd laugh then run off backstage. The guests would be laughing.

Brandon Kleyla, 2000s

Remember Scott, all the girls loved him. We were all in love with him, but he was always so shy and reserved. I remember one night we were closing and he was the lead, and he was so reserved, and I said, "Hey, let's mess with somebody." I forget who the skipper was, it might have been Benny doing the last boat. We took Scott and tied him up to a pole and re-created the auction scene from Pirates of the Caribbean. We had people on the spur line dock yelling, "We want the redhead!" and Scott was totally into it. And the skipper came into the dock and knew what we were doing and he did a pirate voice and the guests loved it.

Andrea Freeman, 2000s

I never loved them or participated in them. They always got done to me, weird sketches. People would act out other attractions, especially Pirates, or other west-side attractions like Indy. There was sort of a catwalk that went over the exit and sometimes we would go over and hang from the rope like Indiana Jones. Trevor did that and he is a huge Indiana Jones geek. He would roll a crappy barrel, it wasn't a scary boulder, and annual pass holders would get it and cast members would get it. Sometimes it just had no punch line to those things. In Jungle you see it and then you are, "Yep, that idiot hanging from the rope is going to help you out of the boat." It was funny and more for us. We really didn't do dock jokes in the day, it was a night thing. I think when it was quiet at night like that skippers did it to entertain each other. You are in that vibe and train of thought you've got to be funny. The jokes in the script, you tell them all day, so it just becomes, no. So you have to do these things to entertain yourself and now the bar is way higher. Your job is to be ridiculous, and now you have to be ridiculous to hundreds of people at a time. You are trying to entertain your rookie buddies, plus the leads that have been there for 10 years, so it's a weird mark to hit.

Ritt Mesee, 2000s

I did have one quiet evening. A steel drum band was across the way jamming. I was on the boat waiting at unload because we had nobody coming so we weren't sending boats. I was dancing along to the steel drum band. Finally I got to move forward to load and got bumped then to actual unload. So I was in the boat that was at unload and now I'm at the dock at unload. This young lady comes walking up and says you dance pretty good, you should be in the parade, and I'm like, no, I'm alright, I just have a few days left here, and she's like, no, I'm in the parade, I can pull some strings and I can get you in the parade. And I'm like, no, I really have to go home. And so she says, okay, well, at least come meet me, this is the party gras parade and we can conga together. So she told me where she would stop for the parade and I met her the next day and she pulls me out and is like, you know who I am, right, and I'm like, yeah, that's why I was standing here. We had a good time just chatting and she again tried to talk me into joining the parade and I said I'd really like to, but I just can't, so that was about the extent of that, but it was a fun experience from just grooving along on a nice quiet evening in the jungle.

Keith Hart, 1990s

My best joke was the Arabic writing on the oasis wall. That was the complaint departments phone number. "If you enjoyed the trip, my name is Brandon, and this is the World Famous Jungle Cruise. If you didn't, the phone number for the complaint department is right up there, be sure to write that down, they'd be happy to help you, they are there 24/7."

Brandon Kleyla, 2000s

I come out, I could read it. I would do my Arabic spiel and at the end I would say, "If you want to contact me, that's my email address right there on the wall," and the people would laugh. "Enjoy my bazaar." There was a girl there named Alley and as we came through one time she had a scarf on her head; before she had done that, I would go up to her and say she is my wife, my number-one skipper of all the land. She started playing along. She would wear a scarf like she was wearing a hijab. So, we would play off it. My favorite jokes were unload jokes.

Tameem Sabry, 2000s

We had skippers that would hide in the trash can by the exit and when a guest would throw their trash in, the skipper with throw it back out. That was a trick invented by a skipper named Sherri. She was so tiny and had skills like a ninja that she could fit inside the trash can and we'd place it right by the exit. And she stayed in there for like 15 minutes. One time none of the guests were throwing anything away, so I took some paper and set it but by the trash can and I asked a guest, "Would you please throw that away for me?" And they did and the trash can yelled, "Thank you!" in this big deep voice. You know how Tomorrowland has that talking robotic trash can? We invented that years earlier at the Jungle Cruise.

Tiffany Davis, 2000s

Every time you come up to unload it was something like a surprise. Some of the jokes I can even say right now. Andy said, "Everyone rise up like bread, no loafing around." "If you like the cruise, my name is Tameem, if not, my name is Matt and you've been riding the Pirates of the Caribbean." I used to know the people working at Pirates at that time, and people would look at my name tag, they thought it was funny. One time people caught me off guard. A skipper would say, "He'll grab by the rear...of the boat." I'd add, "Watch out for him, he's got an elbow fetish." So, people would offer me their elbows as they got out of the boat. Or to pull up and thank the guests for riding on Pirates, and you have someone like David Levy with his keys in his mouth, pretending to be the dog in Pirates. Someone else would do the whistle. Chris Ramirez added to it, he memorized a line from the ride, "We want the redhead, we want the redhead. How much for this wench"? I loved doing the voices. I remember when *Lord of the Rings* came out, I would a joke about the jeep. "Oh, look at my jeep, my precious jeep, my precious." Everyone would cheer. You always get told to follow the script and tell the guests about Walt's dream. But it all depends on the crowd you get.

Tameem Sabry, 2000s

One long running elaborate game played on the dock was skipper tag.

You would get an item or a piece of paper and write "skipper tag, you're it" and the only goal was to not be tagged by the end of the shift. If you had the paper when you clocked out, you lose. But you can't just hand it off and say, "Oh, hello, here's a piece of paper" because people are not stupid, you could get away with it once. You had to make sure it was actually handed off. You couldn't just stick it in their jacket and leave when they have their jacket backstage, it's not fair, they don't know you're playing. One night I was working load and there was a very sweet British family, little girl, youngest of the family is just wide eyed and didn't want to talk, and they were the only ones in the boat at the moment, and I'm chatting with them, and I lean down to the little girl and ask her if she can do me a big favor, big eyes just nodding up and down. I said, "You take this piece of paper, can you hand it to the guy at the front of the boat and say 'Happy Christmas?'" So she goes to the front of the boat, stands on the captain's crate, and she just leaves it and stares at him being very shy. The skipper takes it, being a very ostentatious kind of silly fellow. "What's this, a note for the teacher?" And he opened it up making a big production of it, and reads it out loud, "Skipper tag, you're It!" Falls over laughing onto the captain's crate. I'm still loading and guests are wondering what's going on, so I explain, we have this game..."

A skipper named Dean and I had this elaborate game going on for like two years. It escalated from "tag you're it" to we had to find some bizarre way for it to happen, so we would have everybody on the boat come into dock and scream, "Tag you're it!" I once explained the game to a manager and I filled out a fake guest compliment because the manager would read them and take them over. I made enough clues that it was fake because I used the wrong color parchment paper, the signatures weren't from managers they were from Mickey, and the underneath didn't say "from manager" it said "a talking mouse." So there were hints, and then the compliment on the back said, "Dean, you did such a great job, and tag you're it." And the manager delivered it, she was cool with this, so she put it in a little envelope and handed it to him. He opened it and went, "Damn."

Jerry Whitfield, 1980s

Sometimes a show at the dock took Olympic levels of skill.

Doug Nordquist worked on Jungle Cruise and he was an Olympic high jumper, and he was the only guy I've actually seen jump from the catwalk to the dock without a boat there. He was the only guy, as far as I know, that could do that. He could jump from the dock to the catwalk and back without a boat being there. It was harder to jump back because the dock was higher.

Jerry Whitfield, 1980s

CHAPTER SEVEN

Skippers Are the Worst

Since the Jungle Cruise is the home of cast members whose job it is to be funny, it stands to reason that they could also be a nightmare to work with. Pranks were a near constant event at the Jungle Cruise when I worked there, and from these skippers it seems like that was not out of the ordinary.

We skippers could screw around all night long. The guests and the boats were just a formality; for the most part, we just hung out and screwed around or played jokes on each other or talked inappropriately. I can't tell you how many times we would be talking and one of the people in line would say, "Hi, kids."

Kat Thrailkill, 2000s

I used to go out and mess with the squirter. I would shut it off and then turn it back on as they passed so the entire boat would get soaked. I did it to one of my friends who was really squeaky clean and very pro-Disney. He wanted to work his way up. He comes around the corner and in his boat he has all these ladies with him and they are dressed nice. So we turn it off and he says, "Well, I guess the little guy isn't going to try to squirt us today," and as they pull forward we turn it on and we hear this screaming and everyone got soaked and we were laughing so hard.

Javi Gonzalez, 2000s

There was a lead named Darren. He left me. I went to the island one time in the skiff to pick up some garbage or some stuff that was sitting there and I turn around and he's gone. I was left out there and this is during the end of my first summer, one of my last days working there that summer, so it was one of those last-day pranks. I was wandering around for a while and then I went and laid down in front of the Bengal tiger like I was dead, and I got some laughs. Eventually, I made my way across the island over by the python and the water buffalo and I was able to jump on a boat from there and that is how I got back. I don't think they were coming to get me anytime soon.

Andrew Green, 1980s

This one guy named Jim jumped into the hippo pool while guests were still on his boat. He swam around the boat, went over to the door, and climbed back in.

Jeff Rhoads, 1970s

I had the unfortunate experience of riding in the boat after it was vandalized by an employee. There were sardines hidden everywhere; for weeks, we would find them in the decorations. It was a pretty good prank.

Helen Medina, 2000s

I may or may not have been involved with this prank.

There was another time a few skippers have gone out on safari and I came around the hippo pool at night. And as I approach the dancing natives I see that there were two skippers sitting in the skull canoe with your hands tied up and you were frantically begging for us to come rescue you. I think I made some quick joke and moved on.

Tiffany Davis, 2000s

If anyone ever left a camera in the boat or at the dock, we would take pictures with what was left of the film. However many pictures were left, we would just take photos of each other, and other shots around the Jungle Cruise, and when we used up all the film we would leave it with some lead in case the guest came back to get it. We thought it was funny that if a guest came back for their camera and went and developed the film they would see all these random pictures of Jungle Cruise skippers. That was a common thing we did.

John Verdone, 1970s

When the Indy ride was still being built, there was a little recessed area that was blocked off with bamboo. Inside there was earthenware jars and two skeletons. The back story was they were grave robbers and they fell and died or got trapped. The bamboo grid wasn't there yet to keep people from messing with stuff, and this was the day before Halloween. We grabbed one of the skeletons, climbed over the Indy queue wall, and hid it in one of the bushes which would be the shrine of the sunken city. This would be on a night shift. I said that I was taking a deadhead, jumped off the boat, took the skelleton, and put it in the skipper seat, put a hat on it, put the gun in its hand, drove it around to Schweitzer Falls, and parked it. Then we'd hide, just to see the reactions of skippers as they were coming around the backside of water. We'd wait until we heard the next boat coming up behind us, then we'd gun it all the way through the African veldt and park it on the backside of water and let a couple boats go by, then head back to dock again, take the skeleton down, take another deadhead, back around, and do it again for about an hour. Just putting the skeleton up. Then when the park was closing we took the skeleton up to the radio office, and put it in the chair, put the headphones on it, put a pen in its hand, put a note in the log saying, "We left you a present in the dispatch place, make sure it gets back in the Indy queue." So it sat there for all of Halloween.

Larry Kaml, 1980s

I love the "break time at the jungle" prank. I'd do that as a lead. The first time it happened I didn't know what was going on, no one had told me what the prank actually was. I just heard this announcement by my boat that it is break time, please stop your boat to take your break. So I stopped the boat and started talking to the guests. I told them, "I don't know what's going on, we can hang out here for a few moments and get to know each other."

Tiffany Davis, 2000s

The summer I was there in 1985 the dare going on with a lot of skippers was, can you make it around the river on a deadhead without getting wet. You'd be sitting on top of Schweitzer Falls with a bucket of water or hiding in the bushes with a hose. Phil was like, "I got this, can I take it?" I said, "No, we are busy," but he didn't know we were concocting this scheme so that no matter what happened or what he did, he had to be on the boat, he had this fool-proof plan and was dying to try it out. Finally, we had everything ready to go, and Phil takes the deadhead. He goes off and the boat in front of his boat, we made sure, was a training boat. He pulls up to load and they don't load him, so he's hanging out there just past load. I go up to the next boat and I'm talking to the guy in the boat, and Phil pulls up around the corner and I said, "OK we are taking this deadhead." So off we go; meanwhile, one of the other skippers runs over to the gorilla camp, in there was a spigot and a hose and he is waiting there. I take the deadhead out and I jump out in the shrine, and I run over to the direct opposite to the gorilla camp, because there's a hose over there, too. The training boat, we'd talked to the trainer, and said you have to get to the gorilla camp and stop, do not let the boat behind you pass. So, we had him pinned in at the gorilla camp, and the guy on one side with the hose and me on the other side with the hose sat there for three minutes and hosed him down. Phil's plan was to build a cocoon with the seat cushions, but at gorilla camp you could easily jump on the boat, so the guy jumps on the boat with the hose and sticks it between the cushions and hoses him down. There was a good inch of water in the bottom of the boat when Phil got back to the dock.

A skipper named Dave was also up for that challenge. His idea was to put the boat in forward and then go and make the cocoon thing. As soon as his boat left, I backed up to Trader Sam where you could jump off the boat onto the island. There's a hose where the python is, and I'm standing on the rocks and coming around the corner and there's nobody is driving it and three-quarters speed and it's coming at me. He was in the back of the boat in his cocoon of cushions, so this boat is coming at me and I leap on it, kick the boat in reverse to slow it down. The hose is only so long and I'm holding onto it for dear life, because that boat is starting to slow down and the hose starts to stretch and as the boat slows down, I stick the hose between the seat cushions and hosed him down. Then I put the boat in forward again and headed back to the dock.

Larry Kaml, 1980s

There were certain pranks that also worked better when it was dark in the jungle.

There was a water hose located on the island across from the dock that was the backside of the river. So what you do is you get the water hose hidden behind the bushes. This is better at night and all the skippers' attention is always on the opposite side because that's where the gorilla camp was and that's where the squirter was, so he's never looking at you so if you're standing back there on the opposite side and have a water hose, you can nail him in the back of the head and he never sees who does it.

Jerry Whitfield, 1980s

It was also a common pastime to pull pranks on the guests.

Tropical Imports had the rubber snakes and you would go get one and be at unload and hold it behind your back and drop it in the lap of some-body. One of the guests would start screaming. Just to get them to react.

Larry Kaml, 1980s

Remember when they drained the river and pulled out all the cell phones? They would keep them in the shipping office, so once a month I'd go up there and grab a cell phone and put it in my pocket, and I would have it all day just waiting for the right boat. I would go around and find a spot between gorilla camp or Schweitzer and I'd drop it on the floor, and go, "Did anybody lose a cell phone? No? Anybody?" And I would just chuck it in the river. People would just crap themselves and start looking in their pockets for their phones. It was one of my favorite gags and hard not to laugh. We would get back to the dock and the entire boat would go to the shipping office and complain. The whole boat! That was my favorite one of all.

Brandon Kleyla, 2000s

In Skipper Stories I told the tale of the great prank where the skipper seemed to disappear from the boat. Here is the tale from the perspective of the man who pulled it off.

My first memory of it is when I came around Trader Sam and nobody was there. I knew exactly within the first 10 seconds, because all the guests were like, what? I knew right away, and I turned to the mic and I had a good boat, they really liked it. I told them they are pulling a prank on me, but it's a prank you do to rookies, and I had been there like two years, so I said, you don't prank me, I prank you. I did the reverse of it, I disappeared on them. We went back to Trader Sam, nobody could see us, and I said, alright, I broke character, this is what's happening, we all try to have fun with each other. I think they even liked being part of a jungle joke at this point. They got the whole jungle and those guests at closing— the last thing you do at closing is ride Jungle Cruise, these are die-hard Jungle Cruise fans. I'm venting, "I'm not new! Here's what we are going to do." There was a guest from Japan, right up against the captain's crate, right up front, and I said that I'm going to pretend to sneak off the boat. I'm going to cruise the boat in really slow and I sat right next to the throttle the whole time and I put on this Japanese guy's backpack, his jacket, and his baseball cap. It was like when a movie star is incognito because he puts on a hat and jacket. I'm still wearing my jungle outfit underneath which is hilarious. We pull up to the dock and I'm hoping one of the cast members is going to jump on the boat and stop the throttle. We were going so slow, that even if we did crash it would have been like a bump. Someone jumps up on the bow and immediately stops the boat and all the unloaders are looking in the crates, they are looking up top by the smoke stack, and they are looking right past me and I'm sitting right next to the throttle. Nobody broke or laughed or anything, and four different people supported the whole thing. People I never met, they said, "Yeah, he just jumped out at those rocks." They sold it perfectly, and everybody, me being in the very front, was the last to be unloaded, and they touched my elbow and I walked out the exit past the bazaar and everybody on the boat walked past as well, and all the skippers were focused on the boat. Nobody was looking at the guests. Like it was some weird jewelry heist. They were lifting up the seats and looking inside the engine and I'm looking back at them. So we all go out and we are high fiving and the guests thought it was amazing. They wanted to hang out and watch, but they were getting chased out of the park because it was closing. I sneak back in through the boat house queue and I see everyone is in the shipping office and it's weird because the jungle sounds have been shut off, there are no more crickets, no more of that, it's just somber, and I'm in the queue and I can hear the lead telling everyone, "OK, everyone, we obviously can't leave until we find him." They think I'm out in the jungle on the island and they are discussing who is going to go get me. They were saying, "Do we get a search party, do we tell somebody, do we tell management?" and the lead is trying to handle this before it's gets too big. And I'm slowing moving on the other side of the netting in the closed queue and everyone is circled around and I'm slowing moving, sneaking in like a ninja, and then I was sitting there for about 30 seconds to a minute just nodding. Joey noticed me and burst out laughing and everybody looked at me. It was like a magic trick. That was fun! I never told them how I did it.

Ritt Mesee, 2000s

The skiff was a small boat with an outboard motor that the lead or maintenance would use to get around the jungle in case of an emergency. This skiff was the domain of the lead for decades until the late 1990s when the engine was removed and the skiff was hidden in the Indian elephant bathing pool. The spot where the skiff was parked at the dock is still visible today, just in front of the Indiana Jones FastPass room near the loading section of the Jungle Cruise boathouse. The skiff was put there for work, but skippers had other plans.

We had the gasoline skiff up at the front, so we used to do that several nights a week. We'd go out there and do donuts in the elephant pool.

Gordon Lemke, 1980s

We had skiff races at night. The purpose of the skiff was in case somebody dropped a purse or something in the water and it was floating around, we'd go out and get it, but that's not what we used them for. Cause at night time, a lot of people walk by Jungle Cruise, and it's a fairly dark area and a lot of people thought it wasn't open. I would go out there during Fantasmic or the electrical parade, it's dead, so you are sitting with your free boat and you are waiting and waiting, you need something to keep yourself occupied, so we had skiff races. Time the lap.

Larry Kaml, 1980s

I heard that one of our leads, a guy named Ken, was in the skiff and was hauling ass to a breakdown and the engine died and he sailed right into the waterfall and the skiff sank.

Dave Lewis, 1970s

They threw a birthday party for a skipper named Scott up at JUBA (Jungle Upstairs Break Area). And somebody brought up one of those chrome fire extinguishers and thought it would be funny to shoot him with it. So they did, but they didn't realize that the floor leaks into the Adventureland Bazaar below and it destroyed a bunch of merchandise.

Dave Lewis, 1970s

One day a new guy showed up and he was wearing the khaki costume, and at the time one of the options was a leopard print dickie, a fake ascot. He showed up, wearing it, but nobody wore it. So one skipper said, "It's dickie day," and went over to costuming and came back with like 20 dickies and everybody wore one that day.

Dave Lewis, 1970s

I won't mention names, but I was on a training deadhead for Jingle Cruise with a few skippers and we were done and I'm driving and as I approached the backside of water I hear "oh no!" and two skippers had been sitting on top of the boat canopy and they had to scramble down because the lead was on a boat that was approaching the falls. They almost died and I was laughing so hard, and the lead just stared at me as we passed. I was laughing so hard watching one skipper fall from the top and into the boat.

J'Amy Pacheco, 2010s

There would be people in the jungle that would jump out at the boats or throw things at you, or skippers would go thru the Indy door and try to find a place on the ride to freak you out and you are all jittery to see where they are going to come out next. The guests are looking at you, thinking, *What's wrong with this guy, is he on acid or something?* You are looking behind the rocks and then get tagged by something right in the cheek.

Jeremy Wayland, 2000s

I remember one day somebody dumping a bunch of soap on Schweitzer Falls. I'm sure it's happened multiple times. Nobody confessed, but it was bubbles everywhere.

Rev Vandervort, 1980s

The Jungle Cruise is equipped with real Smith & Wesson 38s that have been altered so that they can't fire real bullets. Guns and skippers who will do anything for a laugh—what could possibly go wrong?

We used to double load the bullets. The rounds for the gun were cylinders like a regular bullet cartridge except with the bullet taken out, but the wadding and the gunpowder was in there. So we would take the gunpowder out of one shell and dump it into a second one so that it was double loaded. And you can hear those bullets go off on the dock, "boom! boom!" And then they finally gave us breakdown ammo, which you would use for 3, 4, or 6 shots. We would double and even triple load other guys' guns, so that they didn't know it was going to be so loud.

Dave Lewis, 1970s

Handling a gun, the Smith & Wesson. It was the first time I'd held a gun in my life.

Andrew Green, 1980s

I remember when we ran out of ammo one time, so we would do the click, click, and the guns empty, so we would pick up a handful of used ammo and throw it at the hippos. That pool is full of ammo, because literally that's all we had was used ammo so we would throw it at the hippos and it would bounce off their heads. The guests loved it; hippos have a fear of blanks.

Jeremy Wayland, 2000s

I would always unload the gun and if the guy who took over my boat didn't check, when he got to the hippo pool he would go "click click" because there weren't any blanks in the gun.

Tom Nabbe, 1960s

When skipper wasn't looking, we would take one round of breakdown ammo, pop it in their gun, and spin the wheel. Why that's funny is the skipper would never really know it was in there, so he'd get out to the hippo pool, and ideally the first shot "pop," second one "boom!" Sometimes other guys would just put all breakdown ammo in the gun. So when the skipper got out there is was all "boom! boom!" It would scare the skipper and scare the kids. One of the other guys figured out how to take it further. The ammo came in these little plastic casings. The primer was on the back of it and you could pry it off, so they'd take a couple of the ammos and dump more gunpowder in it and put the primer back in there so when you shot the gun it was "boom!!" twice as loud as the breakdown ammo. To the point that the plastic would just fly off and melt.

I was amazed for all those years that we actually kept those guns and never really lost them and the fact that they were real guns. What they did was put these copper bushings on the end of them so a real round of ammo wouldn't fit. But they always worried that if they ever got stolen someone could remove the copper bushings and then the Jungle Cruise guns would be used in a liquor store robbery. [Does anyone else find it suspicious that Jerry was so specific about the type of store that could be robbed?]

Jerry Whitfield, 1980s

Once in a while there would be a gun battle in the jungle; you would hear 24 shots. I was on the dock and I was listening to this, they would have gun battles shooting at each other. Multiple gun shots! A common thing was seeing someone dancing around with the natives. I heard stories, people jumped into the hippo pool and stabbed a hippo with their rubber knife and get back in the boat. Most of the gun battles were between boats, one was on land. When you are passing each other in Schweitzer Falls, the gun battle would ensue. Nobody claimed responsibility.

Ken Snow, 1970s

Jungle police is a classic prank where after a boat leaves the dock, another boat goes backwards into the hippo pool to wait for him to arrive. When the victims boat pulls up, the "police" boat flashes its lights and then they arrest the skipper of the boat.

They got me when I was in the hippo pool. They are waiting for me, they pull up and I pull in and they are making the siren sounds. "Pull over, put the throttle down, put down the microphone, your skipper is not funny, we will take it from here." They would tie me up, I would do the walk of shame and be tied to the post. I thought it was awesome, it impacted me in a positive way. It was unexpected, they made it fun for the guests and for the skippers

Tameem Sabry, 2000s

Probably about three weeks into it, we did the jungle police, we would tie the guy to the dock and start whipping him with the lanyards for not being funny.

Jeremy Wayland, 2000s

Another prank was "dead skipper," where a skipper or skippers, and sometimes even guests, would sit in a boat at the backside of water and pretend to be dead. Simple gag, but effective.

At night, when it was slow, there would be deadheads. One night, I had a boat full and was approaching the falls. Coming the other way in the dark was an empty boat with what looked like the lifeless body of its skipper hanging from the canopy, swaying with the movement of the boat as it turned the corner into the rapids. It really looked like the guy hanged himself!

Dave Lewis, 1970s

I remember that skippers liked to do the dead skipper prank at the back of Schweitzer Falls. If you had a deadhead, you would lean over the railing holding your gun and act like you were dead behind the waterfall. You knew the skipper coming toward you had their back to you, so they didn't always see you. Some of them would get so flustered that they didn't know what to say. Dead skipper was fun.

Ton Nabbe, 1960s

This particular version of dead skipper took an amazing amount of effort.

We would take a deadhead out and park front side of water and lay there dead, with a gun in your hand. Then we would elevate it and take two people out, one is dead with the gun in their hand, the other is laying across the side of the boat with their hand dangling in the water. We got up to four, laying dead with gun in his hand, I would be up on the top of the canopy with two seat cushions between the middle seat cushion and the side, I would lay in the canopy and when a boat passed by I would fall off the roof into the boat and just let the cushions break my fall and one guy was hanging from the roof over the side of the boat with his leg caught up in the tow rope, he was upside down submerged up to his waist with this leg sticking out. He took a chunk of garden hose and ran it down his pants and he would breath through the garden hose, the boats would stay there to see how long that person could hold their breath underwater, they were just waiting and waiting with boats backing up.

Larry Kaml, 1980s

One of the rules that trainees were taught was "what happens in the jungle, stays in the jungle."If you saw a skipper on safari doing something silly, you didn't tell the lead. Another rule was respecting your fellow skippers. This meant not taking an extra long break or lunch. People who did faced jungle justice.

If a guy kept coming back late from his breaks, we would just bury him in the boat; instead of doing three trips, he'd take five or six.

Dave Lewis, 1970s

If you maxed, you started jungle justice. You didn't do it very long, because if you jungle justice for two hours, you learn your lesson. Jungle justice for the neophytes. The consequence: four-person rotation, two boats in the dock position and break, and you would make a one-boat, one-dock break rotation and the other boat would be whoever was maxing and it would just go around and around and around. Sorry, you're not on rotation anymore, I don't know who your partner is. They would do it until they caught on and apologized.

Larry Kaml, 1980s

Some pranks involved the now removed Dominguez switch that could keep a boat from reaching the dock, so that the skipper and his crew would have to go around the jungle again.

And then there was where you have the guy throw the rear switch or the front switch and then move all the boats out so he couldn't get back. We'd tell him to go over there and throw the front switch and park your boat over there. And he'd go park his boat over there, but there aren't any other boats so he didn't have a way to get back to the dock. What he didn't know is that we secretly started calling the other boats on the radio because they just started experimenting with the radios. And we'd say, "Hey, take the trip really slow this time around, just milk it for all you can." So there's this guy with all the guests just staring at him standing out there on the cat walk.

Jerry Whitfield, 1980s

The Jungle Cruise is the only place I've ever worked where hazing was an accepted part of life. I managed to avoid it in high school, but at Jungle everyone had to endure at least a little initiating. Generally speaking, those that took it as a good-natured prank were never hassled again. One of the more popular pranks was to dump water on an unsuspecting skipper from the backside of water.

I got hazed at Schweitzer Falls. I hear this rustling from above, I look up, and the next thing I know a bucket of water drenches me and I'm covered in leaves. I had guests on my boat, remember we didn't have leads, so we did all kinds of stuff. So I come back and an older man came up to me and asked if they do that on every tour. They kept me in the boat for another hour because someone didn't show up. I was sticky and drenched.

Jeremy Wayland, 2000s

I remember the animation checks where we would screw with some-body for it. You would send somebody out, they would be new in the jungle, and while they were unloading guests we'd flip the switch and throw the switch to the catwalk and then they would have to wait for facilities to let them back across the thing. We would turn off all the lights in the Jungle while they are out there and just leave them there until somebody decided to let them back in.

Jeremy Wayland, 2000s

There was a lot of bullying at Disneyland. I can only imagine if I worked there at a time of Facebook. People would record us, but those tapes are probably sitting in their garage, but in the digital age, a lot more people would have been fired.

Helen Medina, 2000s

This is my personal favorite, and the most horrific hazing story I've ever heard.

The poor girl that had the cockroach hazing, some of the guys, the ammo boxes had a little top on it so you could slide it off, they had the little grooves so you could slide it back and forward, well, we had two of them, they put one on the girl's boat her very first day after being trained, and she slides the thing open and she is not even looking, and they put a whole bunch of cockroaches in there. The next we know she's got roaches running up her arm. I'm at front load at the time, I hear this screaming and see her running backstage and I never saw her again. The next thing I know there are managers with radios on the dock and I'm sitting at front load. That was one more of the particularly rough hazings that I saw.

Jeremy Wayland, 2000s

CHAPTER EIGHT

This Isn't the Jungle Cruise

A one point just about every area in the park has had to deal with skippers who thought they could take the jungle with them wherever they went. Skippers often don't want to work anywhere else, or if it was their first attraction they just assumed everything was a wild as Jungle Cruise. It isn't.

We don't always get along with the attractions that are near us.

The Indy lead came over one day, and I was in the dock princess position. He told me, "There is a kid that was too short for Indy and he's in tears and so his mom is bringing him over to the Jungle Cruise. Please take care of him." I made a motion with my finger/thumb like a gun and I said, "Take care of him?" And he yelled, "No, not like that!"

Lawrence Janiec 2010s

I failed out of Mr. Lincoln, I'm not sure why, but probably because I didn't want to work there. It was so boring. I failed the test they made me take. I was afraid I would fall asleep on the job. I failed at Canoes because I couldn't dock the canoe properly. I was like 100 pounds and it was too hard to steer. I don't know why they wanted to train me on Canoes, it was not my thing. So from there I learned Haunted Mansion. I worked mansion during the holidays. Mansion was so boring. You just go from station to station. Jungle Cruise was so much better. I'm kind of ADD and the Jungle Cruise was the perfect place for me because you're out there moving around and you're in a boat, then the dock, you are constantly moving. It was the perfect thing for me.

Andrea Freeman, 2000s

People always told me that skippers were a different breed. I never really noticed it until I was sent to one of those Line of Training classes and it was all skippers and we started laughing because we were going to have a good day. Half the class was skippers and the other half was guest relations and Fantasyland people. During training they were talking about security issues and the trainer asked the group, "Now if this happens, who are you going to call?" and without even planning it, every skipper yelled at the same time, "Ghostbusters!" And that is when I realized that the skipper difference is real. At Disneyland we have the reputation of being a bunch of smart asses. I loved having that reputation.

Javi Gonzalez, 2000s

When we all got off Jungle for the summer of 1975, some of us wound up on Haunted Mansion. We didn't leave the spirit of Jungle humor back in the jungle.

When all these skippers showed up as rookies, with their irreverent enthusiasm and need to be funny, they didn't welcome us too warmly. We were doing ticket-taker spiels on the PA like we did back at Jungle. No one did that before and the veteran crew was not impressed.

We would also call unload from the load belt to let them know when something out of the ordinary was happening, like when a celebrity was boarding so they could keep an eye out for them. One guy would call and say he had just loaded a live orangutan in one of the clamshells, or that Spiro Agnew was on the ride. The vets hated that and told him to knock it off. They just wanted to shuffle around in the dark and be left alone. Our jungle nonsense had no place there in a haunted spook house. They were right, but we didn't care.

Dave Lewis, 1970s

One thing we did that really pissed people off is we said that there was going to be a gay pride day at Disneyland, which they didn't do back then. We announced in a newsletter that there's going to be a big gay pride rally down at the canoe dock all day. We did that because the canoe guys thought of themselves as the cool, macho guys. We got into so much trouble for that. I think a couple of managers wanted to suspend us, but they let it go.

Jeff Rhoads, 1970s

I was working a parade shift with this happy, eager, young blonde woman. We were setting up the ropes along Main Street when this morbidly obese couple came up to me. They were both easily 400lbs. The man pointed across the street to the Refreshment Corner restaurant and asked me what kind of food they served there. I was busy setting up poles and the restaurant was barely 30 yards away, so without thinking I started to say, "Why don't you walk across the street and find out yourself?"

I was about halfway through that sentence when my parade shift partner literally leapt in front of me and began to describe the menu items of the restaurant. The heavy couple walked away satisfied. She looked at me and said, "What were you doing? You can't say that! Where do you normally work?" When I said, "Jungle Cruise," she leaned back in horror and said, "Oh god! Go stand over there and don't talk to anyone. Skippers are the worst."

David John Marley, 2000s

And of course, every skipper thinks that the rest of the park is jealous of us.

I think everyone wants to be on Jungle Cruise, but not everyone is, so they can be jerks about it. I had a lot of friends who worked in Innoventions and Tomorrowland. They always talked smack about the Jungle Cruise, but they all admitted that they wanted to work there. They all hated their jobs and we loved our jobs and they saw us as goofballs. Then those super strait-laced Disney people like my ex-boyfriend, they hated us. They were all about the show and bad show.

Andrea Freeman, 2000s

Skippers had no respect for anything, including Walt Disney's apartment.

Someone made a copy of the key to Walt's apartment, and it was like, are we supposed to be up here, yeah, it's all cool. Someone, somewhere has a camera full of pictures of everybody just hanging out at Walt's, desecrating his apartment. But we had two or three copies of that key made and it was just a known secret that we had the keys for the apartment, Splash Mountain, Thunder Mountain, and some other things. There was a spot backstage by the boats where if you went by the drywall they had a little thing for it and they had all the little keys, but those keys opened everything. We always talked about the keys to the kingdom. It was all back there and it would get us into everywhere. So we would hang out up there where all the VIPs would be.

Jeremy Wayland, 2000s

For Jungle, we were a bit obnoxious if you are not part of the group. We all took the shuttle to the third stop and I remember, just to shock people, after everybody got up, this one skipper would just take a big whiff of all the seats, and to the last two people and the driver of the shuttle, he'd say, "After all the people leave, I love to smell their seats,"and this doesn't work on paper but if you knew him, you are just, "Yep!" You have to know him.

Ritt Mesee, 2000s

CHAPTER NINE

Guests Are the Worst

There wouldn't be a Disneyland without guests, and that's the problem. Each boat is a unique collection of people from literally all around the world. Jokes that work with one boat won't always work with the next one.

It's painful when you do a joke that you've done a thousand times, and it always gets a laugh, then realize, in this one instance you made a terrible mistake.

I had Wings Take Flight (the Canadian Make-a-Wish Foundation) on my boat one afternoon. The entire boat was the dying kids and their adult sponsors/parents. At the start of my spiel, after safety, I opened with, "How many of you this is your first time on the Jungle Cruise?!?" (people raise their hands/cheer) "ME TOO!!!" "How many of you this is going to be your last time on the Jungle Cruise?!?" ("ME TOO!" is what I normally would say). So I said that, and all the kids raised their hands.

Lawrence Janiec 2010s

When people in my boat wave to the people exiting Indiana Jones, I like to tell the Mitch Hedberg joke, "You shouldn't wave to people you don't know because what if they don't have hands? Then it's like you're saying look what I've got." One time I got halfway through saying it and looked down and noticed the little girl right in front of me only had one hand. Oops.

Reese Gordon, 2010s

One night, my foreman asked me to go fix the line and close front load. I wasn't as familiar with how to do it as I should have been. A group of guests were at the entrance and I thought I knew what I was doing, so I had them follow me to the boat as I repositioned portions of the railings and reconfigured ropes. We entered at the rear load entry, weaved our way all through the entire line, and emerged at the front load entrance to the line. The group laughed, thinking it was part of a joke. I nervously laughed with them as I tried to remember the correct moves to put the line back the way it needed to be.

Dave Lewis, 1970s

People, especially at night, would walk up the exit and want to get on a boat. Every skipper is trained to see them coming and send them on the right way. One time this group came toward me at the exit and they were determined to get on the boat. I put my hands up and told them this was the exit and this man said, "No habla Ingles" (I don't speak English) and they kept walking toward me. I replied, "No en Espanol es no," and immediately the man said, "Ah, come on, man!" in perfect English without any hint of an accent.

David John Marley, 2000s

At the unload area there used to be the yellow letters in the ground saying "exit only." Every single day people would walk up to me and stand on the exit sign and say, "Is this where we get on the ride?" Finally, as a way of answering people, we would just take off our hats and start brushing away at the part of the ground at "exit only," just being total smart asses.

A skipper named Charlie and I were standing at unload. We just unloaded the boat, nothing going on, and a man and a woman each wearing dark sunglasses and bright canes with red tips come up to that area. They stop for a second, you can see they're thinking, and I hear the man say, "I think this is where you get off. I think the entrance is that way." And they turn and head toward the entrance with their canes tapping away. I look at Charlie and I said, "Did we just see two blind people figure out that this is the exit and all those other idiots who can see perfectly well couldn't figure it out with the giant letters painted on the ground?" That was most ironic thing I've ever seen.

Dave Lewis, 1970s

We had this thing called running the squirter. Depending on the group and how hot it was, sometimes the squirter accidentally got ran and you forgot to stop for it. A lot of the funniest things I've ever seen on Jungle Cruise happened with running the squirter. We had a guest who's really not interested in the ride, his family dragged him on. So, that day I come around the corner and I just was not thinking about that squirter because I was too busy talking to these people. I came up on the elephant and it came up and about the time I realized, "Oh, crap," and this stream of water came up and hit the guy in the back of the head. Everybody on the boat laughed and this poor guy was sitting there and I'm like, "Oh, I didn't know that was supposed to happen." But that was running the squirter and a lot of times people did it on purpose. It was pretty funny.

Jerry Whitfield, 1980s

So I'm sitting at the dock on load; Brad was at the back. I'm telling people to move up to the front of the boat near me and I'm trying to move people around to keep the boat balanced. And I'm saying things like, "Hey, lardo, come over here. Hey, lumpy, move closer to me." And Brad is laughing because I don't realize what I'm saying out loud. I was fat shaming them. So from them on everyone called me Lumpy.

Dave Lewis, 1970s

I was at rear load one time and we're getting ready to load the boat and I asked how many people are in this party. The dad in the group stops to think and then he turns around to look at the people in his group and he counts 1-2-3-4. Then he asks his wife, "Where is the baby?" His wife says, "You were supposed to get the baby." And then they yell, "Oh my god, we have to get out of the line!" And they run to get their baby which they had left in the stroller. I couldn't believe it was real. I know Disneyland can be really distracting and that you can you lose yourself, but you'll lose your children? They came back with their baby and I put them on a boat.

Working load was always the best because you could talk to people while you're waiting for the next boat to come up. I remember one night this lady looked at her boyfriend and said, "It's amazing how they make this place look so nice. I mean it's nighttime outside and it made it look like nighttime inside here, too." And all I did was look at her boyfriend and turn around. He said, "Oh my god, honey, we're outside." And she was amazed. It was a bit awkward. I think she was tired. I think it speaks to how powerful Disney is at creating environments.

Tiffany Davis, 2000s

I had a guest sitting next to me who was on Facebook Live and they were talking loudly and they were right next to me. He was like, "We're here on the Jungle Cruise and you can see all the plants and over there is Indiana Jones." I try not to make fun of people because I'm not sure if I could get away with it. If someone calls something out to me, I might comment on it, but I never try to make the person the butt of the joke.

J'Amy Pacheco, 2010s

I didn't make this joke up, but I told it on a boat with guests. "How do you tell the difference between a female zebra and a male zebra? Well, female zebras are white with black stripes, and male zebras have a penis." Yes, I told that on a boat with guests during park hours.

It was a bachelor party, private cruise, they were all really drunk, I figured I could get away with it. Of course, they just lost it with laughter. The downside, though, was the entire rest of the trip they were all like, "More penis jokes! More penis jokes!" I had to tell them to shut up so I wouldn't get in trouble.

Lawrence Janiec, 2010s

I get in the boat, do my safety spiel, load the boat, I pull to the rain forest, and this black lady screams at the top of her lungs, "Stop the boat, stop the boat, stop the boat." She is screaming! I can still see the dock, I ask her if she is okay, she reaches into her purse, pulls out her shower cap, and puts it on because she saw the rain forest was coming. She literally said, "You are not messing up my weave!" That is a quote. Folks on the dock were wondering what was going on, we were close enough to the dock that they could hear what she was saying, people were crying (from laughing). That's how far we made it from the dock.

Brandon Kleyla, 2000s

So I get in the boat and I'm at unload and we have a wheelchair group, and they get in the boat. It's like a party of 25. Huge family. They are all black. They take up one side of the boat. I'm like, great, no problem, hey, how's your day, okay, great, moving on. We go to load and load the rest of the boats. And for some reason, I had one side of the boat black and one side of the boat completely white. I kid you not. So it was weird and everybody at the dock is just giggling at the childish stupidity of this visual. The crates in the middle were empty. I'm thinking this is silly. So we're going through and I'm doing my thing and they are kind of laughing, the black side of the boat is not laughing at anything. I'm thinking I got good stuff, and I always did my Don Rickles style where it is very dry, and I would not hesitate to turn around and just pick on you. People liked it. So I'm thinking this is weird, and we get around to the gorilla camp and the gorilla is holding the baby gorilla out. The elder of the black family goes, "Hey, it's like Michael Jackson," to his family, like Michael hanging the baby out the window. They kind of chuckle. It was the quietest boat I ever had and I'm thinking what can I do to salvage it. We get to the totem with the rhino and I'm coming around the belt and I go, "Folks, the Jackson 5 are here today performing, it's a rare opportunity they are right over here, it looks like they are in a bit of a pickle, but I'm going to point them out to you, so I point to the totem pole and go, there's Tito, Jermaine, and up on top there's Michael." Which of course is the old white guy up on top. Everybody on the right side of the boat is terrified how the left side of the boat is going to react. There's a beat, and the left side loses their minds, funniest thing they have ever heard, at that point they laughed at everything I said. By the end they were screaming, applauding, and so they unload the boat and everyone on the left came up and shook my hand and said, "This is the best trip we've ever been on." The lead asked what I did and I said, "I don't think technically I can tell you; it's not bad, but I don't know if I want to take the chance."

Brandon Kleyla, 2000s

Disneyland is the happiest place on earth, and sometimes that brings a lot of pressure with it to make sure everything is perfect.

I was on unload, this man with a very heavy Australian accent, had lots of chains and lots of jewelry, he had gotten wet on the ride and started yelling at a skipper. "Look at this!" and the skipper just said, "Yeah, I know you have a lot of jewelry." The guy just got angrier.

Helen Medina, 2000s

I've been hit by guests twice, once at front load because I would not let the woman in with the soda that she had just bought. So she hit me. The other was because I fired the gun in the hippo pool. SOP is hold up the gun, fire the shots, the person sitting right next to me where the gun is sitting in the holster was like a concert violinist and was very protective of his hearing, so he slugged me and as soon as we get back to the dock, he's all fired up and he's talking to the lead, and the lead is like, "Did you hold your arm straight out?" "Yes, I followed SOP, and by the way this guy hit me." And the lead was like, "Alright, you assaulted one of our cast members, you just need to walk away."

Larry Kaml, 1980s

One time I took guests out on the jungle I would get back to the boat and everybody gets out but one guy. He looks at me and says, "I want to ride again." I told him that he's welcome to, but he has to go back through the line and pay for another ticket. And he says "I'm not getting out of the boat, I'm not waiting in line again." I said, "I'm sorry, sir, I'm going to have to ask you to get out of boat," And he says no. So the unloaders called security and they came and got him out. I move forward filled up with guests and took another trip. When I come back to the dock I see the guy sitting off to the side and there are security all around him and they're carting the guy off. My friend said, "That guy was waiting for you to come back around because he was going to clean your clock." But security took him away.

Dave Lewis, 1970s

I used to wear this stupid hat that had pineapples on it. I wore it and at the Indy queue I saw a lady wearing the same hat, and I was insulting her, but it is okay because I had the same hat on. The people in the queue didn't know what was going on, but the boat did.

Helen Medina, 2000s

Busy people didn't listen as much. At times like that, I felt like I could do whatever I wanted and that people were distracted. At the end of the ride, I would thank every part of my body, "I'd like to thank my legs for supporting me, my arms for always being by my side." I also loved to point out if a boat did like me. I'd say, "I'd like to thank those that enjoyed the trip and laughed, both of you. Your checks are in the mail. For the rest of you, there is a brand-new perfume shop on Main Street you should visit called "Sense of Humor." It smells pretty funny in there."

Brian Vestal, 2000s

I had lots of annual passholders who would come and request my boat. I was overly committed to working the Jungle Cruise. There were people there who were phoning it in and didn't care, but I was really happy to work there. There was a sweet little lady passholder who always asked for my boat. I was always really happy to see her. She'd walk up to the exit and ask for me. I loved being there and making them laugh.

Andrea Freeman, 2000s

One time I saw this guy who had broken his leg and he was on crutches and trying to get on the boat. As he goes to unload, he puts up his crutches so he can get into the boat. And just as he makes his move the boat shifts away from the dock and the guy falls straight into the water, his crutches, too. He was okay. It was one of those moments when half of me was thinking, "Oh my god, no," and the other half of me was thinking, "Oh my god, that was so funny"

John Verdone, 1970s

A guy who was paraplegic and had a motorized wheelchair came to unload. He was very independent, flops himself onto the dock, and scooches into the boat. In that two-inch gap between the boat and the dock, his keys to the wheelchair fell in the water. So we got the net and tried to get them out, had to push the boats out of the way. We couldn't find them. So we had maintenance come over to hot wire his wheelchair to get it to go.

Larry Kaml, 1980s

I remember this one guest, and hurting myself on Jungle Cruise. No one else got hurt like this before. You remember the FTDs, the Fat-ass Transport Vehicles. They come right up to the exit area and load up over there, because they can't fit through the line. We had this lady who was 800 lbs, with a husband about 130. We had them over at the boat, and she sat dead center on the boxes, but the second she sat down we could literally hear the bottom hit the guide rail. We couldn't put anyone else on here, her centralized weight is literally pushing the boat right down onto the rail. So we sent her around, she looked like the Queen of Sheba, because it was just her and her 130 lb husband, with her sitting in the middle. To get her out of the boat, we had two people pulling the bars in, one on each of her arms pulling up, and I was one of the guys in the back pushing against the backbone. That fat roll came over each of my arms. The second she hit the dock the boat flipped back the other direction and I ended up getting tossed into the rail right into my back and onto the deck. That hurt and that whole boat...it kind of bent the side rail, that's how bad that reaction was. Too much weight in one little spot.

Jeremy Wayland, 2000s

The park had been closed for at least 15 minutes because we had closed the boathouse entrance and were tying up the last boat at the dock. As we stood there chatting, we heard this crash of trash cans being moved and/or knocked over in the boathouse. Seconds later, these three teenagers come walking through the line all casually and then complained when we told them that the park was closed. One of them wanted to argue until our lead said, "Why do you think the rope was up at the entrance and trash cans were blocking the door?" With that they left.

David John Marley, 2000s

It was at night, we got a boisterous group, and that's fun and the whole trip when just fine, so I turn around coming up to unload and I'm doing my spiel. I said something about odor or gun, and the fellow that was part of the group, who was sitting in the middle seat up front, he stands up, and he has a cap gun and he fires it at me. It was a very light charge. I was so stunned, I should have grabbed the guy and called security. I was stunned. I didn't jump or scream, I just walked off.

Ken Snow, 1970s

It was a hot, busy night. I'm on the boat and the guests are loading when a large group of women from Australia sat up front. As they filled the boat, I decided to use one of the load spiels designed to inspire efficient loading: "Forward ladies, forward ladies [pause] I love forward ladies." Well, it seems these ladies were just that. They all moved forward, and one straddled the middle seat, faced me, and opened her shirt exposing full naked breasts. "You asked for forward ladies, and we're here!" she said in her Australian accent. Nobody else but her friends and I could see while she settled in and made herself comfortable for the trip. The load skippers on the dock didn't know what was happening and wondered if I was ever going to leave. I was totally embarrassed and uncertain of my next move. So, I simply turned my back to her and the rest of the guests and took one of the quickest trips around the river I have ever taken. They had a blast and she left knowing she had gotten the better of a Jungle Cruise skipper.

David Schoenwetter, 2000s

Children are a great source of comedy on the Jungle Cruise.

I love all of Jungle Cruise so much, it's hard to narrow down. I love how people are so willing to go along with the show and get immersed in this world. I once convinced a boat load of kids between the ages of 7 to 13 that not only are the animals real, there was a very real chance that our boat might sink. It got to the point that I had to calm them down and tell them they were safe. I love how people get into it, especially kids. My favorite pastime at Disneyland is convincing kids that there is magic everywhere. I convinced a kid that the light-up balloons were powered by balloon fairies and that when the light goes it means they went back to Pixie Hollow for more fairy dust. And to the kids it made perfect sense, that's how willing people are to jump into the show.

J'Amy Pacheco, 2010s

I guarantee you that this is the cutest story you are ever going to hear about the Jungle Cruise. It's late August, and the crowd has died to nothing, school is about to start. The park was still closed on Monday and Tuesday when I worked there. So at the end of summer it was just dead, especially in the evening, there were no annual passes back then. Nobody was vacationing from out of state, so it was really dead, especially at night. It's Sunday night, school is starting the next day in a lot of places. If you remember night shifts on a slow night, the fireworks are getting ready to go so no one is coming in. It takes 15 minutes to load the boat because so few people are coming in. The first four people in are this family, mom, dad, sister, and a five-year-old boy. I say to the family, "Where are you from?" and they are a local family and the mom tells me that the boy is starting kindergarten in the morning. Tomorrow is his first day of school. I say, "Timmy, that is fantastic! What are you going to take in school? Algebra, trigonometry, chemistry? What are you taking?" Timmy waits one beat and says, "I'm just taking a lunch box." I literally dropped to my knees. It was so brilliant, you could not have scripted that. The rest of the boat didn't think it was as funny as I did.

John Verdone, 1970s

One time it's night and I'm in the boat at load and this guy gets on the boat with a toddler and he sits right in the back all alone. And I tell him, "Excuse me, sir, we have to try to fill the boat. Could you please come on down to the front?" I keep saying things to try to encourage him to move up to the front, but he just ignores me. Then the guy takes his kid, puts him on the back of the boat, pulls down the little kids pants, and holds on as he pees into the river. I'm watching, the two loaders are watching, and our foreman is watching. There was nobody in line then, so no guests saw it. I was trying to think of something to say without getting myself in trouble, so I just said, "Well, I think the water level just went up a little bit." It turned out he didn't speak English and he was from a culture where that was a completely acceptable thing to do.

Dave Lewis, 1970s

I once took a trip with a puddle of urine in the boat. We were on a trip, and a kid was screaming he had to go to the bathroom, so we unloaded the kid and his mom, and I see this big yellow puddle. We called the lead and he looked at the puddle, he looked at the full boat of people, and he yelled, "Hit it, Skip!" I drove the trip with a puddle of pee, all the guests kept looking at it. The guests saw the whole thing, the kid screaming, the wet spot.

Helen Medina, 2000s

Another time I was pulling up after just having been unloaded. It was a slow night around closing time and I look up and here comes a kid, maybe 12 or 13, running at full speed and he splashes right into the water. The two loaders rush over and get the kid out of the water. They ask him what's going on and he says, "I'm trying to get out of the park. My bus is going to leave me behind, and I thought this was another way to get to the main gate. I didn't see any water, it was just black, I thought I can just run through there." He thought it was just more pavement.

Dave Lewis, 1970s

Kids were my favorite. Sometimes I would pick a kid up and use him as a human shield at the attacking natives. Or I would take off my skipper hat and put it on a kid's head and yell, "They only want the skipper! Take him! Take him!" The hat went down over their eyes and they couldn't see and that was funny. If a kid really liked the ride, I would make a big deal out of it and tell everyone, "We made it out alive today because of our hero!" and have them applaud for the kid. If there was a kid who looked like he wanted to get involved, I would bring him up to the front of the boat and let him steer. I would just chat with them. Sometimes, if I had a kid that liked to talk, I'd let him go on, but you still have to do the Jungle Cruise, so I would interrupt and say, "Hold on a second, I have to work. Hey, look, a tiger!" and then go back to the kid and say, "Anyway, what were you saying?" I tried to entertain everybody in the boat and get them all involved. You know how Pixar movies have elements that are for everybody? There's some stuff that is for kids and some jokes are clearly for adults? I tried to have that type of humor.

Brian Vestal, 2000s

I used to grab a little kid and let him steer. That would be the longest 8 minutes of the kids' life because I would rip him apart. "Okay, when we get up to the waterfalls here, I need you to go left, we need to make a shortcut to the left, and we'll get through there." Then I'd say, "How old are you? Didn't you hear me I said left, what is your problem. I don't even know where this goes."

Brandon Kleyla, 2000s

One of the most consistent problems at the Jungle Cruise is hecklers. For some reason, guests will get on board and convince themselves that they can out-funny someone who does it for a living. Every skipper has a story of dealing with hecklers to varying degrees of success.

I had one lady on the boat sitting right next to me, and she didn't speak English, She was being super loud and very obnoxious. She was telling the people around her all about the Jungle Cruise so loudly that I had to turn up the volume on my microphone to be heard over her. So we get to the elephant pool and we get to the squirter. I walked to the back of the boat, the squirter comes up and just hoses this woman down, It was like a fireman hit her with a hose, Then I walked back to the front of the boat and resume the tour. She was laughing and laughing. We have these greasy rags we kept on the boat to clean off the guns. I gave her the greasy rag to dry off with. That will teach you to disrupt my boat.

Dave Lewis, 1970s

When I had a heckler I liked to just give them the mic and say, "Okay, you do it," and then I would just drive. I found that they would very quickly get shy and then hand the microphone back and quiet down. Once I had a heckler that was funnier than I was. He kept saying punchlines and things that I hadn't thought of. So I began to ask him, "Okay, what you be saying up here?" They had been on the Jungle Cruise so many times they'd heard every single joke so they knew some super funny ones. Once we had a former skipper who worked there for years before I got in there and I gave him the mic and let him do a guest spiel. Occasionally, we would let guys do that if they convinced us they used to work there and they knew what they were doing. A lot of the time these guys are pretty darn good because they were doing jokes we've never heard before.

Dave Lewis, 1970s

This is the story I tell when I'm drunk at parties. I lost my voice for a while at Jungle. I got these things on my vocal chords and they sent me to TDA, the land of filing, and I was miserable. So miserable. And then they sent me to costuming to sort laundry and it was awful. This went on for three months. I had three months of these busy work shifts. There was one time where I spent the day literally shredding papers. So when I finally get cleared to go back to Jungle I had a night shift. I was so excited to be back. I used to stop by Jungle and say hi to my friends. I was so excited. I got on my first boat and this kid was heckling me and I was pissed. I started to mess with him. I loved messing with guests. His parents were so embarrassed. They were visibly horrified that their kid was a little jerk. He was saying the jokes out ahead of me and making fun of me and I punched back a little bit. It was miserable because this stupid kid was ruining it for everybody. He was ruining my first trip back and I was pissed. I stop the boat before we get back to the dock. It was nighttime, so I had my spotlight and I pointed it at him and said, "Can everybody raise their hands? Can everyone point to the ceiling? Can everyone point to that awful man in the back who ruined our entire trip?" And I told him that he ruined the magic of the trip for everyone and ruined my first day back and he would never amount to anything. And everyone was laughing, then I pointed the spotlight on him and everyone was laughing and his parents stood up and laughed and clapped. He just sat there like a typical adolescent who thinks he's too cool and he doesn't care. Then I pull the boat up to the dock and the manager Paul was there in his Big Thunder costume and he just says, "Freeman, out of the boat," and I thought I was going to get fired on my first day back. He walks me up to the Adventureland office and says, "Do you know what you did? Did you know I could write you up or fire you right now for what you did? I won't because that was hysterical. Well done. Please tell everyone I yelled at you." Somebody wrote about it on a Disneyland message board I later found out.

Andrea Freeman, 2000s

There was another time, too, someone on the boat was not safe and not listening to me, being very disruptive. I was at the elephant pool when it first started and when we got to the African veldt, it just collapsed. I called it in, I stopped the spiel, I drove all the way up, and I had security escort him out of the park. He was in his teens. He was cursing during the ride, and I had little kids on the boat, and I was just not having it. And he was looking at everyone around him. Not needed at all.

Tameem Sabry, 2000s

My first heckler was right up front, and trying to ruin every joke. I leaned over and said, "Hey, I know this isn't your first time, but it's everybody else's first time, chill." And he kept going, so I said, "Dude, I've got two radios and this one will get you escorted out." And it totally sucked the oxygen out of the entire boat and the rest of the trip really blew, but I can't concentrate when you are finishing my sentence for me.

You get these kids telling all your jokes, and I'm like, "Dude, here's the mic, need a spotlight? You think you can do better?" And they get three jokes in and then they can't do it anymore.

Kat Thrailkill, 2000s

This chubby little white girl was sitting next to me and she knew every joke and she let me have it at every opportunity. She kept telling her dad, "Dad, this guy's not funny." I guess she was around eight or nine years old. We get to the gorilla reaching for the banana right before Schweitzer Falls and I do some lame joke about the gorilla and the little girl says to me, "Hey, is that like looking in a mirror?" People on the boat laughed and clapped, and I thought, "Okay, I'm gonna get you back, little girl." Looking back on it now it wasn't the best thing I could've done, but I had been working a very long shift and I was tired. As we get to the hippo pool, I tell everybody, "It's okay, folks, they're only dangerous when they blow bubbles and wiggle their ears." Then I looked at the little girl and said, "Is that like looking into a mirror?" The entire boat just gasped, but her dad started laughing really hard. She didn't say a word after that.

Javi Gonzalez, 2000s

Another time there was this guy who was on the boat with his friends snd he was repeating my jokes and making other jokes, so I said to him, "You must ride this ride all the time." And he said, "Yeah, once a week." So I said, "Wow, you're a virgin." Everyone laughed at him. He laughed it off, but his friends laughed so hard.

Javi Gonzalez, 2000s

The biggest category of hecklers are those that had been on a ride a ton and knew the jokes and wanted to shout out the punchlines or do jokes with you. I enjoyed hecklers, it was a challenge for me. You could tell at load if someone was going to be a heckler. I would use this as a opportunity to do jokes that they hadn't heard, or do the same set up and then change the punchline. I tried to get them on my side or at least have fun with them. They were all at Disneyland, so maybe they were expressing their love of the Jungle Cruise in that way. So I tried to turn their fun to my advantage. Give them joy. It didn't always work, but I tried.

Brian Vestal, 2000s

There were always times when these things break, or the animation has timed out, and we had to just sit there, and every second you sat there the people would hate you more and the kids would get sassy...it's just cardboard, it's plastic, it's broken. "It's not broken, he's just disillusioned."

Helen Medina, 2000s

Most of my hecklers seem to think it's funny to challenge me to try to be funnier than I am. But I have a microphone and they don't. I also work here and they don't, so I have the advantage. I've never had anyone really bad. It's mostly just guys seeing if they can challenge me, but it's my 25th cruise of the day and I don't care. I don't get hecklers that often, I mostly get people who try to talk over me, but I'm loud so they have to work for it.

J'Amy Pacheco, 2010s

I had a multi-step process for dealing with hecklers. I tried to figure out what they wanted and went from there. Some didn't realize they were heckling, they just thought they were part of the show. You had to be nice to people like that because they were just having fun and didn't realize they were being rude. Others just wanted attention, so you'd give them a little, and they'd usually settle down. The worst were guys who were mad because you made their girlfriend laugh. Guys would get really jealous about that. It was a very primal anger with these guys.

David John Marley, 2000s

I was really glad to be there at that time, because this was pre-annual passholders, so you didn't have repeat guests, and it was also pre-social media and recording, so you didn't have YouTube. People weren't that savvy, they just had this expectation that they were going to have a good time. They didn't have the jokes memorized and there wasn't the pressure that you have nowadays where you have annual passholders that go every weekend. We didn't have those pressures, so it was much more fun.

Gordon Lemke, 1980s

However, good guests can literally make your day.

I put in for vacation in July, my wife and parents were going to Europe, and Disney said you can't go on vacation in July. I tried to plead my case, but they said, "Sorry, it's the summer you don't get vacation." I was really upset, I walked out of there with my tail between my legs and got back to my boat, grumpy mood, being a disgruntled employee at that point. The whole boat ride, I didn't turn around once, I purposely sat on the seat, turned the wheel in the wrong way, did my spiel and in a total monotone voice I said, "There's a bush, there's an elephant, there's a water buffalo, we're coming up to Schweitzer Falls." Did the whole thing deadpan because I was in a grumpy mood. Came back to the dock and I did my Steve and Ben Dover joke. "Up ahead at the docks are the Dover twins, there's Steve Dover on the right and you guessed it, on the left is Ben Dover." The whole boat erupts in applause, totally broke my whole funk, that just knocked me out of the funk and I had to laugh at myself for being such a curmudgeon. Then I get a call that my wife had called the office and said, "What is it with you Gestapo guys?" So, they called me up to the office and they said, "Okay, Dave, we're going to give you your vacation, but you have to promise never to have your wife call us anymore."

David Schwab, 1970s

Sometimes a guest will complain about a joke. Who would ever encourage a guest to go complain about the Jungle Cruise to City Hall?

I actually did get a complaint from a mother in law. We were not allowed to use the mother-in-law joke and a mother-in-law comes up and says, "You did not use the mother-in-law joke tonight," and I was like, please, please, march right down, my name is Keith Hart, please go to city hall and complain that I did not use the mother-in-law joke because that is the only way we will get it back. [The mother-in-law joke came back.]

Keith Hart, 1990s

I once got a guest complaint because of the bad sound system in a boat. The sound system is bad. The speaker in the back does this demon warbling sound before it totally cuts out and I had to calm a woman down who was mad that she couldn't hear anything.

J'Amy Pacheco, 2010s

The only place I ever got a guest complaint was at the backside of water. You know how the boats pass each other at the backside of water and sometimes you can converse with the other boat. There was this commercial that was popular at the time. We had this bit where one skipper would ask, "Hey, do you Yahoo?" and then you'd both sing, "Yahoo!!!" and I got a guest complaint that said, "I don't think employees of the Walt Disney company should be endorsing certain internet service providers over others." I still have it. I had to get a coaching, and the manager thought the whole thing was silly, but she had to remind me to stay on the script. I really wish I knew who did it. I would have loved to watch them walk into City Hall to complain. Who would be that angry about it? Maybe they just got hired by Google.

Brin Vestal, 2000s

Here is a story I was afraid to share in the first Skipper Stories.

This is the tale of how I got a guest complaint and a guest compliment on the same boat. It started with the worst heckler I ever had. He was this high school kid who yelled out, "Show me your tits!" when we passed the Indy queue. I was stunned, no one had ever talked like that before, but I shut him down. He was wearing a Dead Kennedys t-shirt, so I thought I would show him I loved that band, too, and I cracked a joke about us having "A Holiday In Cambodia" and he just stared at me while this middle-aged man in the back yelled out, "Yeah! Dead Kennedys!" It turned out that the kid didn't know about the band, he just liked the shirt. He tried to heckle me three more times, but I shut him down, and he seemed to take the message for a minute or two, then he felt the urge to try again. He was eventually quiet for about three minutes, then at the backside of water he just went nuts and started yelling things at me and guests and he clearly thought he was so cool. He had one friend with him who laughed at everything he said. I floored back to the dock and at this point I lost my temper, and I just unleashed on him in the most cruel way as we were pulling up to the dock. As we docked, I remember saying, "Look, I know your parents don't give you the love and attention you so clearly need, and that's why you act the way you do, and dress the way you do, but please get some professional help, don't take it out on us." He then began to cry, and then I made fun of him, over the PA, for crying.

I said, "You like to yell and cuss and try to look cool by heckling, but you can't take it, you're just pathetic, get off my boat." I was so focused on him that I didn't realize I had 40 other people on my boat who were sitting in stunned silence. I had gone way too far. As you could guess, he went straight to City Hall and complained. They bought him dinner, gave him a few backdoor passes, and he left. (If I had been smart enough to have told my lead, then City Hall would have been ready for him and told him to go away.) A manager was waiting for me when I finished my next trip. He was angry with me, but we talked, and nothing was put on my record because I threatened to quit. I was normally a hyper but nice guy, but this time I was agitated and angry and the manger could see something was wrong. I literally threw my ID card at the manager and told him that if this incident goes on my record then he can walk me out right now. I'd rather quit then let that kid ruin my record. (I know it doesn't flow logically, but I was really mad).

A week later the middle-aged guy showed up at the dock and gave me a Dead Kennedys CD that he bought for me. He had also gone to City Hall that night to compliment me. I got a guest complaint and a guest compliment on the same boat trip. (If that kid, who is now a young man is reading this, I really hope you got help.)

David John Marley, 2000s

Although women have been working at Jungle Cruise since the mid 1990s, they still encounter occasional resistance from guests.

I would hear while you are at load, people saying in the cue, "I hope we don't get her boat," you would hear it, so there was a lot of pressure to do a really good job or get so angry that you really don't care and do a bad job. I hated that pressure and I hated that they had the nerve to say that, sometimes at load they wouldn't get in the boat, they would step out. I think it still happens.

Helen Medina, 2000s

Although recently we've had a bunch of boats, this happened to a couple different female skippers. There were men who were getting into the boat and they would say, "I don't want to get into this boat, it's got a female skipper," and the loader would say, "You get on this boat or you don't get on the Jungle Cruise." I haven't had that experience, but I know a lot of female skippers that have had that exact moment of someone getting on their boat and thinking that they are not going to be funny. One of the most brilliant things I'd ever heard was one skipper had this happen to her and later on the guy laughed at one of her jokes and she said, "Oh no, no, no, sir. I'm not funny, you're not allowed to laugh."

I think part of it is that when people think of the Jungle Cruise they think "boy" and when they think of Storybook they think "girl" because that's how it was when it opened, and there is still a ways to go especially in the marketing of the Jungle Cruise. It's always been "a funny dude will take you on a trip." You never see any girl skipper merchandise, which is a personal soapbox of mine. You know those tsum-tsum plush toys? I complain about this so much that my mom actually bought the skipper one and made it into a girl. So I have the only piece of female skipper merchandise. My mom sewed on pigtails and put on eyelashes.

J'Amy Pacheco, 2010s

Sometimes the guests don't know English.

I remember having boatloads of people who didn't speak English at all. Usually Asian, but I still did the spiel. I knew other skippers would make it a deadhead, but I never did. I knew that they tended to get freaked out by the squirting elephant.

Vince Fragasso, 1980s

It might have been dry but very animated, especially with the non-English-speaking boats. You have to be animated because they have no idea what you're saying.

Keith Hart, 1990s

Usually, with the tour groups that didn't speak English, there was more yelling and screaming and waving my hands. That seemed to work well.

Jerry Whitfield, 1980s

Occasionally there are bilingual skippers who can still entertain the guests.

I used to have lots of Spanish-speaking tours, and if the boat was all Spanish speaking, this one skipper would take the boat because he could do it all in Spanish. So, if I had a boat that was all Spanish speaking, I would try to get that guy to come and do the trip.

Tom Nabbe, 1960s

My favorite thing in the whole world was when I'd have a boat of non-English speakers. I would have so much fun with them. I would point at things and make them look and take pictures and I would go into crazy detail and then start saying nonsense words about unicorns and stuff. I'd point at random plants and get very excited and get them to all take pictures. It was so fun because they had no idea what I was saying and they'd be looking at me very intently, and I would pantomime taking pictures just to see how many random things I could get them to take pictures of. I liked to see what the most random thing I could get them to photograph.

Andrea Freeman, 2000s

Taking a chance nobody on your boat speaks English doesn't always work out.

One guy did a spiel when he thought nobody on the boat spoke English. He even asked is there anybody on here who can speak English and nobody raised their hand. So he did all kinds of crazy things. He looked at this old lady and said, "You know you're the ugliest old lady ever seen in my life," and other stuff because he was sure that nobody there could understand him. It turns out there was a couple of people on the boat who could speak English, but they just were two shy to raise their hands and they went to City Hall and complained. It became a big deal.

Dave Lewis, 1970s

Sometimes you'd get a boat of people who didn't speak English and I would see what they got excited about and I would feed on that.

Brian Vestal, 2000s

I loved the tour groups because they don't speak English so you can talk about your whole day. I'd go, "And today I had to pick up the dry cleaning and I had to do this..." I would literally talk about my high school, and stuff like that. We'd get to the natives with the spears and they go "whoosh" and everybody—a Japanese group—would go "whoosh" and they were copying me the entire time, and it was kind of funny because they got off the boat and go "whoosh" and they were doing the bows. At the beginning of the tour, I would ask, "Does anyone speak English? I'm a big red tomato!" No reaction. I did have a British guest come up to me and say, "That had to be the strangest tour I have ever been on in my entire life." He was Japanese, but had a British accent. I was laughing my butt off.

Jeremy Wayland, 2000s

CHAPTER TEN

Like a Boss

It is a rare place in the world where workers exist who love their boss. While most skippers love their leads, the skipper who is essentially the onsite supervisor, it is the ever-rotating series of managers that cause the most friction.

I could see the managers had a little different way of handling the Jungle Cruise crew, like it was a bit of a chore for them. To have to walk all over Disney and then to go, "Oh, okay, we've got Big Thunder, Indy, and oh… Jungle Cruise." They had a different attitude about the Jungle Cruise.

Ritt Mesee, 2000s

I think the worst thing was the bureaucratic crap that Disney would throw at us, the new regulations. When they would come down on us for script stuff. I remember that they were doing ride alongs to make sure we were following the script then they would hassle you about it. They took all the fun out of it. They had a right to regulate us, but they really tried to kill the fun.

Andrea Freeman, 2000s

I wish they would pull the reins back at Jungle a little bit. Not make a crazy unsafe free-for-all, but loosen up and let people have fun. It gives the guest an experience that they can't have anywhere else.

Javi Gonzalez, 2000s

The other thing I didn't like is when they really came down hard on following the script. I was there as an employee, but sometimes they would randomly come down hard on us. I learned early on that if I just wanted to have a positive experience, I can't do anything super off-script at the dock, so I learned to build it up. I didn't want to get management's attention for my antics.

Brian Vestal, 2000s

I remember it being a world of three-ring binders. Up in the Adventureland office they had all of these three-ring binders and everything was written down and I felt like we were so far away from anybody who could make a decision to change anything with where we worked. There was the sense that everything had to be done by the book. And decisions about how the Jungle Cruise operated were being made by people way, way, way up the chain. Like even the guys that were the suits in Adventureland were not making any of these decisions. They reminded me of a manager at a Denny's, they were just following the rules put in place decades earlier.

Andrew Green, 1980s

All of the supervisors at Jungle Cruise could be divided into straw hat and felt hat people. The felt hat guys didn't like me because I didn't follow the rules. The straw hat guys always knew they had to give me a written warning for whatever it was I had done, but they felt bad about it.

John Verdone, 1970s

I remember in summertime, management would say, "Okay, this hour we are going to try and hit our number," and if we did, they'd bring us a cake. They would run the numbers on a little chalk board.

Gordon Lemke, 1980s

In the more than three years I worked at Disneyland I was late one time, and this is the story of that day. I was always afraid to be late, so I usually got to work early. The nice thing about it was I was more relaxed, I could chat with my friends before my shift started, and often the lead would have me start sooner than scheduled because someone always wanted to go home early. One day, traffic was worse than usual and I knew I might be late and by the time I was on the CM shuttle from K Lot, I knew I was going to be late for the very first time. On the shuttle with me was a newish skipper who was not fitting in so well, mostly because he was always late. We hustled across the park and made it to the dock. The lead nodded hello to me and looked at the other skipper and said, "You're late, that's 1.5 points." Instead of apologizing or begging for mercy, he said, "What about David, he should get a point, too!" The lead looked at me and then back at him and said, "David has been here for over two years and has never been late before, and will probably never be late again. Whatever happened to him was clearly beyond his control. This is the third time you've been late this week." The skipper was fired a week or two later for swearing on stage and I never forgot the kindness of my lead and was never late again.

David John Marley, 2000s

I want to tell you about the time we broke the load record for an hour. We had a supervisor named Joe Petaluga. There was no incentive to move a lot of people to the Jungle Cruise. I think we were doing like 1200 people an hour. So Joe comes down to the dock and bets us that we can't get 1800 people in an hour. He bet us a keg of beer. That got everybody excited. So we were putting more people in the boat than could comfortably fit. One guy was so good at it he actually got twelve people to stand in the boat, too. He just loaded the boat up and yelled, "Hit it, Skip!" When he came back around some of the people were still standing in the boat. It was like the New York subway. So we have 1800 and we were very excited. The manager looks at us and says, "Well, now I know you can hit 1800, so you'd better be hitting it all the time."

John Verdone, 1970s

From time to time, and with varying degrees of success, managers will try to crack down on the Jungle Cruise. The common denominator is that the managers are usually new and have never worked the attraction.

There was still a sense of what happens in the jungle stays in the jungle. Me and this other skipper got in trouble once. It was a Santa Ana wind and a bunch of sticks had flown onto the dock, so we started sword fighting, for just like two seconds. The boat was by Trader Sam and by the time it reached the dock we put the sticks down and were ready to unload. Someone reported us to management and we both got "safeties" for it. I was so pissed, nobody said anything, they just ran to management. We eventually learned who ratted us out. This was around 2010 when things had really changed. What was weird is that it was the older skippers who cracked down the most. One skipper had done all kinds of wild things when he was a skipper, but as a lead he cracked down hard on people. I understand that he was under a lot of pressure from management, but at the time people were upset because he had been so wild before.

The attraction went from being a place that was really fun with a lot of camaraderie, that you were a skipper forever, to a mentality of micro-managing, with managers riding boats all the time. They cracked down on everyone. When they started cracking down on the Tiki Room, that is when I knew it was time to quit.

Javi Gonzalez, 2000s

I have a slew of written warnings, none of which are for actual job performance issues. They're for things like "John will not cut his hair" or "John is drinking coffee on the *Mark Twain* in the sight of guests." I think I have a record for how many written warnings I've got. I actually got a written warning once for having too many written warnings. The manager called me into his office and I thought, *What's wrong now, I didn't do anything.* They handed me a written warning for receiving too many written warnings within a certain span of time. I wore that one with pride. All of my warnings were just for screwup stuff. I was just a kid having the time of his life. I didn't like authority. If something was going to be funny, I would always opt for that.

John Verdone, 1970s

Sometimes the leads were like, "That was funny, you were hilarious, but you can't ever do that again." The leads were interesting to me because they were at the weird place of being blue collar but also like establishment. They had to balance both, but they came from being a ride operator, nobody hires in as a manager, they were one of us. The leads are the ones who would rein you in, but they were there so they had a respect for it. Kind of like, but you are not going to get away with that for a long time. Like Gerry had been there a long time as lead, the Lorne Michaels of SNL, he was just there, that was him. He would see something and not laugh out loud, but just comment about it academically in a way and like it. But he would say that's not going to work: "Between us that is awesome, but legally I have to say something to you." To me, the leads were always torn between let's have fun and let's not get fired.

Ritt Mesee, 2000s

Some leads were more popular than others. First, the legenday Gerry.

You didn't want to disappoint Gerry, and if he came up to your boat and told you to to kill that joke, you would never do that joke again. One time I totally slayed this joke and Gerry looked at me and said, "If you're going to do that joke, do it right, or just don't do it around me."

Javi Gonzalez, 2000s

Don Chapman was a popular lead during the 1980s.

He would never say "skip," it was always, "Move it up, guy." He would put his foot on the bow of your boat and say, "18 inches, guy, want me to show you 18 inches? I'd show you 18 inches, but it hurts when I fold it in half, move it up."

Larry Kaml, 1980s

Being a lead at the Jungle Cruise is like being stuck between two worlds. On the one hand you are still a ride operator like everyone else, but on the other hand you are expected to do whatever management tells you to do. A lead has to be a bridge between these two worlds while also making sure the attraction runs smoothly.

It was kind of a pain, but I would jump a boat every once in a while. I got bored and the guys looked at me like I was crazy. The day shift was a different animal because they had a lot to do. You get in, sign the books, set up the rotations, fill out the op sheets, and then we had a labor sheet to fill out. Then we had a gun log and then I would do the rotation sheet for the night guy coming, and we also had log books so we had to write log book entries.

Jerry Whitfield, 1980s

My first experience as foreman came one slow night when the actual foreman left me in charge so he could leave early. I guess he wasn't feeling well. Knowing I would now be in charge of all the skippers and the operation of this famous ride caused my bowels to need evacuating ASAP. I ran to the bathroom, took care of things, and ran back.

Unbeknownst to anyone, there was a mix-in that night. It was a group of square dancers. They expected a few hundred. It turned out to be more in the few thousands. Here I am, first time filling out time cards, the OP sheet, doing a changeover, etc., and I get bombed. The line is out the ying yang and I have to add boats without enough people. I have to ask people to extend. I have to get in a boat myself. It was a colossal nightmare.

The next day, supervision asked me why the OP sheet looked like chimps had been coloring on it. When I told them, they understood. I guess from that experience they figured I could handle pressure and I wound up with more foremanships. Fortunately, another skip with some lead experience helped me through it. I'll always be grateful to him.

Dave Lewis, 1970s

It was great, you didn't have to spiel. It kind of depended on the time of year it was, working summer time and it's pretty hectic, trying to get as many people through as you can. Also, it depended on if you were the opening lead or the intermediate lead because then you were just the lackey for 7 hours and you had that one hour of fame and glory before the closing lead came on. Usually, if you were the intermediate lead, you did guest control and just hung out there, park strollers, take ropes up and down for 7 hours. And you got to be in charge. I really liked being night lead because it was pretty chill. During parades, nothing is happening. It was fun because you hardly saw supervision at all. If there was a problem they were there, but for the most part you didn't see a lot of supervisors around because they didn't want to know what was happening.

Larry Kaml, 1980s

I was supposed to come in just working a short parade shift and I ended up getting moved over to Jungle Cruise to be the lead and then I had to work the whole shift which I wasn't too cool about. The other lead thing is the skiff; if I got new people and their spiels were way out of control, I'd get in the skiff. I would go out after they left the dock, and especially at night, when they couldn't see me. I'd sit in the skiff and hear their entire spiel. Then I'd come around and park the skiff and he would go around again. Then he would come back to the dock and I would say, "Hey, I heard you had this line about blah blah blah," and he would ask what happened, did a guest complain? I'd say no, just be careful and understand that there are certain things that you can and cannot say on the ride and I don't want you to get in trouble. It was sexual innuendos. He would just drop his head and say okay and go to his position.

Jerry Whitfield, 1980s

As a lead, the best part of working the Jungle Cruise was the other skippers. As rewarding as it is to work with guests, it was almost more rewarding to work with skippers. I had skippers come to work and tell me that they wanted to call in, but showed up when they found out I was the lead. I wanted to create an environment for skippers to be free to express themselves to me. I wanted to be a place where skippers could have fun. We kept it safe, but I wanted to be able to push the limits and that's very important at Jungle because being a skipper is draining. So it was great to create an environment where skippers felt charged and excited to be in a creative environment. Making my cast members happy to be there was more rewarding than helping the guests have a great time, because I knew that if the skippers were happy the guests would be happy. To me, my job was to serve the skippers.

You've heard the old saying, the day lead's job is to keep the jungle moving, the line moving, keep everything going smoothly and the job of the night lead is to keep the skippers out of the trees. It was so fun, everyday was different, I never knew what was going to happen. I was always this nice person and there's always people who wanted to walk all over me. I hated it when a skipper would flat-out lie to me. I knew other leads and managers who would blow it off and say these were just kids, so who cares, but when they lied to me I took it personally. Once I was in the jungle fixing something and a skipper drove by and said something that was completely inappropriate for the Jungle Cruise and later I asked that skipper, "Hey, when you are in the elephant pool, do you do this joke," and he looked me straight in the eyes and said, "No, I would never say that." It was like a dagger in my heart. I wasn't that kind of lead who would say this is being documented right now. Skippers were always afraid that everything was being written down. It's sad that that's how they felt it was. I used non-OG jokes, but I would never lie about it. So that was hard, they were like my kids, even those with more seniority than me. It was like family, but sometimes you wanna slap your brother around, you know? They are in a very unique group of people. Being there is certainly different than being a lead someplace else, like Main Street vehicles. Those cast members have been working for the company for decades, so they're not trying to impress anybody, not going to do anything just to get a laugh. They just want to do their job right.

Tiffany Davis, 2000s

I was lead once and a manager called and told me that the park was slow, so I had to send three people home. I asked literally every skipper if they wanted to ER (early release), but for the first and only time in my life, no one wanted to leave early. I kept asking because I couldn't believe that no one wanted to go home even an hour early. When the manager called back and asked how many I'd sent home, I told him, "Zero, nobody wants to go." He then said, "Well, pick three people and send them home." I didn't think that was a fair way to treat people, so I said, "Disneyland scheduled these people these hours and they showed up to work them; it's not fair to send them home to save the company $60. Disney is a multi-billion dollar company, I think we can afford it." That was how much money would have been saved if I'd forced people to go home early. All my skippers got to stay.

David John Marley, 2000s

After the Russian Revolution of 1917, communist leaders removed managers from the factories since their ideology taught that these managers only got in the way. The result was total chaos and a loss of productivity. For a brief period in the mid 1990s, capitalist Disneyland executives thought they could save money by removing leads at every attraction, and experienced similar results.

It was different because without the leads the managers never showed up. I didn't know we had a manager in the area until I was 2 or 3 months in. Without leads, we got away with bloody murder. Absolutely bloody murder. It was a much freer environment out there. Everybody maxed on everybody else. The trainers would basically set the shifts for everybody, they'd come in and write up the whole thing. I think there was a general lead for the area, but they were never on the ride. You could just sit in the shipping office the whole time on your break, and that's what we did, but nowadays it's bad show. But I'll be honest, without the leads everyone got much more risque with the jokes.

Jeremy Wayland, 2000s

Not all managers and leads were popular, or good, or even mildly qualified.

There was so much hiring prior to the opening of Disney California Adventure. Casting had to hire some people that historically may not have been considered for roles, both union and non-union. Some people who had impressive guest service skills in restaurants or retail were terrible guest service managers at attractions. They hadn't come up through the ranks, so they had trouble coaching others when they themselves couldn't spiel, operate the ride vehicle, etc. One manager froze when speaking in front of guests, got lost walking backstage or inside attractions, and panicked when the trains backed up at Big Thunder. There were a number of managers like that. Managing at Disney is a tough yet extremely rewarding job, adding up to far more than 40 hours a week. It's just a whole lot easier for everyone if you have lived the life of an hourly cast member and know the rides before trying to manage a crew. It unfortunately took a serious accident and a number of near-misses before every manager had to be trained on each attraction they managed.

David Schoenwetter, 2000s

I remember once the lead had screwed up the rotation and I did 11 trips before I got a lunch break. He sent too many guys to lunch. I was mad, but I couldn't do anything because I was stuck on the boat.

Andrew Green, 1980s

A friend told me that one night Jungle was 101 (not operating) because there was no power to the entire west side and we couldn't run our boats because the animals couldn't work. So an Adventureland manager (the "Enemy of Fun" mentioned in *Skipper Stories*) walked into City Hall, laid down in the back, and said, "I'm gonna hide here for a bit and listen. You guys are about to be really busy."

Karen McGuire-Vogelvang, 2000s

I was at the front load and there was only one load open, the rear load, and I had a spontaneous nose bleed, so I started calling out for the lead, and he just ignored me and said, "It's not time for your break yet," and walked away. Then eventually Saul brought me out and checked on me and took care of me. Good leadership!

Helen Medina, 2000s

One lead pisses off the other leads because she'll rearrange the shipping office, she'll move the oars and stuff. She is bad. It's one of those things where when we find out she's the lead we all try to ER (early release).

Once a boat died at Trader Sam and instead of using the boat at unload to back up and tow the boat forward, she went backstage and pulled on a new boat to tow the broken down boat to the dock.

Anonymous, 2010s

There was this one lead who everyone liked, but I hated to work with. He was super nice and very gregarious. He was always funny and loved to talk to guests. The problem was, it was nearly impossible to get him to do his job as the lead. If there was a guest concern, he'd be gone.

Once we needed him in the shipping office for an angry guest and he was at front load making small talk with other guests. I sent two people over to get him and finally had to do it myself, and he was so engrossed talking to kids and doing silly voices he couldn't manage the ride. If he wasn't at the dock and we had a downtime, we wouldn't call him until we had resolved it, since he wouldn't be over in time and would probably make it take longer.

Anonymous, 2000s

They brought in a lot of mangers during the Paul Pressler/Cynthia Harris era with no theme park experience. They didn't come up the ranks at Disneyland, so they didn't get the attitude. You could tell who they were right away because they just said "no" to everything. They were mostly worried about keeping their jobs, so any idea was a bad one. Since most of them had worked in retail, you could tell they were used to firing people all the time. They didn't seem to understand that Disneyland invested in its cast members and it was more than just hitting a budget goal.

Anonymous, 2000s

Jungle Cruise leads kept track of the day's events in a large ledger called the log book. Each shift the lead would take a moment to write a paragraph or two about the day's events.

I think Disney saw a lot of liability. The whole idea behind a log book was to say okay, this is what happened, but they became like these big narratives of the skipper's day. It could have been somebody's fantasy adventure, depending on who was writing it. I think at some point the company realized that all this stuff might hurt them during a lawsuit if a lawyer got his hands on a log book and read through it.

Jerry Whitfield, 1980s

I hated it when you were on the dock in a boat and you said something and then you'd see the lead go write in the log book. You didn't know if it was about you or not, but it drove me crazy. They would never show us what was in it.

Anonymous, 2000s

I got to be an emergency lead at Jungle a few times and the first time I did it, I grabbed that lead log and started reading. I was convinced it was full of gossip and slander and other fun things. It was so deadly boring. Sometimes it was a list of good hourly counts, crowd size, the weather, people who'd been warned for going way off-script. One lead had been an animator for *The Simpsons*, so he never wrote anything, just drew a picture to represent the day.

David John Marley, 2000s

I worked a lot of night shifts and we had a lead who used to be an animator for *The Simpsons*. There is a lead log where you write down the things that happened that day. I don't scare easy, insects don't bother me, I don't get startled easily, and I'm not fazed by a lot of things. I'm sitting there and I'm unloading a boat and I have my hat on and I'm going through my whole unload spiel. I can see from the corner of my eye something drop down. I look and it's a huge spider staring me in the face. And I just lost it, because I'm wondering whether it's a brown recluse, a black widow? What the hell is this thing and I screamed, I mean I screamed just like a little girl. I have never done that in my whole life. I screamed so bad. Everyone on the dock was laughing at me, all the guests are laughing at me, it was so funny that I got scared by this thing that I ran off the boat. I don't care, dude, I ran off the boat. The lead documents this, animates me *Simpsons* style, on the boat with the spider coming down and me freaking out. It was a real spider. I remember him documenting and drawing, and I asked him what he was drawing. I look and it's me. He said "That's you and it's going in the book." I wish I had that picture. It would have been the only picture of me in my Jungle Cruise outfit. I don't have any pictures of me in costume for Jungle Cruise.

Tameem Sabry, 2000s

Sometimes Disney executives will come to the Jungle Cruise and inadvertently cause panic.

There was one time when we got an unexpected visit from the resort's president and vice president, Michael Colglazier and Mary Niven. We immediately loaded them on the nearest boat and sent them on their way. Now the skipper had no idea who they were and as they left into the jungle, we all started sweating. Even the lead, who is normally a calm, quiet, direct person, was scurrying around the dock looking for every piece of trash he could find and was picking them up. Very soon their boat came back. I unloaded them and turned to tell the skipper who they were when I saw that she already was being told and with tears in her eyes she said, "No, it wasn't!" She turned to the lead and asked, "Am I going to get fired?" He looked right back at her and said, "No… not immediately. He needs to send an email to her. She needs to send an email to somebody else and you'd find out in about two weeks. Move it up, Skip!" Her face was priceless. She still works here, by the way.

Eddie Agin, 2010s

I had a manager who rode my boat and I got in trouble for a few of the jokes that I did. You're at the gorilla camp where you would see the big explosion. As we approach that scene, I would say, "Oh my gosh, everyone look, there's Ariel, the Little Mermaid is here with us today!" And then the water would just explode and I'd turn to the boat and say, "Fish sticks, anyone?"

Javi Gonzalez, 2000s

Skippers are great at taking a good idea and running it into the ground. Here's my tale. There was this old joke that we started doing when *Pirates of the Caribbean* came out in 2004. The joke was, "In honor of the new movie, if you go over to the Pirates of the Caribbean ride, they will pierce your ears. It only costs a buck an ear." Some skipper took that joke and added, "I'm kidding, this is Disneyland, it will cost you $35 and ear." So I started doing both of those. After the Haunted Mansion movie starring Eddie Murphy came out, and promptly bombed, I added this line, "And if you go over to the Haunted Mansion, in honor of their movie, they will give you an apology." A week later a lead heard me say it, laughed just a bit, then came over to my boat, and said, "That was funny, don't ever say it again."

David John Marley, 2000s

Being a manager at Adventureland has to be one of the truly thankless jobs in the universe. Most cast members are horrified when they do something wrong or upset a guest. Some skippers seem to revel in it.

Dave comes and it's his second day as manager. I think Dave is one of the most stand-up men, he is Jungle in the purest sense. I'm a bit of an ass. He comes down there and I always had a problem with authority, and he comes down there and I'd just done a trip, and Andrew was in the boat in front of me. He would also go very slow, so I'm kind of riding his butt on the tour. He would start a joke and I yell and finish the joke behind him. Well, Dave comes down and he goes, "Jeremy, you know I think it is bad show that you are going around the jungle and going so fast, you need to slow it down and give the guests an experience." I said, "All my guests are laughing and I haven't had any complaints, I've been doing it now for three years, I'm the longest skipper here right now." "But it's just good show, slow it down." "Slow it down, you got it." So I load up the next boat and ask, "You guys ready for a good tour?" Yeah! "You ready for a long tour?" Yeah! Fifty-three minutes later, I come back into the dock area. I had six boats behind me, I heard them idling out there, I hear the radio calling me, did you 6 shot? But I just ignored it, I didn't stop talking for the entire 53 minutes. I told the history of the thing, I answered questions about Space Mountain, I did everything I could, and they were all laughing, and behind me I could see a train of boats. I was mad, because a manager that has been here two days is coming up to me and telling me to slow down because this is bad show. By the time I get back, I get a rousing applause and the whole dock is full; the line went from 10 minutes to 45 minutes. They did a triple unload, the front load, one boat in the middle of the catwalk, one boat right there, and the one boat at front load because we were so backed up. I go, "Slow enough for you, Skip?" I got moved to Tiki the rest of the shift and for the rest of the week I did Tiki. He couldn't write me up because technically I followed instructions, nobody complained, and the next week he had to give me a compliment because one of the guests went to City Hall to report. I will never forget that.

Jeremy Wayland, 2000s

Managers? They rotated around a lot and I never understood them. I think the managers want to make sure the guests are happy and satisfied, no liability shit happening. I think the original west-side managers we had when I hired in were very fair and they would look the other way, then I feel like they had a management shuffle which Disney does, and they brought in all the east side managers. East side was like red state vs. blue state. They were a lot more "what would Walt do." They were a lot more rigid in the sense of park operations and I think they just didn't understand what weird anomaly the Jungle Cruise was. So the east-side management would come in and start holding people more strictly to certain rules. It was east-side managers I didn't vibe with. The west-side managers let me do my thing, but let me know they were there and not to cross the big line whatever that would be. But the east-side managers didn't judge things by situation to situation, they said this is the Disney law and this is what we are going to enforce and that's it.

When I left in the summer of 2002, the tone of the whole attraction had changed. Starting from the management, I don't resent it, they were just doing their job, but they didn't get it whereas the original west-side managers got it. It made the west-side managers look pretty good. So, it is kind of like the kids book where the teacher has a bunch of horrible students then she goes sick for a couple weeks, then they have a horrible substitute teacher, then it ends up being her and she was in costume the whole time. Then they are like, "Oh, we are so sorry we were jerks to you." Management, they got on me a lot but they couldn't actually indict me on anything because I didn't get guest complaints. If I got one, it was rare; all my jokes even if they were pushing it, they weren't offensive. They were coming from a place of pain or there were skippers that were totally LOG, but they went totally on script but had low energy about them and would get complaints. It's like, what did they do? They didn't do anything; she just seems awful and unhappy. Then they started to do jokes about the animatronics, but I never told them in the tone of I hate my life and I hate my job.

Ritt Mesee, 2000s

CHAPTER ELEVEN

In the Tiki Tiki Tiki Tiki Tiki Room

While the Jungle Cruise opened with the park in 1955, Walt Disney's Enchanted Tiki Room didn't open until 1963. They've been linked ever since. Skippers were often cross-trained at the Tiki Room and for decades getting trained at Jungle Cruise meant being trained at Tiki, too. Even today, usually the first day of training at Jungle Cruise is spent at the Tiki Room. It's only been during the last few years that people, usually veteran cast members, have been trained at Tiki but not at Jungle. Sometimes due to the physicality of working the Jungle Cruise skippers get injured, and are only allowed to work Tiki. Whatever reason brings them there, skippers are sure to bring the jungle with them.

I tend to fall asleep when I'm bored, and one night I was working Tiki. I started the show, and I'm leaning back on the stool that is by the control booth, and I fall asleep. Not until I hear the standing ovation do I realize that I've been asleep and everyone is standing but can't figure out where to go because I haven't opened the exit door yet. They didn't open automatically then, you had to hit the button.

Dave Lewis, 1970s

During the 1960s and 1970s, the Tiki Room and Treehouse were considered to be one attraction.

We used to seed money on the beds and fountains at Tiki and Treehouse. You'd go in the morning and you'd go up to the bedroom and toss some coins onto the bed and if you were really good you'd take a dollar bill and fold it like a paper airplane and set it on the bed as well. And over at Tiki you'd toss coins into the fountain. At the end of each day we'd take the money and we'd save it and use it for a party at the end of the year for the crew who worked there.

John Verdone, 1970s

I was a lead at Tiki one summer. Tiki Tree was a rotation, summer of early 90s, you just go and do the same show over and over. You wake up when the storm hits. The only creative outlet I had was the log book. I would sit there and write these really fanciful logs, and it was the story about the Tiki show, when Jose says, "I wonder what happened to Rosita?" So I made up this really complicated backstory about who Rosita was. Every day I would write a new chapter, Rosita was in love with Jose, but Jose's evil twin brother Rodolfo would play upon her affections and she ended up living on the street. It was Fritz who came upon her living on the streets and told her to come back because she was the original bird on the bird mobile. Rosita says no, and she runs off into the night never to be seen again. So every time Jose asks, "I wonder what ever happened to Rosita," a tear trickles down Fritz's beak.

Larry Kaml, 1980s

Every attraction has these log books. They were really thick books like old-time ledgers. And the Tiki Room was the best one. You were supposed to write about how the day went and what other events happened, any significant events. This is how you communicated to the next shift. It became a great work of creative writing; people would write all kinds of wild stories in it. During Tiki shifts it was fun to go back to the pages and see all the crazy things that people had written. It vanished one day and nobody knew what happened. Somebody stole it or management took it, but it was gone.

John Verdone, 1970s

Tiki Room terrifies me. Training Tiki is very short, maybe three hours. I started one show, and I didn't even know that it was my PA, and it was my first time speaking in front of a group of people at Disneyland, so I was terrified. I still don't feel comfortable there because I only did that one time. Tiki to me is so much more intimidating than Jungle Cruise. I'm not as familiar with it. I will always remember how terrified I was of the Tiki Room.

Maureen McLandrich, 2010s

I'm not sure that I ever got trained at Tiki, I think I was just sent over there. The guy showed me how to do it and that was it. It's not exactly complicated; you just push a button. However, I was there during the very brief time they decided the people working at Tiki should be part of the show. The job used to be you push a button then you go to the break room and read the newspaper for 15 minutes. But someone decided that during the part of the show where they sing, "Let's all sing like the birdies sing," that the attractions host or hostess should go out and lead everybody in singing, and reach out to the four different sections of the audience. It was horrible.The music was playing so you really couldn't do anything, you just kind of did this sing-along. I never saw a single guest decide to sing more because we were out there running around singing. You can only face one quarter of the room at a time, so half the time people were looking at the side of your back. But most of the time they were not looking at you, they were too busy looking up. It lasted for maybe a month. I think nobody would go do it.

John Verdone, 1970s

I knew the Tiki Room. I loved it. It was great. We had the white pants and the neon orange shirt. So I would do Tiki and I loved Maynard, and I watched him and what he was doing. And if people watched me, it was because I watched Maynard. I loved working the Tiki Room. I don't know if it was allowed, but I would come out and do an interactive thing with the show. I would dance around and grab a kid and dance in a circle with them. I saw Maynard do stuff like that. I had this little pre-show I would do in front of the Tiki Room doors and I would announce the upcoming show. Part of my spiel was to say that the birds were friendly and not surly. I would get kids excited about the show.

Brian Vestal, 2000s

Another legendary skipper who loved to work the Tiki Room was the late Andrew Peterson.

He loved those birds. He posted on his Facebook page, "I hit birds with a stick for a living."

Brandon Kleyla, 2000s

I worked at the enchanted Tiki Room for the *Pirates of the Caribbean* premier and nobody came. I guess if you were there to see a movie premier you didn't want to waste your time at Tiki. I just did the greeter and watched the red carpet. It was really awesome.

Tiffany Davis, 2000s

The Tiki Room used to be a three-man rotation: one person working the turnstile, one person in the show, and one person on a 20-minute break. It was fantastic. Then management changed it to a two-person rotation, and they'd send a skipper over to give you a 10-minute break. During my last two years there, they usually only had one cast member working Tiki. You would start the show, then run back out to help greet people, answer questions, help handicapped guests, then run back in to exit the show, then bring in the next group. Good Jungle leads would send over people to give you your break or a lunch, but you often had to call over and remind them that you were alive.

David John Marley, 2000s

When they started cracking down on the Tiki Room is when I knew it was time to quit. A long time ago it used to be a three-man rotation, then they made it two, then they came and said that you can never sit in the Tiki Room office under any circumstances. Managers would hang out by the back exit of Big Thunder to watch us at Tiki. It was a lot of the union leads who worked there, so maybe that is why Disney cracked down on them, but they were watching us all of the time and it became less fun.

Javi Gonzalez, 2000s

One lucky skipper has had the chance to work the Enchanted Tiki Room on both coasts.

I got to work the Enchanted Tiki Room in Florida for one shift. It was a cross-utilization shift while I was working for Adventures by Disney. They had us all go out for a day and work a location that didn't have any safety sign-offs required, so I got to work and watch that show. It was fun to work there. The cast members were super cool and wanted to hear about how our Tiki Room worked because it was different. I got to wake up José on two sides of the country.

Tiffany Davis, 2000s

My mom and my dad fell in love in the Tiki Room. I don't know much about the details. Imagine if your brother married your wife's sister, two different families, but married, so that's kind of how they met in New York and they went to Disneyland in California, they moved out here, my mom's family, so that's where they fell in love, in the Tiki Room. Several years later I'm born and my dad passed away and guess where I'm working? The Tiki Room. Working Disneyland was very therapeutic for me, because I'm working where my parents fell in love, and my sister worked in Tiki Room, too. I love working Tiki when I can. It was relaxing for me, even though it was boring. Just to sit and wait for Jose and wait for all the celebrating and coming out.

Tameem Sabry, 2000s

This story isn't funny, it's tragic, but once a guy died during the show. It happened to a buddy of mine. He was in the Tiki office reading the newspaper and a guy died and nobody knew it until the show was over. My friend went out to open the next show and he saw everyone huddled around this one guy.

Dave Lewis, 1970s

We used to play a game called "Jose like me better," which I played with Kipp. This is a wonderful game and works better with a boy and a girl, but you can use it with anybody. You spend the whole time outside as greeter, both of you, and you make it clear you are fighting over Jose's affections. "Oh, Jose told me last week that I'm his favorite and he loves me so much, and he tells me this every time I work this shift." And he'd say "No, Jose told me that I'm the best." And you go on for as long as you can so that when someone starts the show, and they say they're going to wake up Jose, the other person comes bursting out with, "No, no, I'm Jose's favorite, so I'm going to wake him up!" Then obviously he picks a girl so you walk away with, "Ha, he likes me better." I loved playing this.

Siobhan Armstrong

You're supposed to speak Hawaiian in the Tiki Room, not Spanish.

I was training new skippers. This was my first group. Two gals that were very different from each other. Elizabeth's grandfather had some design input on the Tiki Room, so I figured she was a sure thing to pass her PA, etc. Nope. She was too terrified to spiel in the boat even with no guests. We ended up recasting her to Indy where she thrived. Anyway, we were training at Tiki and it was Elizabeth's turn to do the opening spiel. So I hand her the mic and this is what happened. Elizabeth: "Hola!" This was followed by complete silence except for me and her training partner. I was crying I was laughing so hard. But I figured she'd catch the mistake and make the adjustment. So, with even more vigor, "Oh come on, you can do better than that. Hola!" Still silence and confusion except for one lone voice from the far side of the theater. "¿Como esta?"

Kipp Hart, 2000s

Not everyone enjoyed working at the Tiki Room.

I didn't appreciate Tiki because I wanted to be in the boat. I felt Tiki was a punishment, and I always thought that was a good place if you were starting to get hoarse and lose your voice, that was a good spot to go, or if you were sick or not in a good mood, that was always a good kind of purgatory, but just being put there, I didn't like it. It was a lot of you standing there with a lot of guests coming at you asking questions about Dole Whip. And you hit a button and that was it, that was your half hour. It just made the day feel like it was 20 hours long. You weren't part of anything, you just hit a button, and I felt like anybody could be there and at the same time I also felt there were a lot of people on Jungle that didn't like being in the boat and spieling, and why not give them that? I loved being in the boat. I loved it.

Ritt Mesee, 2000s

CHAPTER TWELVE

Work Life

How did skippers feel about working the Jungle Cruise all the time? This chapter is a collection of thoughts of what it was like to work there in good times and bad, rain or sun, with good guests or a boat full of people who didn't understand a word you were saying.

This is a whole little weird frat anomaly within the Disney corporation itself. It's so golden and G-rated all the time.

Ritt Mesee, 2000s

When you hire in, there're guys that were there three or four years ahead of you, and they're still around. These guys were like gods. You look up to them in awe. What I didn't realize until I left the park was that to the group behind you, you were that guy. This is always true. The new people look up to these cool people, who are not really cool. I'd love to see where these people went with their lives. It was like high school, but at Disneyland everyone was at the same socio-economic ladder and when we left the park we went our own ways. Then we kind of go back to our roots. Some guys end up driving a bus while others become a VP of some huge corporation. We had this link, this commonality, that we were funny. We were all those kinds of guys. That was my fraternity. I wasn't in one in college, but I had my Jungle Cruise friends.

John Verdone, 1970s

I had a lot of seniority by the time I got there, so I already worked with a lot of these guys, even the old-timers knew me from my character days. So I wasn't treated like a newbie.

I enjoyed the routine of it. You took three trips, then you spent some time on the dock at a position and then you took a break, got back into a dock position, and then back into the boat. I really enjoyed that routine. I also really enjoyed driving the boat. It was different because on the rafts and the keelboat you actually had to steer them, at the time the Jungle Cruise boats ran on rails underneath the water.

Tom Nabbe, 1960s

Other attractions are about amazing effects, and jostling, and Jungle Cruise is about as analog as it gets. The ride is making fun about how ancient it is, that's where the jokes are. I think that's the beauty of it, where you had a deprecating view of Disneyland, it's part of what makes something more charming anyway. A good comedian will be judgmental and opinionated about stuff, but self-deprecating first, and it sets you apart from just being a judgmental dick versus I'm just judgmental including myself. To have this happen at Disney where everything is so elevated and refined and expensive, I think it's important and adds perspective to the whole character of the park. When you go on Jungle Cruise you get to sit for 10 minutes and the line is short and it's funny; everything else is Lucas effect, craziness, then there is Jungle Cruise. And it is the people that make it and the culture shifts, too. I think I hired in at a really interesting time, but I think I saw I came in on a down slope, it was calmer, and it got more managed and became swallowed up by the more Disney-ness.

I found it interesting that an average Joe could go in there and you'd have to audition for it as an actor. The amazing pros and cons are that you have some amazing people in there that wouldn't have gotten in there, but you also have a lot of skippers that clearly don't want to be there.

Ritt Mesee, 2000s

So there are two types of guys. I always felt this construct is fascinating. When you went to wardrobe and you worked the Jungle Cruise, did you choose a straw hat or a felt hat? I think people were picking those based on their personality type. The straw hat guys were the guys I liked. They were the irreverent crazy guys, and the guys who were more strait-laced and buttoned-up they got felt hats. I have no proof of this, but I believe it with all of my being. So I think the hiring process for the Jungle Cruise should be simple: there should just be two hats on the table. Tell people to pick a hat. If they pick a straw hat, they get the job. If they pick the felt hat, they have to work somewhere else in the park.

John Verdone, 1970s

I didn't ever work another attraction that wasn't Jungle related. Tiki Room or Treehouse. The misfits...even if you go to church there are some kids in the back that are not into it. Disney culture had an old-school, east side, Fantasyland kind of Disney, and Jungle Cruise was its counterpoint. As much as we were misfits, it was an accepted, refreshing counterpoint. Everyone in the park got it. Even if there were people that said either I want to be there or I don't , we always sat in the back of the shuttles, the riffraff in the back. You see your standard cop, clean-cut, button-down, Boy Scout-looking police officer. Then you see one of those renegade, Denzel Washington kind of bad cop or you see military and they are very military. It was a little more lax in the way that everyone had their Disney badge on and we were like, meh. We are still going to do the job, but he had our own rulebook. And I liked being in that zone.

Ritt Mesee, 2000s

I worked with this one guy who had the worst breath. You didn't notice it while talking to him, but if you shared a boat with him the mic would have this horrible smell. It made me gag. So I started keeping bleach wipes with me and once just told him that I had a cold and needed to use my own mic. He was a super-funny guy so I don't think anybody wanted to tell him.

Anonymous, 1990s

One day I got to work and we were really understaffed. It was the lead, Gerry, two other skippers, and myself. The Jungle Cruise can have 18 or more people working when it's really busy, and in the morning we usually have seven people for the first hour, but on this day we only had four. So for the first hour we only ran one boat. We had to move the two other boats at the dock backstage to make room. One skipper was at load, one skipper was on the boat, and the third was at unload. When the boat came back, Gerry would come out and help unload, since that requires two people. While the boat was in the jungle, he was busy talking to scheduling about getting more people in. It was hard work, but a really fun bonding time between us.

David John Marley, 2000s

There is a great picture in the shipping office of everybody backstage right by the gas pipe that says no smoking and everybody lighting up. Everybody smoked on Jungle Cruise at that time. I didn't smoke, but everybody smoked.

Jeremy Wayland, 2000s

One of the most common words that people use to describe the experience of being a skipper is fraternity. Here are some examples.

Being a skipper means you are part of a fraternity. The Jungle Cruise always felt like a fraternity with females. Meanwhile, people that work at Disneyland are part of a very cool club that almost anybody can join, but skippers were a special fraternity within that club. It's unique to be able to tell people that you are a cast member at Disneyland, but being a Jungle Cruise skipper is more elite. Jungle does have more outgoing personalities. If you're working attractions at Disneyland, you have to be a bit of an extrovert; being at Jungle you will sink without that ability. We've seen it happen. We've seen skippers fade away and never cross those rocks again.

Tiffany Davis, 2000s

I would get in trouble and skip classes at college. I would call into scheduling and ask who's on the crew today. If I liked what I heard, I would just turn my car out of the parking lot. So I ended up missing a lot of classes to go do Jungle Cruise. I didn't really have a frat kind of experience when I was in college. When you think of going to college and it's going to be huge and open up your mind, and I went and it was quiet and buttoned down. Jungle Cruise was where I got that satisfaction where you feel like you were part of the community. People at Jungle Cruise wanted to be there, unlike some of the other attractions. I had to go through all this corporate conglomerate to get hired and I lucked out on getting Jungle Cruise by accident because the guy next to me didn't show up. I would have left if I didn't get that job.

Ritt Mesee, 2000s

I love the camaraderie among the skippers. What we do is very unique and very special to Disneyland. The closing crew is like my family. I don't work that many day shifts, I work nights. And I think nights are more fun. The skippers know when you have a bad day and will help you have a better day. That is great because in other attractions they don't have that same sense of camaraderie. We keep that funny attitude with each other as well. It's a much more laid-back working environment, which I love. The people who work there know how to take a joke. The banter in the joking back and forth is what makes the Jungle Cruise really fun.

Maureen McLandrich, 2010s

It was my second day at Jungle and I was at the shipping office with Kim, Eddie, and Mike. Kim and Eddie were doing something stupid about how they couldn't see without their glasses and Eddie, who I didn't know at this point, turned to me and said, "Are you blind, too?" and I just blanked and said "WHAT?" really loudly and Mike turned to me and said, "Yeah, she's gonna be fine here." It was such a heart-warming moment and I knew I was in and I used the worst joke I'd ever told. That summarizes what it was like coming in, how welcoming everyone was. My enthusiasm wasn't seen as weird, the attitude of everyone seemed to be "cool, she wants to be here! Let's welcome her and give her the best experience possible."

J'Amy Pacheco, 2010s

It's one of those attractions and we've seen so much turnover on the attractions, people seem to be made for it, people who grow into it, and then there are those that don't want to be there, it's not their fault, but they don't have the same energy. When you have someone that generally wants to be there, I say bring them on.

Jeff Bautista, 2000s

It was just kind of the way things were. Storybook was all female. Disney's spin was that these are characters in the show so the skipper is a male character. It's a holdover from *The African Queen*. I remember we had this joke we were doing for a while. We're pulling away from the dock, we would get the people in our boat to make fun of the people that were still in line. We'd chant things like, "We're on the boat and you're not," and then we yell "Neener Neener Neener." A couple of days later, I don't know who wrote it on this big board in the back, it was probably Don Chapman who was the lead, but he wrote, "Jungle Cruise skippers are men and men do not say Neener Neener Neener." So that joke was quickly struck from the record.

Andrew Green, 1980s

At the end of the summer everybody jumped in the water. They did the same thing over at rafts, everybody went swimming. Of course the edict came down that if you go for a swim at the end of summer you will not be rehired, but nobody cared. I don't know if Disney ever did that or not.

Tom Nabbe, 1960s

You cannot live or die with any boat. If you get a good boat, great, pat yourself on the back, but you are going into a next boat. You cannot carry that funny over, you cannot carry that humor over, you cannot carry that vibe over from boat to boat. If you find a boat that is not laughing, do not push the extreme, do not tell risqué jokes, we all had our non-SOP jokes that we went to, and I said if you are not feeling it, go SOP, and go do the next boat. I see too many skippers that try to make everybody laugh as opposed to giving the tour itself. They would push the extreme and that's how they get a guest concern or a complaint. It is about reading your boat. If you've got 19 people laughing but three in the back giving you the dead eye, don't push it trying to tell the Pocahontas joke. As soon at that boat got out, I never gave them a second thought, never thought about the people, and just went to the next boat. I'm here to shake the pixie dust off you, you are going to get as much out of this ride as you put into it. If you enjoy it every day, you're going to have a fun time. But at the end of the day, this is a job, you are not a stand-up comic.

Jeremy Wayland, 2000s

I remember sleeping on the back boats before a shift, getting there early and sitting out in the jungle. Jungle in the morning was one of the best experiences. You got out there and you are eating your Egg McMuffin and you're sitting in the shipping office and you are just sitting there and someone tells you, "You are going in front load." Oh, fuck you, everybody...

Jeremy Wayland, 2000s

Working at the World-Famous Jungle Cruise is a bonding experience that transcends time. I have talked with skippers who worked at Disneyland in the 1950s and we swapped stories like we had worked together.

You hear about how the presidents have their own president's club because they know what they are going through; it just like that to me. It was something that we all get even if we worked different periods, we all know there's going to be one group of people that will always get you. There's going to be moments when you can't bring yourself to be entertaining in any sort of way, you are just having a bad day. There're other days when you are just being silly and you throw caution to the wind. Some days you are emboldened. We all have experienced that range of emotions, that was always my favorite part. And we are all beasts.

Jeff Bautista, 2000s

The one thing that is really cool is that Jungle is a family. I know every area of the park says that, but at Jungle it's true. Some people loved Seaside, but you didn't see them very often and Fantasyland was like a bunch of little families. People who came in together and stuck together. But with Jungle you can meet someone that you've never seen in your life and they will have your back and you have theirs. It is such a supportive group. From leads to people who have been there for two minutes. It's something I haven't seen at any other attraction.

The workload is different. Fantasyland classics is all about efficiency, but Jungle is about making people laugh. So you ride boats and tell guests funny jokes and encourage them.

J'Amy Pacheco, 2010s

I remember at the time hating things there, but I also remember some of my best times and best friends of my life I met over on that ride. I remember trying to ER a lot or get shifted over to monorail or trying to go out with one particular girl, or you try to avoid her so you go over to Indy for a little bit, and then you dated an Indy girl and it didn't work out so you go back over to Jungle Cruise, and hating it at the time, but looking back, I remember one night was a Grad Nite and we are all sitting on the boat and prepping and sharing tales from high school and I'm looking around and we all got out drinks from the place by the manager's office. One of the guys got the key to the soda machine and brought down a whole bunch of sodas and we're just sitting on the boat sharing stories and I remember rocking out in the boat and the jungle is around and thinking this is my happy place.

Jeremy Wayland, 2000s

This bond wasn't random, it was something deliberately created and maintained.

Kaz telling us "What happens in the jungle, stays in the jungle." Upstairs in the attic of the Enchanted Tiki Room or sometimes on the roof by the ABC camera. Key to the story is that she was instilling the culture of the Jungle Cruise to the next generation of skippers. At every other attraction, people write statements and complain to managers; at the Jungle Cruise we proudly took care of our own. People who showed up and loved to write statements didn't last too long.

David John Marley, 2000s

I've never had a job like it before or since. A place where you could be totally in the moment yet out of the moment at the same time. It's hard to explain. It was such a cool place. I love the camaraderie of the place, even after you leave the park. I mean, I never worked with you, but I feel like I did, there is this instant connection that Jungle gives.

Mark Mendoza, 2000s

I think it was the fact that it was a giant playground that you show up, looking like Indiana Jones, I would wear a German map bag around my chest and I would keep the maps in the map bag for the kids. I had my leopard print around my hat. I think it was just the fact that I get paid to go to Disneyland, which is pretty great on its own, I get a six shooter, a boat, and I get to drive around the jungle. That's pretty bad ass.

Brandon Kleyla, 2000s

It was still a tradition that all of the skippers parked at the third stop at K lot. If you parked anywhere else you would just get yelled at and shit on the whole time. Every skipper knew you had to park at the third stop.

Javi Gonzalez, 2000s

The challenge of being a theater person, someone trained to be in front of people and engage them. When people walk into your boat, you throw out a couple of jokes to see what they are going to respond to and tailor your spiel, so it was a challenge as a performer to try and read my audience. It has prepared me so much for being a teacher. You do the same thing with your classroom. I like being on and being the center of attention.

Larry Kaml, 1980s

It seemed to be very clicky and political. I showed up and just wanted to have fun. I remember one day I rolled in and I had made my animal band, I got my ass reamed. Not by the leads, but from the guys who had been there forever. "You don't do that, you earn that." Nobody told me, so I said, "You guys need to calm down, this is Disneyland, just take a deep breath." From that point on, up in scheduling if I saw what guys were there, I said if he's there that day, I'm just calling out that day, I'm not dealing with it. Mainly it was only three people, but I said, hey this is Jungle, beside your trips aren't that good anyhow, so just calm down.

Brandon Kleyla, 2000s

I had this one shift that was just terrible. It was the longest night of my life. And since I told Disney I'd work 7 days a week I was on my 30th day of working during my first summer. I got a late break for lunch, the fireworks are going off, and I wanted to kill myself. I see Jeffery and the lead chatting and I'm so done, but the person at load, Ashley, knows how tired I am and sent me on a deadhead. As soon as I cleared the Indy queue I put the boat on its slowest speed and I lit up a cigarette. I didn't pay attention to anything. So after that, anytime I had a deadhead it became a smoke break. Smoking in the jungle was such a surreal experience because the animals look so fake just sitting there in the darkness.

Mark Mendoza, 2000s

I know most people would say the camaraderie between the skippers and that was certainly part of it, but for me it was the performing aspect. I really loved being front of a crowd. I love to tell jokes. It wasn't my life's calling, it was a summer job, so the shine, the excitement, never wore off. I work two nights mostly. I discovered that if I volunteered to work the midnight shifts I would often get weekends off. Working night shifts meant they would often send you to work parades so you do fewer trip,s but I also like working at nights because there was less pressure because the attraction was much less crowded.

The camaraderie aspect was important, but it was kind of a bifurcated experience between some of the skippers. There was a big group of us that were college students going to some elite schools. We were just there for the summer kind of in and out, and then there were the full-time employees, and their long-term career prospects are very different from our long-term career prospects, and they weren't as welcoming to those of us that were clearly just going to be there for the summer. I recognized that there was a full-time group of people that worked there and they realize that we were all just short-termers. A bunch of the guys that I worked with were pre-law or pre-med; one guy was pre-engineering, so they just had a different mindset.This is just a fun summer job so when people give us crap we really didn't care. We didn't care about the politics of it all, having the lead get mad at you never bothered me. I mean, who cares, because in three months I will be back in school. I wasn't gunning for the big promotion, I wasn't trying to be a trainer or a lead. That didn't matter to me. I was always a good kid. I always got there on time, so I never had any trouble or run-ins with the leads or managers.

Andrew Green, 1980s

Imagineer Gordon Lemke went from working in foods in Disneyland to attractions and noticed a difference in camaraderie in the two locations.

In foods, everybody worked til closing, so we would go out and do stuff. We used to explore the park or go out to the beach or whatever. In attractions, everybody got off at weird 15-minutes increment, so you really had to work to get even three or four people to go out, where there would be 8 or 10 of us that would go out in foods.

Gordon Lemke, 1980s

One thing that most guests and even cast members don't understand about the Jungle Cruise is that it is a physically demanding job. It's not just standing and talking or pushing a button while seated at a control panel. Working Jungle means having one foot on the dock and one on a rocking boat while you help people in or out of a boat. You will catch people, have them fall and so on. Then you have to drive a boat and entertain people. An eight-hour shift at Jungle Cruise is exhausting.

It was very physical. People didn't talk too much about that, but if you are working unload you not only had to squat, you had to reach down and get the cushion below where you were squatting, so every minute you were doing a full squat, grab the cushion.

Gordon Lemke, 1980s

They're insane, you have to be wacky, and about 7 degrees off of true north, to be able to work there. People that aren't a little crazy and work there for the summer quit, or they are there for the summer and ask to be trained somewhere else. They thought it wasn't for them. They were in the boat for 8 hours a day and if you are not somebody who wants attention, then you are going to burn out pretty quickly. And I found that my experience at Jungle Cruise prepared me to be an elementary school teacher a whole lot more than getting my degree at Chapman University. It's the same thing; you've got a crew of 30 kids, and you've got to entertain them and connect with them, make sure they are going to be paying attention to you. The only difference is the 8 minutes versus 10 months. You are a Jungle Cruise skipper for 10 months. Same crew.

Larry Kaml, 1980s

I remember the first week of summer when everybody's coming back to work. Everyone would lose their voice. Everyone would get sore throats and lose their voice together. It was hot, we hadn't been talking that much, so our voices were not spiel ready yet. It was a muscle that you had to get back into shape. Plus, we all got sick because we were sharing microphones. We used to have these big spray bottles of bleach. It would take all of us at least a week or so to get our voices ready for the job. What other attraction at Disneyland requires you to use your voice that much? It took awhile to get the rhythm back, to get the timing back for the jokes.

John Verdone, 1970s

The worst things were the days you got sick. The first two months, you got sick because of the humidity because you are touching elbows when you are loading people into the boats. I hated touching people's elbows. I have mild Asperger's, and I have to do these different exercise to be socially adept or aware, and alcohol helps me sometimes, but touching people was the thing I couldn't do. I would do this ghost thing where I'd be a half inch behind their elbow. I'd get caught every once in a while, and then I'd touch it. It was the most awkward thing. I didn't mind helping an older person, but if you were an active fit individual you can get yourself in and out of the boat yourself.

Jeremy Wayland, 2000s

It did take a skill to drive those boats. Yes, they were on a track, but how you loaded you always had to load the front first so that pushed the boat against the dock, cause if you rear load first that would pull it away and that would add more danger of dropping people into the water. Nowadays they have a rope and rollers. If you weren't loading well, they could pull away. If the whole rear load sat down first, and the front load hadn't started, there was a huge gap. That took skill and around 1983, they added that fin on the rear guides, so you couldn't derail as easy. There is a big piece of metal that pushes it down, so usually in the hippo pool if you go fast then slow, that wake lifts you up in that S curve right before you stall, so you would derail. If you wanted to, you could do that. We had the boats without the governors on them, much easier to derail.

Gordon Lemke, 1980s

Some people would say to me, "Wow, being a skipper must be really easy job." And I would tell him, "You try doing three trips for a while, see how well you do." Other cast members thought we just talk to people for a living; they didn't realize the effort it took to do it well. And that we were actually performing. People think it's easy but it's actually very tough.

Javi Gonzalez, 2000s

I remember we had a contest to see who could take the most trips, and I was the last girl standing, but it was a bad idea. My voice was shot.

Andrea Freeman, 2000s

I remember one day I did 37 tours in a row. I went to the bathroom real early and stayed in the boat for 10 hours straight. Cause someone told me, again young and stupid, someone told me they once did a 16-hour shift and I said that I could do that. Stupid!

Jeremy Wayland, 2000s

I was primarily 70 hours a week in Jungle. I made the mistake of checking the "overtime is okay box" in scheduling and man, that's rough. Open to close and you are just, "Oh my god." It's very much the definition of, "Ah, I was young." I had a good time, I have no complaints.

Brandon Kleyla, 2000s

Working in the rain was okay because I had worked at a golf course where we had worked in the rain. What I didn't like was spieling when your throat hurt. When you didn't feel good physically. When you want to ER but you can't because everyone else already has. You get a cold that lasts a couple of weeks and not just days because it keeps getting passed around from sharing microphones.

Dave Lewis, 1970s

Rainy days were fun for me because I remember coming around and loading guests and they are saying, "Oh, the seat's wet." I'm like, "You are dripping right now, that's your problem, sit down." I remember coming around the piranhas one day and it was just pouring and windy and felt like one of the skeletons in Pirates. The wind was cranking, and the rain was coming in sideways, and it was hailing—there was hail bouncing off the boat.

Brandon Kleyla, 2000s

It got to a point where we had been stuck on that ride for so long that we hated it. Everyone had nodes on their vocal chords, they were sick all of the time. Those mics spread disease. We'd spray them all with Lysol, but we'd all get sick. Nobody wanted to work the Jungle Cruise. Even people that didn't know the Jungle Cruise didn't want to work the Jungle Cruise.

Dave Lewis, 1970s

There has to be some term for when a skipper goes cold, when they lose their passion for the attraction. They lose that spark. That happened to me that second summer. The first summer every trip was fun and new, but that second summer for some reason was off. Lauren rode my boat and asked, "What happened? Where did your heart go?" I kept my back to the guests almost the entire trip. I didn't even notice. It was a wake-up call for me. I think what happened was that I had been trained at Big Thunder Mountain and Columbia and you've eaten the apple. You've seen good and evil. You see the sarcasm and the cynicism of the cast members and I was only 17 and I was very impressionable. Whatever everyone else was doing, I was into. At first I was excited to be one of the few guys at Jungle that was thrilled to take a boat. I let people bump around me. But some skippers began to say, "Oh, you're *that* guy." So I tried to fit in and became cynical like the other skippers. It's funny because you don't want to be that way. You want to love it.

I think there were times when you would get that way. I think it was dealing with the guests. "Wow, the guests are so dumb." When you start talking that way, you start to believe it and you miss the opportunity to fill these guests with joy. I think there were a lot of guys who had both sides to them, but I don't think I realized it. They would talk bad about guests backstage, and I let that affect me onstage. I had people bump around me all the time, and I'd have extra long breaks. I remember being allowed to bump around people in your rotation, then they stopped it near the end of my time there. You start out at your unload position and the guy there would say, "Bump around me." So you'd go to the guy in the boat and he'd say, "Bump around me." And then I'd just go back upstairs to the break room. It was strange to have that happen.

Fred Martin, 1980s

You got to the point where you just had enough Jungle; it works you pretty hard. It's one of those jobs where we actually have to work.

John Verdone, 1970s

On an average eight-hour shift, a skipper will do around 25 trips. That means that after a while the spiel becomes automatic and if you are not paying atten-tion you can take a ghost yrip. This is a trip where you remember leaving the dock and then nothing else until you come back to civiliztion.

You go into robot mode sometimes. Once I was doing elephant bathing pool jokes and I look up and realize I'm in the hippo pool.

Kristin Labok-McGuire, 2000s

You get back to the dock and you think, "Where did I go?"

Karen McGuire-Vogelvang, 2000s

I'd been working on my Ph.D. dissertation when I was a skipper. Some days I would bring the manuscript to work and edit it during my breaks and lunch. One day my brain was focused on the book and I walked right onto the boat and started spieling. I remember when I came back because it was the only standing ovation that I ever got in three-and-a-half years. People all stood up and applauded. This couple came over and took their picture with me and were like, "That was amazing, thank you," and I just stood wondering what the hell just happened. I still have no idea what I did, not a clue.

David John Marley, 2000s

What you are thinking about is what I called the "tune outs"; you are talking to someone and they go, "Oh, I just got here," you were thinking you were talking to a guest from three trips ago. You just go with it. You do so many trips in a day you just don't care anymore. The only thing that brought you back to reality was that coming back to the dock was the flashing light and Trader Sam. You throw it quickly into reverse before you derail the thing.

Jeremy Wayland, 2000s

Being tall is usually awesome, but at the Jungle Cruise it comes with a challenge that most tall people have to expect, hitting your head on things, in this case, the boat.

One of the questions on the application at Disneyland is your height. As my paperwork was being processed, a guy from casting said, "You made a mistake on your form. You wrote that you were 6'4" and I can tell that you are 6'3" and three quarters." I told him, "No, I'm not, I'm 6'4!" I'm tall and proud. He replied, "I can tell that you are not 6'4," which is good because people who are 6'4" are too tall to work at Jungle Cruise. So, you're 6' 3" and three-quarters, right?" I got the clue and said, "Right."

About a year later a manager brought a really tall guy to the dock, like 6'8," and asked me if he was too tall to work there. The guy really wanted to work Jungle, so I told the truth, that tall people are pretty good at not banging their heads on things. I always had to stand with my legs apart so I wouldn't hit my head on the top.

David John Marley, 2000s

A lead named Jasen did me a huge favor during this most recent downtime. I told him that when they tied the canopies off to leave with the ropes facing down so the skippers can hang on to them. I asked him if they could not do it that way because it was tough for us taller skippers, and they made that change to every single boat. Now they're tied off above the bar, so it's not rubbing your head and messing with your hair a day long.

Kipp Hart, 2000s

One of the only reasons I'll tell a story about a fellow skipper is because Luis is the one I credit with breaking me out of my non-friendly shell. He called me out on the fact that he would try to make friends with me, but I wouldn't make friends with anyone unless they'd been there for a few months already. Due to the high turnover rate, I stopped making friends with new hires, because I figured they'd be gone in a few weeks and I'd never see them again. Luis changed my outlook to be more accepting of new skips.

Lawrence Janiec, 2010s

On Jungle, time would just fly. One day you'd have 20 boats with about 45 people per boat, on a four man, that's 1,000 per day. I started doing math in my head, that's like a million people have heard my stupid jokes. Like I had control of their lives for 10 minutes. Totally bizarre. I'm not an extrovert, I went to school, and my sister is in theater, but I'm a behind-the-camera kind of person, I don't like getting up in front of class speaking.

Ritt Mesee, 2000s

I'd say 2001 is when they put the governors on the boats. I could get that thing throttling. I can't remember the name of the boat, but I could gun it so much that I'd create a wake that I could throw the other boats off. I had just the right amount of people, and I'm just speeding around Indy going like a bat out of hell all the way around on the thing, I didn't pause, I ran the squirter, I ran right through it and missed it. I was good.

Jeremy Wayland, 2000s

The sporadic cynicism that some skippers would have about the attraction, the park, the guests, and it would sour the guest's experience. You can do it in a dry way, but you are still there to perform. I think it was a wasted opportunity to have some fun. I stopped short of telling people how to do things, but you could tell when someone was phoning it in. This is the Jungle Cruise at Disneyland! How can you not be excited?

Brian Vestal, 2000s

One time I wore the wrong nail polish and my boyfriend got really mad and told me to take it off and we were on a date, not even working. I know people didn't like how relaxed we were at Jungle Cruise. Our drama wasn't as vicious as it was at the rest of the park. Jungle was more chill, we had a weird code of silence.

I liked that every day was different. It depended on who was working and what guests you got. It was never monotonous. It was always fun to come into work wondering what was going to happen that day. What are the guests going to be like today? I wonder who is working and what crazy things can you do. I liked looking at the roster and seeing a name, like Trevor, and knowing that you were going to have a good day. It was fun, especially when I was the only girl, when it was me and a bunch of guys. It was always rowdy and fun. The ratio of guys to girls was always heavily leaning toward guys. The guys would always be pulling jokes on each other. It was so fun. There were only two people I didn't like working with. I loved making guests laugh, but it was mostly seeing your friends and having fun with them. I always hated working another attraction that I tried to switch back to Jungle. Those three months that I was on vocal leave were the worst three months of my life. It was just awful. I was bored out of my mind. I loved Jungle because every day was different. Even on days that sucked and every boat was full of people who wouldn't laugh, at least I got to hang out with my friends. No matter what was going on in your personal life, you could come to Jungle and be silly and it would make you happy.

You have to commit to doing the whole thing. Even if you had a crappy day, you had to give a great show. There was so much pressure in my life and I worked so hard and Jungle was an escape for me. It wasn't real life. You could come and just play. And everybody was always great. You could tell when people didn't like being there, they didn't last very long. They would move to another attraction. Jungle Cruise was the land of misfit toys. Everyone was a little different and a little weird and we all fit in.

Andrea Freeman, 2000s

Ramadan is when you don't eat any food or drink or chew gum; you don't even think about sex. It's that intense, from sunrise to sunset. During Ramadan, I always worked the swing shift, meaning my lunch time was right around sunset, so I would say, "Hey, I need to have a break at this time," and I would explain it and say I hadn't eaten yet, and then they would they say, "Courtesy," and I would say, "I just told you," 8 trips in and I'm just saying fuck it, I would just start bring food on the boat and start eating, I don't care I'm eating onstage. There came a time when I had had enough. It was definitely up there as the worst thing.

Tameem Sabry, 2000s

When I worked at Jungle Cruise I was finishing my Ph.D. In history and teaching at a few colleges part-time around Orange County. Working at Disneyland is what kept me sane as I tried to finish my degree, work on a book, and hunt for a full-time teaching job. Since I wanted to be chill at Jungle, I never told anyone that I was a professor. To them I was just David. One day a lead comes up to me while I'm on break and says, "Are you a history professor?" And I confessed and asked him how he knew. He said, "A bunch of people have come by the shipping office asking if Dr. Marley is working today, and you're the only person named Marley here." My secret was out. A co-worker heard this and said, "Oh, good. I'm glad you have a real job. I thought you were too old to work here full time and too young to have already retired." Soon after, someone named me "Dr. Skipper," and the name stuck.

David John Marley, 2000s

I did this thing with a penny where I would wedge it in the mic to keep the mic on for the entire time. It wasn't fun to be holding that thing down for 8 minutes at a time. So when I left the dock I would wedge the penny in so that I could be more free with my hands and it was a piece of flair sort of thing. It became so routine for me, I would put it in, take it out near Schweitzer Falls for a bit, then put it back in, then take it out again at the dock. One day there was a memo telling us that we couldn't put pennies in the mics because they were always on and it was burning them out and their circuits. It took me awhile to be able to stop using pennies. It was like quitting cigarettes. I like to follow the rules, it wasn't a defiant thing, I would leave the dock, and I used to leave a penny on one of the dials on the boat's control panel, and I stopped leaving them there so I wouldn't put them in the mic. And inevitably I would come back from Trader Sam and I would have a penny in the mic. I was like Smeagol with the one ring; it just kept showing up. It was such a part of my thing. Tiffany Davis was the lead most afternoons, and she would get so mad at me when she saw me with these mystery pennies. It took me awhile to quit the penny.

Michael Libby, 2000s

I always loved what I felt was Walt's heart, that Disneyland was a good place, a place where you can bring your family. There were some people at Disneyland, not just at attractions either, that felt like it was a giant high school. People would love to gossip and be snarky and make fun of annual passholders and make fun of how excited people got about the park. But you can't look at Disneyland as just your workplace; we were making magic everyday. So I never wanted to do anything that would ever mess with people's experiences there.

Brian Vestal, 2000s

When you go to the ticket office there is a log book and it's opened up and it simply has names and the date. It is the list of every skipper before you that has been trained on that attraction. You've been trained as Jungle Cruise. So I'm signing the book with the very same skippers that had been there from the very beginning. It was the time when they started to do Jingle Cruise, adding enhancements, explosions, and piranhas, cause it's not *the* Jungle Cruise that got me, so for me signing that book, it was special because it wasn't just signing the book of everyone before me, it was also the same book that my sister signed.

Tameem Sabry, 2000s

My wife asked me the other day if I missed working at Jungle. I said yes, and she asked whether it ever got old. No, because every 8 minutes was new. Yeah, I said the same stuff, but none of the reactions were going to be the same, the guests aren't the same, and I'm playing off of them.

I don't know what's going to happen. I never got tired of it, even after 70-hour weeks.

Brandon Kleyla, 2000s

Some Disneyland cast members work all year long at the park while others are only there for the summer and holidays.

What was interesting about being seasonal is that I would finish up classes in Santa Barbara on Friday and I would be scheduled for a shift on Saturday. I had no update training or anything. I would just show up and jump in a boat, having not done it for 3 or 4 months. I can't imagine they do that nowadays. I was fine after a couple of trips around the jungle.

Vince Fragasso, 1980s

There was always the canoe guys vs. the Jungle Cruise thing. The difference was athletes versus actors. The guys in the Jungle Cruise were more the comedian/actor/entertainment type crowd, with a geeky quality that goes with it. And then the canoe guys are more the knuckle-dragger guys. I hear this from my wife, because my wife and I met at the park and we got married. She told me that people thought the canoe guys were always cooler and thought the Jungle Cruise guys were geeks. Well, whatever.

Jerry Whitfield, 1980s

Here is what fascinates me about the people at the Jungle Cruise. There were people like me who took to it naturally and had that kind of personality. Those became my closest friends at the Jungle Cruise. Then there were people who clearly shouldn't be there, often times they were As or Bs which meant they have been there a long time. It was the only place where there were hours for some of the older guys. People that were irreverent were the ones I liked the most.

John Verdone, 1970s

CHAPTER THIRTEEN

Celebrities Are People, Too

Jungle Cruise skippers have a unique relationship with guests, and that includes celebrities. A skipper will spend more alone time with a Disneyland guest than will any other cast member, which is sometimes the problem when those guests are VIPs.

I had the president of China on my boat. I forget his name [Li Xiannian]; it was the summer of 1985. It was only him and his party and skippers told stories that there were snipers in the jungle to protect him. They had me empty my gun and I couldn't take it with me. It was pretty cool. I got a picture with me and him.

Vince Fragasso, 1980s

I had Hugh Hefner with two bunnies. He didn't look at me once and it seemed like he really didn't want to be there. The bunnies also looked like they could care less.

Andrea Freeman, 2000s

When Hef and the bunnies were backstage, every XY chromosome disappeared. They left safety positions and said, "Hey, you got this, right?" Oh sure.

Kat Thrailkill, 2000s

One time Steve Martin came by the park and was hanging out in the Adventureland break room to see Wally Boag. Everyone went up to meet him, and I was stuck in the boat. Back in those days he was the biggest comic and we were all trying to be like Steve Martin. We would do these "wild and crazy" spiels and do every punchline and every joke.

George Trullinger, 1970s

A skipper once had Jimmy Fallon on his boat and afterwards Fallon said to him, "Oh, you were kind of funny," so the skipper said, "Oh, good, one of us was." Not everybody can throw that back in their face like that.

Anonymous, 2010s

I had Marvin Hamlisch on my boat and he was an easy audience. He laughed at everything. By the time he rode my boat I knew that I wasn't the funniest skipper out there, so I didn't let it go to my head. He was the only celebrity that I had at the Jungle Cruise.

Dave Lewis, 1970s

I once had Wilmer Valderamma, from *That 70s Show*. He was a great guy. They loaded him in the back, he had a group with him, and we had other guests on the boat. I never looked him in the eye. I tried to not give him celebrity treatment, and I'm sure that's a good thing. He came up to me and talked to me about it afterwards. I tried to be super cool about it. I told him I was a huge fan and tried for 8 minutes to not look you in the eye, and analyze what jokes to tell. He was really gracious.

Ritt Mesee, 2000s

Diane Keaton would come and request my boat. I never officially met her, she never said two words to me, but she took my boat once and smiled and laughed and then a couple weeks later she was back again, and I forget who the lead was, but I was told Diane Keaton is back, get in your boat. So I'm assuming she said that she wanted the guy from last time, don't know how they'd know, but she got in the boat and we did it again and she would smile and laugh, then at the end she would smile and nod and be on her way. I want to say that is the only one that sticks in my head. That was funny, she never said anything, just smiled, nodded, and off she goes.

Brandon Kleyla, 2000s

Tom Hanks and Jackie Gleason had done a film and I saw an interview with Gleason where he said that Tom Hanks had the best comedic timing of anyone he'd ever worked with. That is high praise. A couple of months later I had Tom Hanks and his family on my boat and I was nervous and I got cotton mouth so bad! It must have sounded like firecrackers going off around the park. So we get back to the dock and his wonderful wife came over and thanked me and then Tom came to me and said, "That was a lot of fun, you have great timing. The jokes are kind of stale, but you were great." I don't think I slept that night. Other skippers heard him and it was the best day.

Ron Robledo, 1980s

When they opened Star Tours they had a big party for it. The park was open from 10am Friday to 10pm Sunday straight on through. They brought in a lot of people from Star Wars. So Mark Hamill is there, and all these celebrities have security details, but Mark didn't have any of this VIP treatment, he just wanted to enjoy Disneyland with his family, so he ditched his security and he was going around and standing in line just like everybody else. He didn't want any back-door VIP treatment. He ended up on my boat, sitting right next to me. It just so happens as we are coming by Trader Sam, they are taking a boat off so I stopped. And I asked, "Does anybody have any questions, anybody, any questions." Mark wanted to know how many times a day I did the ride and how many times I'd been on Jungle Cruise. So just a down-to-earth guy.

Larry Kaml, 1980s

Will Ferrell was on my boat and I didn't recognize him until halfway through. He was dressed really casually and I felt like I wasn't funny at all. He came up afterwards and said, "Good job." And I said, "I'm not funny, you're funny," and he just looked at me and walked away.

Andrea Freeman, 2000s

I had Andy Dick on my boat once. I didn't know who he was, I just knew he was a celebrity and about half way through the trip I heard him lean over to one of his friends and say, "She's really funny." When he got off the boat he began to walk away, then turned around and looked at me, came back over, stuck his hand out, shook my hand, and said, "You know, you were really funny." The other skippers had to tell me who he was and that what he said was a good compliment because he was a comic.

Tiffany Davis, 2000s

I had Adam Sandler on my boat once and I said to myself, "Javi, don't try to be cute, just do your jokes." He had a plaid [VIP tour guide] with him. I tried to keep it OG. It was cool and he would laugh at some of my jokes. When we were in the veldt he said to me, "Hey, buddy would you mind if we skipped the gun?" So I didn't use the gun when we got to the hippo pool. He had his kids with him.

Javi Gonzalez, 2000s

Sometimes skippers will fight over a celebrity.

I had Tom Morello from Rage Against the Machine. I kicked a rookie out of his boat for that one. I saw that he was getting on the boat and I got on and told the skipper to get out. He hated me for that, but now we're friends. We still are friends. Morello was a really good dude.

Javi Gonzalez, 2000s

There was a skipper by the name of Patrick and he's a big boy. I only saw him run once the entire time I knew him and that was when Weird Al Yankovic came to the dock. This big guy sprinted from backstage, ran onto the dock, and said, "Nope, nope, I'm taking him, he's on my boat."

Javi Gonzalez, 2000s

What's it like to lose out on a celebrity trip?

I had Brian May from Queen on my boat, but he got stolen from me. I had just pulled up to the dock and this other skipper knew Brian May was going to be on my boat so she hopped on my boat and said I'll take a trip for you. And then I realized she did that because he was getting on the boat so I just sat down and stayed in the boat. It was an old-timer trying to take advantage of me being a rookie. So Brian May and I got to chat.

Tiffany Davis, 2000s

The favorite guest that I ever had on my boat was Ken Shamrock. I will always remember the trip I took with him. He was an original MMA fighter, hall of fame, the original UFC fighter, and he was also a pro wrestler. He was with the WWE in the 1990s as the "World's Most Dangerous Man." He had just lost a fight to Tito Ortiz, and his face was still beat up. I see these people on the dock with jackets that said "Team Shamrock" and I walked over and told them what a huge fan I was and so they asked to take my boat. He didn't have a plaid with him. So I got to meet him and he was super cool. I threw out a few wrestling jokes and he and his people laughed. Afterwards I gave him some cut-the-line passes. I got to take my picture with him. It was so cool.

Javi Gonzalez, 2000s

Dave Foley went through the line with people incognito and we had this woman come up to the dock, steal our pen, steal our rotation sheet, and run after him for an autograph. And here's Gerry going, what do you do?

Kat Thrailkill, 2000s

At unload there were a bunch of skippers and a group of people. I was doing my regular routine. A skipper said, "Let me take this trip for you," but I had time to do one more trip before my break, and I loved being in the boat, so I said no. He was insistent that he wanted to take my boat.

So they load at no-mans land and I move up to load and nobody is loading the boat. I hadn't bothered to look at the three people in my boat. A loader yells, "Hit it, Skip," and I joke with the guests:"Sorry, folks, these guys are new, they don't realize that you have to put people in the boat." The loader yells "HIT IT, SKIP!" So I take off and as we roar off into the jungle I see it's Jennifer Love-Hewitt sitting really close to me looking super cute and wearing Mickey ears. She was there with her friend and a huge security guard. I got nervous. They started taking pictures with each other and I tried not to engage them too much, but it is weird because there were only three people. Then she told her friend, "Let's listen to him," so I started performing and she was laughing and touching my arm. As we get back to unload, it was like a scene from a movie. There was a crowd of male skippers standing there and as soon as we saw them, they scattered. But for some reason they all had jobs that required them to be on the dock. One guy was pretending to mop the dock. At unload her friend's sunglasses fell and I bent over to pick them up and as I handed them to her my hand began to shake and she smiled. After I got off the dock all the male skippers came over and hit me on the shoulder and were asking questions. She was very nice and very cute.

Brian Vestal, 2000s

Cindy Crawford was probably my favorite celebrity because I was too shy to talk to her, but I talked to her kids. I look at her daughter now, who is a model, and I remember her when she was so little. You go through the spiel—is this your first ride, what's your favorite ride—and a skipper named Heather comes up, and I'm talking to the kids, and she says, "So what's your favorite ride?" and they said, "Well, this is our first one," and she goes, "And you chose us first? We're touched." I said, "Yeah, in the head," which got them all laughing and having a good time. There's such a sense of responsibility—whose boat do I put them on; no, he's going to squirt her; no, he's going to leer. Of course our resident lesbian was the one who ended up getting Cindy Crawford.

Kat Thrailkill, 2000s

Once, I had Turk, the gorilla voiced by Rosie O'Donnell in the cartoon *Tarzan*, on my boat. Turk and her handler got on my boat at the exit, and I had to be reminded of Turk's name. They sat in the front and guests got on my boat. Turk mostly sat there, until I got to the gorilla camp and then I started yelling at her, "What did you do! You told me they wouldn't mess anything up!" and she put her hands in front of her face and tried to hide. The guests laughed.

David John Marley, 2000s

I had Nicolas Cage. It was late one night and I was about to head to break when I notice a group come up to the exit. I ask the plaid, "How many," and they say, "Four." I look through the four—one...two...three...and Nic Cage dressed in a long trench coat and wide-brimmed fedora tilted down strategically over his face and eyes. I lean over to the lead: "They're going to need a private boat." To my joy she said, "Do you want to take it?" I gladly leapt at the opportunity. I leaned in to the next boat and said I was commandeering it. I get in the boat and realize the skipper didn't leave, she was sitting there right next to me. Then they loaded Nicolas Cage's group. So there I have Nicolas Cage and family trying to hide out and focusing on that and not me or my jokes and on the other side I've got a friend of mine, fuming that I got to take this cruise and not her. Nick finally loosened up around the Indian elephant bathing pool, out of public view, but the fellow skipper kept fuming. It took her a long time to forgive me, maybe not entirely still, but that is the story of how Nicolas Cage nearly tore apart a friendship.

Eddie Agin, 2010s

Eddie Murphy, big security, he had such a large entourage that it took two boats. This was an evening and I was off before he arrived there, so I just hung out. When the boat went out with Eddie, a buddy of mine and I ran off to the dancing natives and took our shirts off and danced as he went by.

Larry Kaml, 1980s

Do you remember the show *Saved by the Bell?* Screech, the nerdy guy, played by Dustin Diamond, he was like Mr. Disneyland and would come several times a year and treat the cast members like dirt, and be just, "Hey, I'm a celebrity," but people were like, "Who are you again?"

Larry Kaml, 1980s

We had this celebrity come up to the back door with a very new tour guide and she didn't quite know what to do, and none of us could figure out who this guy was. So I'm in the boat with the mystery guest. (It was a private boat.) Dude has long hair, and sunglasses, a wife, another female companion, a bodyguard and two children with long, long hair. The tour was going really good, but the bodyguard was creeping me out, he was really edgy. We get stuck at the unload area right behind Aladdin's Oasis, and apparently they had a paparazzi following them around all day and he snuck into the oasis where he could get a really good shot, and we couldn't move because the unload ahead of us was taking so long. The bodyguard stands up, the tour guide stands up, I move, and the little boy yells out, "He's there again!" and he's angry, and I felt bad because you come to Disneyland to have fun and enjoy yourself and that's absolutely the worst possible thing to happen to have someone tracking you down whether it's a paparazzi or a guest. I couldn't do anything and the bodyguard is getting angrier and angrier and we finally pull into the dock and Bill is the unloader and is trying to tell the guy to sit down because we are still moving, and I told the tour guide she could stand because she's a cast member but technically not with attractions so technically no, but I'm trying to middle ground it. Part of my responsibility is to keep the family safe. So the bodyguard attacks Bill and says, "You need to move, you need to move," and Bill says, "No sir, you need to sit down." And he leaves bruises on Billy's arms as he physically moved Bill out of the way. Apparently security had been waiting for him to do something like this all day, so they removed the bodyguard from the park. The family stayed, but the bodyguard did not stay because he physically assaulted a cast member. Not ok, but I also get why. So Bill had the story and the photos and he said, "Look I got all these bruises..." It was then that I realized the celebrity was Bono! His wife was trying to pass me money while all of this is going on. Bono was cool and I liked his family, but his bodyguard was just a mind trip. I think this happened in 2008, and it was Perez Hilton that bought the photo, of course it was, and it was a story about how he was cheating on his wife with these girls in a hot tub. They juxtaposed it with me in the photo turned around with my super long hair, trying to stand in front of him, to block the photographer, it is very clearly me. Security went after the photographer, but I think they missed him, not sure. They had problems with him all day and had been tracking him. He had done this before and knew where to hide.

Siobhan Armstrong, 2000s

Celebrities and fake celebrities.

When Michael Jackson came to Jungle Cruise he came with either Macaulay Culkin or Emmanuel Lewis. He had child actor friends with him when he came in and then there was another guy who was a Michael Jackson look-alike who would sneak in the park. He fooled the people at the main gate. He'd say he was Michael Jackson I think it took him about two or three times of him doing this before they figured that out.

Jerry Whitfield, 1980s

Celebrities who were supposed to show up and didn't.

I was supposed to have Schwarzenegger because he was in the park, and they opened the park two hours early just for him and his family. And they had a radio schedule on where he was supposed to go. A buddy and

I were there, opening, and we wanted to come up with a two-person bit and we had this tag team thing all worked out. They were short on time, so he skipped Jungle Cruise and went over to Indy.

Larry Kaml, 1980s

Just because you're famous doesn't mean skippers know who you are.

I had someone on my boat and to this day I have no clue who she is. She got a deadhead with a plaid and she was hiding her face from the guests on the dock but I had no idea who she was. Some skippers were in the shipping office trying to figure out who she was, but they didn't know. At the end she took six pictures with me, which was weird because they didn't listen to a single thing that I said. It was a bad boat. One person would kind of listen and everyone else was talking or trying to comment on the jokes. I think they might have been drunk, which didn't help. So they didn't hear a single thing I said. When they got off they said, "You were great." She looked familiar to me, but we could not place her. It was a weird boat. That is my only celebrity. They took so many pictures I've tried to see if they have been posted anywhere, but no luck. None of the other skippers knew who she was.

J'Amy Pacheco, 2010s

I had supermodel Rachel Hunter on my boat and I didn't recognize her until the ride was almost over. Her group got on the boat at the exit with a plaid. The group consisted of four adult women and their kids. Because I had a plaid, I figured one of them must be famous, but I couldn't figure out who it was. As I did the trip, I took turns looking at each women and still nothing. Finally, we were coming to the python and water buffalo and I cracked a joke that made her laugh really hard, and as she laughed I recognized her. She didn't have any makeup on. As I passed Trader Sam and headed to the dock, I noticed that every male skipper was standing on the dock, trying to look nonchalant. They congratulated me on taking her for a trip and I didn't tell them I didn't know who she was until literally seconds before she got off the boat.

David John Marley, 2000s

Or even care who you are.

To be honest, at the time I didn't really pay attention, I would have somebody say, "Oh, you had such and such," and I'd go, "I did?"

Jeremy Wayland, 2000s

CHAPTER FOURTEEN

It's a Real Jungle Out There

The Jungle Cruise might be the most Disney place in Disneyland because it is something artificial that has become real. There are no natural jungles in southern California so Walt Disney had one built and over the decades this fictional jungle became real. The plants were real and even the animals and insects were real. Well, some of the animals were real.

It's weird when you are in a park with 80,000 people and you are alone in a boat in a huge jungle. It's kind of its own oasis. You go through this huge parking lot, go through the park and swipe in to get your costume, you wait in line, it is worse than the DMV, then you end up in the jungle where it's quiet and calm, and every few minutes you hear a boat pass by. It's like its own national park within a park. If you had a graph for the amount of people in the park, like for density, the gungle is about a fifth of the whole Disneyland park. To think there are only a few hundred people in there and they're all separated. I loved it, it was its own separate thing.

Ritt Mesee, 2000s

I'd love my guests to imagine that I was a real skipper driving about the real jungle, and I think that translated well for the guests in my boat. That area seemed like the most isolated area in the park, and it's about a football field long, from the snapping crocodile to the Indian elephant bathing pool. That section along the Cambodian shrine was the most isolated part of the entire jungle. You never see boats ahead of you. It's a garden that we got to live in and it was the most beautiful place to be.

Fred Martin, 1980s

I liked when nothing was going on and the jungle was open and quiet. I liked it because the jungle was all yours.

Helen Medina, 2000s

When I worked there the orchids in the rainforest were real. They had a few artificial plants, but it was mostly real orchids.

Tom Nabbe, 1960s

One night a skipper and I had a conversation with a guest who was convinced the entire jungle was fake, like the tree at Tarzan's Treehouse. The man assumed that the entire jungle consisted of fake trees and bushes. We stood in front of the entrance to Jungle and tried for five minutes to convince him that they were real plants, but he didn't believe us. Finally, my friend said, "Yes, the plants are all fake. The leaves are this special kind of plastic that start out green and slowly turn yellow as they age, then they are replaced with new green ones." The man said, "I knew it!" and proudly walked away.

David John Marley, 2000s

Since Jungle Cruise was an outside attraction, a skipper had to be able to handle the elements.

It was pretty hard working at the Jungle Cruise in the winter when it was damn close to freezing outside. You had to talk about the lush tropical rainforest that you're going through. I enjoyed the summer costume when we were in go aheads and short pants and a shirt and straw hat, versus the khaki costume with the leopard skin ascot.

Tom Nabbe, 1960s

My personal favorite was rainy days or nights, when it was pouring rain and nobody wanted to go on the ride, and we'd just drive our boats around. If you know your plants, the jungle is amazing. I used to do this spiel where I just talked about the plants. I didn't mention the animals at all. I would go on and on about a dead log and ignore the animation. I called it the "vegetation spiel" and some of it was factual and some of it was bullshit. Some of the guests would look at me funny because they were expecting me to comment on the animals, but I would ignore them.

Jeff Rhoads, 1970s

After a big rain storm, the ground was nice and muddy, there was this really nasty wind and stuff, the trees that are 50 feet tall are swaying back and forth, I'm working unload, we are looking up at the trees and hoping one of them doesn't fall over, and 30 seconds later we hear this crack and we see this tree coming toward us. It was so big it landed on the unload dock and there was a boat parked on the catwalk, and it just took the boat out, it didn't sink it, but it destroyed the canopy. We were down the rest of the day, we couldn't bring any more boats in. So all the boats have to back up to load, unload, back up to load. Fortunately, we had the front switch where we could put it onto the catwalk and unload the boats.

Larry Kaml, 1980s

It wasn't my story, but it happened to a lead. She would go out on very windy days and would knock over bamboo. It was a perfect opportunity to knock over bamboo and shut the ride down.

Helen Medina, 2000s

A guest got hit on the head by a branch, but didn't tell me until she was getting off the boat. It was past the backside of water and I saw the branch come down and at first I thought it was a snake because of how it moved. It scared me. So at the dock she came up to me and said, "I just want you to know so you don't get sued, but you should remove that branch. It hit me. I'm fine, but it hit me." So I called a lead over, who normally doesn't work Jungle Cruise, and they didn't know what to do. I told the lead to let me take a deadhead and wait for two deadheads behind me and then we will be good to go. It will be enough time to clear the branch. We go out to the spot and we're breaking branches off and it looks good and we see boats in the jungle. So I think everything is fine. I get back to the dock and see that the lead has closed the attraction and emptied the line of guests. They had me go upstairs to write a statement and when I came back down 15 minutes later the attraction was still closed and all the experienced skippers were just standing there because the lead hadn't said to open it back up. We were down for 45 minutes that day for no reason.

J'Amy Pacheco, 2010s

We had situations where on a windy day, it gets clogged up or the pumps are turned off because the screens would take all the stuff. I remember once I am rolling up to Schweitzer Falls and I look around and it's off. I say, "Oh well, but it's off, well, it's Sunday and we are always dry on Sunday." That's an old term for a place that didn't allow the sale of alcohol. I used it the entire day.

Ken Snow, 1970s

The jungle is home to some real wild animals that don't care that children are watching.

I liked to let kids drive the boat when that sort of thing was allowed. It was a great experience for them, their family, and the rest of the guests if I could catch their comments, reactions, and our interaction over the audio system in an impromptu way. As they say, "out of the mouths of babes." It kept me on my toes. I got some grief from other skippers for letting kids drive because it was making my trips longer, like 9 or 10 minutes. Anyway, I pick a kid and we pull away from the dock with me carefully showing "Jimmy" how to steer. At that point I'd say, "Don't worry, Jimmy, this boat will 'track' just fine." Winking at the guests when I said the word "track." It was my way letting them know we were actually safe on a track. It also set the stage for the multiple levels of comedy I liked to use. So off we went and the kid is pointing out stuff, talking into the mic with me and having fun. All of a sudden these two ducks come flying through the boat canopy startling everyone and landing in full view. One duck then jumps on the back of the other beginning a scene of very aggressive duck sex. There was head pecking, wing beating, and tail feathers flying. I mean really rough. At that moment Jimmy screams into the mic, "He's killing the other duck!" Being a witty trained skipper, I say, "No, it's just Donald...and he sure loves Daisy." Everyone laughed and I felt pretty good about myself when a gay-sounding gentleman from the back yells, "Um, Jungle Dave, don't you mean Donald really loves Daffy?" I hadn't noticed that it was actually two male ducks having sex. Compelled to answer the question I said, "Well, I guess it *is* the happiest place on earth!" and roared off.

David Schoenwetter, 2000s

We actually have wild cats that go after the rats. And we have these ducks. You could always tell it was spring when the ducks would hatch. You see these ducks and it was my second boat ride and I had Kaz as my trainer. I see a family of ducks with six ducklings following after it, and they are heading right for me and I'm like, oh my god, these ducks are going to die, and you are not supposed to slow down, so what do I do? No, you're in the Nile you have to floor it, so we did, and I remember driving over the ducks and looking back as they all popped back up. It was so traumatic to this day. I always feel for the babies, so when I see the cats, I'm like, what about the baby ducks?

Tameem Sabry, 2000s

The jungle would be full of baby ducks. A baby duck would hit a wave and it would just throw it into the wall, it would ride the wave and hit the wall. You come around and see a baby duck just floating. So we would take them up to Schweitzer Falls on the little patch of grass up there and we had a little duck burial ground. We would take little spoons and dig a little hole and put the little ducks in there. By the end of summer, we had 12 little ducks up there. I would love to have had a boat go by with the guests seeing the skippers with their hats over their hearts and heads bowed. "What are those guys doing?" "Oh, it's a burial."

Brandon Kleyla, 2000s

One time I was helping the A lead check something on Catalina, better known to skippers as Spider Island because of the large variety and quantity of spiders known to inhabit it. I was waiting for him by the step-off rock when I saw him quickly run down the island into the boat followed by a quick, direct command: "Drive." "How was it?" I asked. "I turned over a rock and there were about a million black widows."

Eddie Agin, 2010s

I would try to do as many pull ups on the bars as I could and I remember doing it and a spider went walking right across my wrist and I had a welt right across my knuckle where it bit me and it was huge.

Jeremy Wayland, 2000s

My very first safari as a lead was a night shift. I was a brand-new lead, this young kid, and somebody told me that the water buffalo by Trader Sam are not moving. I had all this confidence. I'm the lead, I can fix this. I hop on the boat and I made the executive decision that we would not shut the ride down. I can do it covertly enough that nobody would notice. It was at night, so it was much easier to sneak around. I get dropped off on the island and I start making my way over and this is before they had installed any footpath on the island. When we went on a safari you took a stick with you or piece of bamboo to push the spiderwebs in branches out of your way. So I'm out there in the dark and all I can see are different prints left by the horticulture teams, kind of leading me in the direction that I needed to go. I have my flashlight and I'm following the footprints and then they disappeared. I take the flashlight and I pull it out to look around and as I scan around I see there are cobwebs everywhere. It was like *Indiana Jones and the Temple of Doom.* There were spiders and cobwebs and it was terrifying. I started to cry and I couldn't move because I felt surrounded by all of the spiders, and I didn't know how many I had just walked through. So I cried and I thought maybe I can't be a lead and that lasted for maybe a minute and I snapped myself out of it. I fixed the problem and the second I got back to the dock I ripped off the giant coat I was wearing because I was convinced it was covered in spiders. I was stepping on it and I was screaming "check my back, check my back." Other skippers had no idea what I was doing.

Tiffany Davis, 2000s

I remember the rats and there is definitely a snake out there. I had been out there before, right by the gorilla camp, and I saw something. I get on the boat and the trainee is giving their spiel and I'm not listening, I'm looking for the snake, and then I see the thing, I see the tail and it's got the markings on it, there was a snake out there. There are a lot of rats out there, you go out at night, you see the rats going across the river like it's a damn exposition. They leave little wakes behind them as they are swimming across. I remember a girl skipper was giving a tour and the rat fell out of the tree and landed on the boat. She starts screaming. Next thing I know she comes to the dock, boat barely stops, and somebody jumps on the boat to throw it into reverse, she never even paused it. By the time she leaps out of the thing because the rat is running around, and the guests are jumping out at the same time, the boat is still coming forward, you see this rat running around, a facilities guy takes off his coat and smacks the rat on the top of his head, picks it up in his coat, and walks off. I'm thinking, well, guess that's done.

Jeremy Wayland, 2000s

This is, perhaps, the best story about how real Disneyland's jungle has become.

I have a story about how my current job working for Adventures by Disney relates to my work at the Jungle Cruise. We were going down the Amazon rainforest, and sometimes we use these little motorized canoes very similar to the Jungle Cruise boats. They have a cover on them and often, depending on the group size, we'll have two of these boats and we will go up the small tributaries of the Amazon. There were times you would be in this boat and you would look up at the canopy and you would swear you were at the Jungle Cruise in Anaheim. So the Amazon rainforest began to feel like home to me because I spent much time there at the Jungle Cruise. And I actually do some of my Jungle Cruise jokes while we're driving down the Amazon River. How smart Walt Disney was in his foresight to make sure this looks like a real jungle and that you were on a real safari. He wanted people to really feel like you were in the Amazon rainforest. I can say first hand that the rain forest in the Amazon and the rain forest in the Jungle Cruise are hard to tell apart. It validates for me how real the Jungle Cruise is.

Tiffany Davis, 2000s

CHAPTER FIFTEEN

3 Shot, 4 Shot, 6 Shot

Accidents happen and even though the Jungle Cruise is a technically simple attraction, the boats can break down from time to time. There is a simple system for communicating problems in the jungle that involves shooting the pistol either 3, 4, or 6 times. What happens after the downtime starts is sometimes the most exciting thing a skipper will encounter all day.

A 3 shot is a mechanical breakdown of the boat. It is rare, but it happens.

I three shot one time in *Hondo Hattie*. The engine just died and I tried everything I could to get it to restart, every trick, so I blow the air horn and the lead shows up on the boat. He hops onto the boat, pushes the start button, and the engine roars back to life. He just looked at me and the guests on my boat started saying she tried that, she tried that. Later that day I had another three shot in the same boat, but this time I got it to start back up.

Tiffany Davis, 2000s

I remember the very first trip I had on training. I got the *Zambezi*, was having some trouble, and it had to do with the oil pressure. So you go into the jungle and it would die. You couldn't get it started again, so I gave a three shot, they come and tow you in and put it back in the boat storage, an hour later they say it's good. "Larry, you're going to be in the *Zambezi*." Three or four times around, bang, bang, bang, "Okay, we will take you back to the boat and we will fix it." An hour later it's back on the river again. "Larry, it looks like you're on *Zambezi*." I went 3 or 4 times with three shots on the *Zambezi* that day. That was my first shift off of training.

Larry Kaml, 1980s

I had one three shot. It died at the African veldt. This boat had been trouble all day long and it would go really slow and the engine made weird noises and I knew it wouldn't be long before it broke down and sure enough it died right there at the veldt. Maintenance came out and the guy hopped on my boat and just did one quick thing and the engine roared back to life and I just looked stupid.

Javi Gonzalez, 2000s

There was one night, near closing, when I was in the hippo pool and suddenly realized my boat wasn't going anywhere when I throttled. It shook a lot, but it had absolutely no speed whatsoever. Clearly something had caught on the prop and I was stuck. So I initiated standard procedures, I stopped the boat, I was near the skull canoe, and fired three shots into the air. As I did, I heard a rustling sound near the skull canoe that was heading for the hippo pool. I was then towed back to the dock. As we arrived, so did the training group from backstage. They were on safari in the same scene that I three shot in. They then bolted toward the hippo pool when I fired my shots and tried to blend in. That worked momentarily until the next boat arrived in the hippo pool with their lights on and apparently a little boy in that boat asked, "Who are they?" The skipper behind quickly shut off her lights.

Eddie Agin, 2010s

One time a 3 shot almost caused several boats to collide. This is also a story of how non-Jungle Cruise cast members don't understand skipper culture.

One day I was going around, and I was in the elephant pool and I heard three shots. I always tried to stop in an area where animation wouldn't stop. They'd hear the gunshots, and I didn't want to stop where some kid would see the monkeys not moving, that would break my heart, so I'm in the elephant pool, I hear the shots, I do the squirter, I do everything, then I stop right before the gorilla camp, that little patch. "Sorry, folks, we have to stop for a minute, there's some trouble up ahead, so we are going to sit here for a moment." Austin is in the boat behind me, and 30 seconds later, I'm vamping up and I'm talking, here comes Austin around the elephant pool, top speed, back to me, yelling, screaming, spieling, being Austin, his normal crazy self. I'm going "Oh shoot, oh God," he can't hear me and I'm literally reaching for the gun. I'm going to fire three shots, because he will hear it. Finally, he turns around and he sees me, and I had one hand on the throttle and one hand on the gun, he sees me, slams it into reverse, no boats hit, no boats even touch, but he triggers the squirting elephant, it comes up and just destroys the back of my boat. Peoples hats are being blown off their heads, they are soaking wet, drenched. At that point, I'm just leaning over my wheel, tears streaming down my face, dying in laughter as was the rest of the boat. Anything can go wrong on that ride and nobody cares, the guests love it. It's the one attraction where that could happen, and everybody goes, "OMG, I had the best Jungle Cruise ever. I actually got hit by the elephant." We got back to the dock and we had to do a double unload, and I get around and there are people in my boat that are soaking wet, don't ask questions now, if they want re-ads, give them whatever they need, I'll explain when I come back. I go around and do another lap, come back around and the lead gets in the boat. I explained that Austin didn't hit, nobody got hit, both boats didn't get hit, but I explained that guests got wet. The lead said the guests didn't complain at all, but there were some cast members on the boat that turned us in, and they weren't even west-side cast members, they went and complained. The guests had a great time. Neither of us got in trouble, but it was funny fellow cast members were ratting us out.

Brandon Kleyla, 2000s

4 shot is the rarest and the most frightening, since it means a medical emergency is taking place, whereas 6 shot is the only shot that a skipper will probably get in trouble for firing. This means the boat has come off the rail either in the front or back, or sometimes both. Generally speaking, a skipper won't get in trouble if the front guide derails, because it means they probably hit a submerged object. A rear derail almost always means the skipper slowed down where they shouldn't have and the wake lifted the back of the boat off the rail.

I worked with a guy named Chris, a really nice guy. He and I were working unload one night, a good evening, it was pretty slow. So we're leaning on the boat that was at unload and we just start gently rocking it, then we start pushing it backwards and forwards harder. And I said, "I wonder if anybody has ever derailed a boat right here by doing this." And he said, "No, the rail is really high right here, there's no way you can derail the boat here." So the skipper pulls forward to load and we're unloading the next boat and look over and the foreman has the boat hook and he's trying to reattach the front guide rail. So we did it! We derailed a boat at the dock just by rocking it. They pull the boat in the back so maintenance can look at it, and they come back and say it was a bad guide. The foreman had told them that the guide was bad so that we wouldn't get in trouble for breaking it.

Dave Lewis, 1970s

Sometimes the maintenance men think they know what's going on and how to fix it, even when they don't.

I did have a couple six shots. This involved Alden, who had the day shift, and I had the night shift. In those days a lot of the maintenance guys were very old school, conservative in their mindset, and a couple of them had very southern mentalities. The boat was the *Magdalena*, and Alden had the boat during the day, and he had an issue with it derailing somewhere where it didn't usually derail, somewhere between the gorilla camp and Schweitzer Falls. Later I got in the same boat, I got as far as the exit to the rainforest. In both cases it was the front guide. Sometimes it was the rear guide that would come off. So I'm in this boat, full of guests, and this guy comes out with the lead on a skiff, and he's right there laying into me, right in front of the guests about why I keep taking the boats off. I'm pretty pissed by this time, but he just keeps going and going and going and then I think the lead figured this out, too, so this guy put it back on the road and then I also have to suffer through this guy as they're towing the boat. They had so many boats at the dock, I had to go all the way around. We had the rope with the wood on it, goes under the front of the boat, and then they had a piece of wood in a short length of rope and then another piece of wood in there to make sure the boat wouldn't get too much tension. This guy is in the front of the boat, the entire way in, he's trying to hold the guide, because he's figured out that the guide wouldn't stay on the rail and he's laying into me the entire cruise. I couldn't spiel, I couldn't do anything, and I've got a boat full of guests. All the guests get out of the boat and at that point they are all convinced that it was my fault. I got out of the boat, I looked at the guy, I thought for about a fraction of a second how quickly I can push him into the river. I thought better of it, I didn't say anything, I looked at the lead, he knew that I was pissed off, and he said, "If you want to take a break, you can." I sat in the break area and I stewed, but I didn't say a word about it. That guy pissed me off to no end. And later the lead, to his credit, apologized.

Jerry Whitfield, 1980s

Usually at Schweitzer Falls, when you made that right hand turn, the wake of the boat would come back and kick the ass end of the boat up and then the bogey (guide) would fall off, and then you had to six shot. Once the guide lifted off the rail It would fall out of the boat completely. They changed that in the middle of the 1960s. So when that happened the divers had to go in and find it and put it back in the boat. Once they found it, they then had to stick it up through the neck, what we call the traveler, to reattach it and put it back on the rail.

Back at that time we were changing ammo. They were going to start usinge plastic blanks,and they were not very reliable. There were several times you'd just hear click then bang, that type of thing. Trying to get six shots off in a row took forever. You would shoot three times and then blank and then one more time and then blank. They finally fixed the ammo so that it is halfway decent.

Tom Nabbe, 1960s

Another time I went to get another boat, I jumped onto the spur line and threw the switch and I forgot to put it back, so when another boat comes out of the jungle it just starts floating around after Trader Sam, but before the dock. I didn't know I'd done anything wrong. I didn't notice it and I had gone off to lunch and so all of this is going on and nobody could figure out who had done it. So later on that night the foreman asked me, "Was that you that was back in boat storage switching the tracks?" I told them I didn't remember if it was me or not.

Dave Lewis, 1970s

I derailed a boat in storage once. It might have been Gerry as lead. There was one girl that everyone had a crush on, and she was working with me. She said I'll flip the switch for you. I'm not paying attention, I'm staring at her and driving around, and I went right off the track in boat storage. I fired my six shots from boat storage, just for pure comedic value, and it took so long for people to figure out where the shots came from. I'm sitting on the crate with my gun in my hand waving at them.

Brandon Kleyla, 2000s

One night I was working on unload and there was a 12 shot. Started as six, and we are unloading, then six more shots go off. And we were like, okay, what is going on out there. Is it the first boat and we thought we didn't hear them, or is there a second boat out there. We all get in a boat to go see. One of the ladies had bumped off both railings in the hippo pool and was just bumping around into everything. It was a mess. Maintenance went out and brought the boat in backwards. We had to unload it with the window rod between my legs. Taking people out thru the window. The fastest way to get it back on the track was going backwards. So from the time it happened to the time they got the guests back, it was two hours and not one complaint. They loved it. "Oh my god, we got stuck in the hippo pool, they had to come and get us, we had to exit out a window." Greatest day of their life.

Brandon Kleyla, 2000s

I did the typical derail in the Nile because I was speeding and I slowed down too fast, S-curve derail, it was just typical, and that was my response, too. "These are just typical spots." I did assume responsibility by saying I was going too fast. I wasn't paying attention because I was too busy in the act. Then you realize where you are, and you throttle it back and now you're stuck.

Jeff Bautista, 2000s

There was a guy who used to work there and we all called him Wet Willy because he always derailed boats. I think it was day 2 or 3 and my trainer Steve pointed him out and said, "There is Wet Willy, hopefully you won't find out why we call him that." And we are out in the jungle on the Nile and we hear shots go off and sure enough, Wet Willy double derailed at the hippo pool. So Steve has us keep going and we do a boat-to-boat evacuation in the hippo pool. It was the one and only boat-to-boat I ever did and it was in training.

Javi Gonzalez, 2000s

You had to walk past unload and load, and there was this little path between the jungle and the river that you could walk on. It was right by the edge of the skiff storage. There was this big pole sticking out and it was decorated to look like a piece of bamboo. And on those manual switches you always had to put the pin in to make sure the switch stayed where it was supposed to. This is the happened all the time. You'd tell a rookie to pull on a boat, and they would throw the track switch but put the pin in the wrong hole so the tracks switch isn't locked. So the first boat that goes over just rattles the switch and the second boat that goes over derails. Sometimes they didn't notice it right away and they would tear up the bottom of the boat. And that's how a boat got sunk on several different occasions. Another way what happened was this rookie would go out through the track switch and he would get confused and wave the boat forward and the boat would immediately derail.

Jeff Rhoads, 1970s

Thinking about great downtime, one year with El Nino, when the water level would get too high, one morning all the boats had derailed, every single boat. We had to go fetch them and get them back on the tracks.

Helen Medina, 2000s

Some skippers would 6 shot on purpose.

One skipper would out to the hippo pool and say, "Hold on, folks, I think there's something wrong with the engine." He hits a button and you hear that sound, and he says, "Let me see if I can fix this." He flips open the hatch thing, picks up the guide rail, drops it, breaks off two wheels in the elephant pool, and he goes, "Sorry, folks, 6 shot," and that was it. They would disable the ride whenever possible if they didn't want to work because it got too hot or to annoy people, or if they had a bad boat, just lots of different things.

Jeremy Wayland, 2000s

Sometimes you can have multiple types of shots to combine the fun. Here is a case where a 6 shot led to a 4 shot.

Just passing the gorilla, I get to Schweitzer and I was going too fast, it was in the *Congo*, I double derailed, and then right at the turn, the bow of the boat hit the island. When it hit, this lady who had been leaning back, her head slammed into the pole and she started bleeding. So I four shot and I called it in, they say come immediately back to the dock, and I can't because I'm derailed, too, and I can't get back, and she was bleeding and crying, and we had to wait for the boat to evac. They evacuated her first. We were down for about an hour or so. It was a long time. I was in the boat and it was just awkward. If it had been a 6 shot, it'd be okay, but someone was hurt, just bleeding. I tried to keep her calm and they could see I was on the radio. I wish I could have just broke the tension. I usually respond with tension breakers, but I think with that, I just felt like, "Oh crap, what do I do?"

Jeff Bautista, 2000s

Sometimes the people sent to fix problems end up creating more.

We had a six shot in the hippo pool. The guide got really bent and they couldn't get it back on the rail. They had to bring the divers out, and when they bring out the divers, you know we're going to be down for hours. During the downtime, I was sitting in boat storage with Randy and we were talking about the old times at Jungle. He starts describing what the maintenance guys are doing. He begins predicting trouble because he said these second-shift maintenance guys don't know what they're doing. He describes what's going to happen if they don't do what they're supposed to do: "They're going to realize the guide can't go back on, so instead of pulling it off, they're going to try to lift it up as far as they can and then bring the boat back, they're going to get the tracks to switch one, and then hit track to switch two and they're going to get stuck. They're going to have to push the boat back out to the hippo pool and hammer that thing out." Sure enough, it happened as Randy had said. The pole was dragging on the ground and it broke all of the air hoses that run all of the track switches. They had to push the boat back into the hippo pool and then had to try to take the pole out. Then they had to repair the track switches. It took at least three hours just for that part alone. I think we were down a total of five hours. It was funny, because it happened exactly the way Randy said it would.

Kipp Hart, 2000s

Another time was right after Disneyland's 50th anniversary and a boat derailed. It six shot in the rain forest. As were going to rescue it, I got a phone call from Tiki telling me that the Tiki Room was flooding. And then we hear six more shots fired, and there was a different six. That was out by the gorilla camp. I had two six-shot boats and also trapped two boats between them. So I had four boats couldn't go anywhere; meanwhile, Tiki is flooding. It was one of those moments where you stand on the dock and look around and you don't even know where to start first. Maintenance came out and was helping with the first derail. We ended up doing a multiple boat-to-boat evacuation. Just had to go from one boat to another boat to another boat to another boat to get back to the dock. It turns out the Tiki Room wasn't actually flooding, one of the toilets in the bathrooms by the entrance was overflowing. Everything worked out fine. It was just one of those moments where you look around and think, *Well, this is new.* That was the fun thing about being a lead, you never know what you're going to have to deal with that day.

Tiffany Davis, 2000s

A new skipper is often terrified of being stuck in the jungle behind a broken-down boat; however, a seasoned skipper sees it as an opportunity to go off-script and have some fun.

One day the entire attraction was down because there was a computer chip that runs the gorilla camp and it was broken so they had to go get another one from WDI in Burbank and we were closed all day. It was just myself, Don Warner, Shaun, and a couple other skippers hanging out. Don and Shaun and I went out in the jungle and played cards. We were on a boat in the elephant bathing pool just waiting. I think we were there to trigger the sensors when they got it working. It was one of those rare great days where you didn't have to do anything. That went on for a few hours. By the time I came back from my lunch break they were just about to get the attraction going again.

Javi Gonzalez, 2000s

One of my least favorite things was being stranded out there in the jungle during a breakdown. I'd run through my four or five well-rehearsed ad libs, then be out of material. I was on a boat once that got stuck, I was just a passenger, and my friend Rick was the skipper, and he worked that crowd for the 20 minutes we were out there. It was hilarious.

Dave Lewis, 1970s

I was once stuck behind a 3 shot and I had a great crew. I talked for 20 minutes and they loved every second. The skipper in front was brand-new and didn't call it in. She just sat there. So after 5 minutes when nobody showed up I yelled to her, "Did you call it in?" and she didn't know that she had to. She just sat there. I guess she thought it would automatically tell someone. We had to back out of the jungle.

J'Amy Pacheco, 2010s

Once I was on an exit dock rotation without a boat. We didn't have the staffing to do it. I try to come into Jungle Cruise with lots of energy. I drink a lot of coffee, so it was killing me that I had all this energy and no way to get it out of me. It was killing me. So Eddie suggested that I commandeer a boat. I grab a boat and it's fun and we get to Trader Sam and I wait there for 10 minutes and then a boat backs up from the dock toward us and we were out there for 20 minutes and I was doing every joke I could do. Finally we get to move forward and I ask what the problem was and it turns out there was a 4 shot, medical emergency, on the dock and the EMTs had to show up and cart someone away. I was on that dock for 8 hours and the one time I take a trip I miss all the action.

J'Amy Pacheco, 2010s

I'd start doing stand-up and crowd work and mess with people. Sometimes I would start a story and make it up as I went along and see if I could improvise. Sometimes I would make up a joke that didn't have a funny punchline and then sell it as if it was a super-funny joke.

A lot of times it was somebody in front of me that 3 or 6 shot. You tried to keep show spacing, but sometimes you would come up on them. I would talk to the other boat. Sometimes I would get them to all do a sing along.

Brian Vestal, 2000s

One night the lights in the jungle wouldn't go on, so we circled boats while they tried to fix it. We'd had trouble keeping the gorilla camp jeep headlights on during the day, and then they went off and we realized that none of the lights were on. We did deadheads for an hour. Maintenance was trying to fix things. The jungle was so dark. We don't have enough spotlights for every boat and the exterior lights are not that bright.

J'Amy Pacheco, 2010s

The one thing they didn't change was Trader Sam. I used to sit at Trader Sam for like 5 minutes, I would tell all the Trader Sam jokes I had. I loved those jokes, or I would hear jokes from other people like, "This is a net," like they were saying, "This is my girlfriend, Annette, she's a real catch from the internet." Then you start tying in the constrictor jokes. "Oh, he can be a little bit smothering." The food items on Trader Joe's menu like "toe-fu, head-cheese, finger foods." I just kept going down the list of jokes. I would sit there for 2 or 3 minutes. People at the dock would get frustrated and say, "Move it up, Skip."

Tameem Sabry, 2000s

As a new skipper, I would get terrified of getting stuck at Trader Sam. After I had been there for a summer, I prayed that the river was backed up because then I would start riffing and having fun with the guests.

David John Marley, 2000s

Occasionally, a lead would use the PA that could be heard across the entire attraction. However, just because the skipper heard the voice doesn't mean the guests did.

There was a break down and Gerry the lead decided to use the all ride, and said, "All boats hold your position," and I just kept talking. Then I'm sitting there for a long time and we are not moving and I don't know where the break down is, so I'm spieling then finally a little girl asks why aren't we moving, and I told her because there's a boat broken down up ahead. She asked me, "How do you know that?" And I said, "Because the voice of the jungle told me." The mom is starting to get upset and she pulls the girl away from me. We are still stuck and they think I'm hearing voices and they are trying to figure out how to escape, and I'm like, OMG, what do I do? Then Gerry's voice comes back on and says that we can move again. So the entire ride back I kept saying, "I told you, I told you!"

Siobhan Armstrong, 2000s

If the boat behind yours was the one in trouble, you often became the rescue boat. You would unload your guests, take a lead, maintenance man, whatever, and head backwards into the jungle to help your stranded skipper.

We loved to go out to the boats that 3 shot because we would play it up so much and overact heroic stupidity like we were standing up in the boat with the ropes around our chest as if we were crossing the Delaware. It was crazy, but people loved it. We would play into it to make it memorable. "Thanks to me you folks get to go home tonight."

Brandon Kleyla, 2000s

Sometimes skippers will take it upon themselves to fix things on their own.

On Christmas Day 2016, near closing, the call came in that one of the crates full of bells next to the African elephants had fallen into the river. It was far enough to the side for the boats to pass, so we got them past and cleared the attraction. I took my boat to check it out. Sure enough, there was the big crate bobbing in the water. Now by this point it had been too filled with water to heave it back onto land, so maintenance was called to deal with it. In order to get it out of the way, though, it was decided to bring it back to the dock. So the lead grabbed hold of the crate and with me at the throttle, we began proceeding to the dock at the slowest speed possible. In my mind, there were only two faults with this plan. There is a step-off rock on the right side near the hippo pool and then all bets are off when we reach the piranhas. Sure enough, we approach the step-off rock and we have to stop. We try to get it out of the water but it was far too waterlogged by then. So we swing the crate around the back and continue forward. There we were, in the hippo pool with the stars twinkling above. I couldn't help myself, the holiday spirit overtook me. I took hold of the mic, looked back at the lead heaving the crate behind my boat, and said, "Merry Christmas. I hope you like the gift I got you." "SHUT UP!" So we kept going forward until the piranhas. Then we were stuck. By that time the maintenance crew had showed up and they were very upset with us for moving the crate.

Eddie Agin, 2010s

The good thing about being a trainer is that you got to hang out with the facilities guys and they show you all the tricks to get the boat restarted, because I remember one time, I should have 3 shot, we had three boats on the river, I go to the battery and I'm taking them out and moving the guests to restart the battery and literally jury-rigging my boat to get it back to the dock. It died on me out in the jungle. I'm checking the connections and I had a little copper wire filament brush that was underneath the thing and I'm scrubbing it off and I got the thing running again. But I'm making these guests move so I can get the battery out. I'm not 3 shotting it, I'm going to get this boat working again, damn it!

Jeremy Wayland, 2000s

There are other types of accidents that didn't involve using a pistol to signify anything. Some of them were bizarre.

The Tahitian Terrace was right next to us. These Polynesian dancers would come out and do this fire dance and twirled the sticks around while they were on fire. Their backstage area was also where our boat storage was.

One time I was in line at Trader Sam, spieling away, and the torch guys were behind the stage. They were waiting to go on. The one guy lit his torch and he accidentally lit the little curtain on fire. It was the curtain between the stage and backstage. And it just went up! All the skippers were yelling "904," the code for fire since we can't say "fire" on stage. So were yelling "904" and the guests have no idea what we're talking about. Meanwhile, the dance show was going on. I pulled out my fire extinguisher, but I was too far away. A skipper on the dock put it out. He grabbed an extinguisher and ran over there. They never even stopped the show.

Andrew Green, 1980s

Not everyone follows the edict of "what happens in the jungle stays in the jungle."

I bumped into a skipper's boat once by the water buffalo. I told him to be cool about it, but he went straight to management. I was so pissed because I just barely tapped it. He told everybody.

Andrea Freeman, 2000s

I ran out of gas on New Year's Eve. We were open late and they said, "Oh yeah, you have lots of gas," and around the python the boat began to sputter, we were going so slow, and I got around to Trader Sam, doing a bad cruise, and I had to push the boat to get it back to the dock.

Helen Medina, 2000s

Another thing we did that I'm sure was done long after I left was loading a skip's gun for him while he was being unloaded by the two loaders. We'd squat down on the bow, grab the gun, pull out the spent shells, and replace them with fresh ones. It made it easier on the skip between trips, giving him one less task to worry about.

One afternoon, I squatted and was loading the gun. The skipper turned around to see who was helping him and busted out laughing! Unbeknownst to me, the fly on my pants had broken and was wide open. I was going commando that day and my junk was on full display for him and the guests to behold. Once he stopped laughing enough to regain the ability to speak, he told me about it and off to wardrobe I went.

Dave Lewis, 1970s

The greedy gorilla lost his hand one day. Nobody knows where it went. It was just gone. It's not like there are wires sticking out, it was just a black stump. Nobody on the boat noticed.

J'Amy Pacheco, 2010s

From opening day, skippers would joke about the boats sinking, but there were a few times when it actually happened. First off, sinking the skiff.

I was the sinkable skipper. It was really true, I had Schweitzer Falls hit me on the top of my head while I was in the skiff. There was a breakdown outside the hippo pool. I get the skiff, it was a warm afternoon summer, I try to fire up the darn thing, and I choke it, so maintenance gets it started, off we go through the river, reach the boat, and the fellow gets on and says, "We may have to push this." So he is working on it, and then he got it started and off we go past the dancing natives, through Schweitzer Falls, and I start coming up to it and my engine dies. I still have forward momentum, so I'm getting closer to the falls. I am pumping like crazy trying to get this thing started, and now the water is at the front end of the boat. Meanwhile, there is a boat behind me and I begin to hear laughter. I could hear the skipper talking about me, so I move into the falls. In the event of an emergency, there is a paddle in the boat, so I get it and try to paddle away, but the paddle breaks. There must have been a crack in the paddle between the base of the blade and the handle. So, you give it a really deep pull and it snaps, and there I am up a creek without a paddle. I'm half the way covered, and I begin to use my hands trying to paddle away. I'm sitting in the back of the boat, the water is hitting me on top of my head, I'm trying to bail the water out with my straw hat. By that time, I figure that's it, so I stand up and turn around to look at the boat behind me. I put my straw hat over my heart, and down we go. People were taking pictures of me, and I was able to pull myself onto the boat. I was in the front of the boat and I remember doing some of the spiel at that time. We were all laughing. The maintenance guy saw me go down, and anyone that had a maintenance radio throughout the park heard that there was a skiff and a skipper that had gone down. Everybody in the park heard it. I show up soaking wet, they send me out to get changed, they had to send divers out to bring the boat up. I didn't get into trouble because they realized they didn't check the skiff out too well. Me and the skiff didn't get along well after that. There was another time when we did have a breakdown, and the foreman tells me to get in the skiff and I go, "OK," and the same thing happens again, I can't get the skiff started and the maintenance guy jumps it and gets it going. I'm starting to have flash backs. We go out there and Schweitzer Falls is off, and I start laughing. I did have to slink my way back to wardrobe. There were 40 people working on the Jungle Cruise that day. That was my claim to infamy.

Ken Snow, 1970s

One of the leads took a supervisor out on the skiff and decided to play a joke about getting too close to the waterfall, and killing the engine, then cranking it up just in time. Went right through the waterfall with the supervisor, with the attraction open, and the supervisor in a three piece suit.

Larry Kaml, 1980s

There have also been times when an actual Jungle Cruise boat sank.

The best sinking boat story was the boat derailed at the safari camp, where you never derail. The guide hit the shoreline and it bent the shaft, so when maintenance came out to put it back on the rail again, they couldn't get the guide back up onto the rail again. Maintenance, in their wisdom, said they were just going to bring a boat up behind, use a tow rope to tie the boats together and get back to the dock. The maintenance guy said, "I'm just going to sit on the back of the boat and if the boat swings out and it gets too close, I'm just going to push off with my feet." So that's what we are doing, and we made it just past Trader Sam and those rocks by Tahitian Terrace, and the boat swung out and bounced off those rocks and ripped a hole in the side of the boat and it sank.

Larry Kaml, 1980s

This one combines a 6 shot and a boat sinking.

During Fantasmic, when it's really dead, you go take your lunch. I'm up in the break area and I get a call saying there was a 6 shot and a boat had derailed in the elephant pool. I asked if anyone was in the queue, and he said no, so I told him to just shut off the line, send somebody out front, and say the ride is closed. I wander down there and while waiting for maintenance to show, I hop on a deadhead and ride out to the elephant pool to scope things out, and as I make the turn, I noticed something was wrong, because there were only six guests on the boat, but it was sitting in the water a good 8 inches lower than my boat. About that time one of the guests yells, "Oh my god, we're sinking!" I looked in the boat and there was water coming in through the floor. Fortunately, the six guests on the boat were pretty young and agile so I tell them to evacuate. They climbed off the stern of the boat to the deadhead boat and back to the dock, so it's just me and the skipper with the boat, and water keeps coming in and coming in. By the time maintenance got there, there was so much water in the boat they couldn't get it back onto the rail again. So they did what the skiffs did, they tied it off to the boat and brought it back. By the time they get it back to the dock, it is pretty buoyant so they pushed it to boat storage, then 15 minutes later, a maintenance guy comes out and calls me over. I went back there and there's a hole about the size of a half dollar punched in the side of the boat. When the boat derailed, it swung out and hit one of metal frames that the baby elephants are on, and it just punched a hole in the side of the boat. That's why it was a slow leak the watertight walls and the hole in the boat were both activated. Same as the *Titanic*, we can sink three compartments, but once you get to the fourth, it's going down.

Larry Kaml, 1980s

For decades it was a tradition that on a skipper's last shift they got thrown into the river. These skippers went in all on their own, and not on purpose.

In my third week I fell in the water because I was goofing around at the dock. I had taken this big piece of bamboo and I ran up and stuck it on the back of the boat and I would lean on it and use it to lean into the boat and make loud noises and scare the people sitting back there. Once, as I was using the pole to stand back up, the skipper moved forward and I was quickly feeding bamboo as I watched the boat pull away and I fell in right behind the boat. The two things that came to mind was that the boat has a propeller and my trainer Benny had told us that there were leeches in the water, so I wanted to get out as quickly as possible. Meanwhile, the skipper stopped the boat and instructed everyone in the boat and in line to laugh at me. It was pretty funny. The lead was Dave, the rocket scientist, and he was in the shipping office when it happened. He just looked me up and down and said, "Go change your clothes." People made fun of the new guy who fell in.

Brian Vestal, 2000s

Some accidents are caused by guests who are usually not paying attention. This particular story is painfully ironic because in the mid 2010s the Jungle Cruise was forced to tie off their boats as a safety measure to keep people from falling in the water. Still, guests found ways to ruin the fun.

Even when we were roping off, I had a little boy keep sticking his hand between the boat and the dock and I was like STOP. I looked at his mom and told her that he needs to stop. I kept telling him and he did it anyway And it squished him and hurt him. How many times can you tell someone not to do something. I have kids, so I know it's a thousand times. I remember the mom being pissed and I was like I told you he's sticking his arm out and I wouldn't even let the boat do tension, I wouldn't even give them the clear to do tension.

Jen Chavez, 2010s

I did drop one kid into the water when we were loading. We had a little bit of a gap, and the kid was small. Even though I had a hold of his elbow, he dropped down into the water and I lost sight of him for about a second. You tell the skipper so he can shut the propeller off, try to get the dock side people to stand up to help pull the boat away, to grab him out. His parents were fine, everybody was fine, but occasionally we lose people into the water.

Gordon Lemke, 1980s

We had a lot of dips. Back then we had to grab them tricep and wrist and help them into the boat. There were lots of little kids who would miss their step and slip up to the shins into the water, but I'd pull them out. One kid fell all the way in, and it was like magic. Immediately two other skippers push the boat away from the dock and I jumped in and grabbed the kid and handed him to a guy on the dock.

Dave Lewis, 1970s

One time I was loading guests into the boat and I got a hold of the first kid and I got a hold of the third kid, but the second kid squeezed by and he went down. I remember dropping the first kid into the boat and asking the third kid to wait and reaching down and I got the second kid by the back of the neck and pulled him up and put him on the dock. His eyes were huge and his mouth was open and water is rolling out of his open mouth so I took him over to wardrobe and got us some clean clothes. That was interesting.

Tom Nabbe, 1960s

CHAPTER SIXTEEN

Skipper Safari

Going on safari, exploring this natural wonder, is a rite of passage for skippers. Especially at night, skippers were known to roam the jungle to explore or just cause trouble. In recent years, Disneyland has tried nearly everything to stop safaris, even going so far as to threaten to fire anyone who dares go out there. They claim it's too dangerous to go out there, so you can be fired for being unsafe. Being unsafe sounds like a better reason to fire someone than saying that they went out there to look around.

Despite Disneyland's claims that banning safaris is a safety issue, having skippers who don't know anything about the land they are driving around is not any safer. There were leads who allowed a skipper to go on safari as long as they lead was asked permission first. This kept the chaos to a minimum.

Safaris for me were team-building experiences; that's how I looked at it. I formed the best bond, you're thick as thieves, you know you are not supposed to do it, so you go out there, and my first day, I had the squirter turned on me. He got me good and I was stopped there and so it was full on.

I always wanted to try doing that, to safari, just to fool around, I never got to Schweitzer Falls. Once me, Matt, and Adam had gone from backstage to the elephants and for some reason there was a manager out there. I think it was Mark. We were going to exit through the Indy queue, but he was out there, so we were hiding behind rocks until he left and we didn't want to go back the other way, as we can't go out that door, so we went over to the Indy queue and we were just scaling the wall, through the rain gutter trench, and stayed down because another maintenance worker came out, and all our exits were blocked. It was like Mission Impossible. We maxed out at 20 minutes. We never got caught. Mark was looking for people, checking things out. I'm sure it was for guests. None of our cast members would have said anything. We got to jump over by the ancient ruins, we took the rain gutter all the way to the ancient ruins and got back into the park by Indy's exit. We were muddy and slippery. That was my most memorable experience, other than my last day going out there.

Jeff Bautista, 2000s

It was really fun. They were really super into doing those. Do you remember hiding the Simba beanie baby thing? We would hide it around the jungle and boats tried to spot it. I loved it when they would put Simba in the mouth of one of the lions. That was the best; they are basically cannibals.

Andrea Freeman, 2000s

I danced with the natives in my boxers. I think it was for a Grad Nite. I went in and took everything off except the boxers. I ran in and danced with them and the boat didn't know how to react to that.

Javi Gonzalez, 2000s

I remember when trainers ruined safaris for everybody, jumped on the turntable and danced with the natives. Someone saw them, and it was not any of the trainees, but someone saw them and turned them in.

Helen Medina, 2000s

Some less than honest leads made up stories in a effort to keep skippers from going on unauthorized safaris.

They told us that Disneyland security randomly walks through the jungle to check to see if you are out there. I went on safari a few times, but I was just terrified, my heart was thumping because I was afraid that I was going to get fired. I went to the dancing natives and the squirting elephant, but never to the top of the waterfall.

I think it was during the first month that I was a skipper I had a lead that took us to Manhattan Island. We hopped from the dock to the boat then the island and we re-created a scene from *Raiders of the Lost Ark*. He did the first scene where he finds an arrow and tastes it for poison. It was so fun. I talk to skippers now and they never go out there, they are terrified to do it. They can't even imagine doing it.

Javi Gonzalez, 2000s

I did a deadhead a few times and some of the people knew I was going so a couple skippers went on safari. They ambushed me by the attacking natives. I'm on a deadhead with a girl skipper and we are just hanging out having a cruise and for fun I had the gun out. Kriztina was the girl on the boat. We get past the dancing natives right before Schweitzer Falls, and this other guy Ray, who is kind of out there, had gone on safari. He jumped out of the bushes on a hill and the hill was this kind of slope, and I had the gun in my hand and I just shot at him. I had no idea that was going to happen and that is probably the reason I should never own a gun. He was so shocked to be shot at that he almost slid into the river

Ritt Mesee

One time on a safari I climbed through Bertha's cave. This is still when I was a brand-new lead. And inside the cave they have this light that was on a timer, so I turn it on and I go out into the jungle to fix what I had to fix, and before I could get back the timer went off and the light switched off and I didn't have a flashlight with me. That was one of the scariest walks I've ever been on. I was walking into trees and smashing things over. Every time I would reach out to grab something I would scream because I didn't know what I was touching. That cave is really long and terrifying when it's completely dark.

Tiffany Davis, 2000s

Shortly after a huge tree fell down, they started cutting down all the trees. Gerry would be hiding behind one piece of bamboo, and I'd say, "I can see you, why are you hiding?" I can remember taking a trip and facilities would be out there and didn't even try to hide. "Oh, look, that is Bigfoot, his name is Gerry."

Helen Medina, 2000s

We would take the super soakers into the jungle and try to shoot the skipper; occasionally, we would shoot a guest. We would hide on the Nile River right by the gorilla camp, behind the elephant and the squirter. There were some really good hiding spots out there. Someone told me there is a super soaker still out there that somebody left.

Jeremy Wayland, 2000s

Once in a while we would be asked to go out and check on the zebra because someone said he isn't moving. I would go with other people because I went out there so infrequently that I would never remember how to get back out. I would be the guy waving at boats asking for help getting back. We would be working on something and a boat would be coming by, we would just dive behind a hippo or something so guests couldn't see you, then come back up.

Brandon Kleyla, 2000s

I saw the lead on safari the other day because we were having some problems with the gorillas and it was like one of those old Bigfoot photos of him walking between the trees.

J'Amy Pacheco, 2010s

I've been on safari a couple times, never during operation. It's hard to categorize this as safari , but twice I have been out to the veldt with all the skippers. For the closing of Jungle for the new dock and the cast photo, we've had the great opportunity to have a "pop-tart breakfast" out at the African veldt. Officially sanctioned by management, we've led the entire Jungle Cruise cast to the King Kong doors at Indiana Jones and walked behind the Indian elephant bathing pool for breakfast out at the veldt. We've walked around the scenes and see all the animatronics up close and personal. It is really something to see 40 skippers roaming around the veldt.

After a retraining shift for working with the new dock, we had some time to kill. So the head lead decided to take the rest of us willing to do so on safari. We had no idea, because he loaded us onto a boat and just began an informational tour about the plant life. Then we reached the step-off rock for Catalina. He casually said, "Alright. Everybody out." We were all a bit shocked. "Everybody talks about this island like it's some big thing, so let's go!" We walked out to the attacking natives and got to look around them and into the huts. Then we wandered over to an area called C Curve, the curve after the trapped safari and just before the hippo pool. The lead was standing on a tree trunk about four feet across. He began to tell us that that tree had fallen a few years earlier during operation. It was so tall that it rustled the trees by the skull canoe. While we were still in awe and looking, the lead sped away. He did can-yoneering in his free time so this terrain was easy for him to navigate. He got back to the boat, which one of the managers was watching, and while we were all watching, he began to speed away with all the cast on the island. We were stuck there with the sun going down. Slowly, the boat reversed and there was the manager laughing. We all re-embarked and made it back to the dock. Then he had us all grab flashlights and we crossed the boats to Manhattan. We found ourselves among the bamboo. Suddenly, one of the cast members and I found a carving in one of the bamboo stalks. It was two letters followed by "10...?" This immediately had us curious. We took a picture and proceeded back to the dock. We showed another lead who broke down in tears laughing. It turns out that another cast member had those initials and had started in 2010. That was his marking and I joked someday we'll have to go finish it.

Eddie Agin, 2010s

Some people go on safari without their official consent.

On my last day, Keith, the foreman, said, "Let's do an animation check, go get the skiff." So we go buzzing around in the skiff and he says, "Let's check out the island, here is the rope, hop off and tie us off." I was so naive that I hop off the boat and he throws the skiff in reverse and leaves me alone on the back island (Catalina). I walk over to the African elephant and I climb it and take off my shirt and I wave at guests as they go by. It was great to hear skippers doing their regular spiel and then burst out laughing when they saw me. And then I tried to get off the island by jumping onto a boat at the attacking natives, but I couldn't make it. By that time I hear the skiff coming back, so I go back to where he left me and he pulls up to the shore and as I step on the skiff he throws it in reverse again and I'm doing the splits. He then pulled forward so I didn't fall into the water.

Dave Lewis, 1970s

I once went on safari with a lead and another skipper. We climbed over a little hill and were on the railroad tracks. We had to be careful because our lead told us that the engineers would call security if they saw anyone on the tracks, even a cast member. So we walked along the track, trying to get to the elephant bathing pool, when we hear the train leave the station. We started running and running and then ran up the hill to hide. Problem was, the only thing to hide behind were palm trees. I don't know if the engineers saw us, but I know lots of guests did.

David John Marley, 2000s

Chim Chim was a fiberglass monkey in the rain forest. it was a static figure, attached to a branch. One day we noticed Chim Chim wasn't there anymore, so we took a boat out and jumped onto Manhattan Island and walked over there, and it was on the ground, it had fallen off the branch. It had baling wire that had rusted through. So we got Chim Chim and brought him back and thought about notifying maintenance to put him back. Then we thought, no, we aren't going to do that, so we came up with this game that every morning, the opening shift would take Chim Chim and put him somewhere on the attraction and the object was to find him. The ride would open and we would ask "OK, where's Chim Chim today," and the first person who spotted him had bragging rights, but that's about it. We tried to get it in more and more bizarre and difficult to reach and see places. One day they put him on a branch, hanging over the Nile River between the two elephants. They had to climb up a tree to put him up there. So we open the attraction and we wait for someone to say they spotted him. We went for hours and hours, and we thought we'd got them this time. Then we got concerned because no one was finding Chim Chim, so we took a deadhead, and he wasn't where we put him and that was the last time we ever saw Chim Chim. We think he fell in the river and was no more after that.

Larry Kaml, 1980s

A brave skipper might go out into the jungle while the attraction is running in order to fix something.

I had a great experience with Brian in the elephant pool. We had a torn skin situation with the elephant that squirts water and sits in the middle of the elephant pool, wobbling back and forth. We have that skiff in the back so we can take it to fix things. I made the executive decision that we were not going to shut down the ride. I thought we could go out there and fix it really quick. In hindsight, I was a bit overzealous about that. I told Brian, "You're going to paddle and I'm going to repair." He was big and strong, so I thought he could get out there quick. At night there aren't a lot of boats running, so we wait till one goes by and I yell now and we went as fast as we could. Brian had worked on Canoes so I thought it would be easy, but that skiff was a lot harder to steer then we had planned. We finally get out there. I'm holding onto the leg and I'm trying to fix this tear so that nobody can see it. In the distance I hear this skipper named Don, I hear him by the Bengal tiger and I realize we're not going to make it back in time, and before we can move he triggers the sensor for the elephant pool scene. The elephant that I'm trying to fix starts to wobble back and forth and spray water. It totally hosed me down in front of all of his guests as they're going through the elephant pool. It looks like I'm just standing there getting bathed by an elephant. Don makes eye contact with me and I don't remember exactly what he said, but he cracked a joke about how hard of a time those two skippers were having taming those elephants and then moved on. We fixed the thing and I got back, soaking wet.

Tiffany Davis, 2000s

Austin said to one of the leads (while we are unloading), "Hey, I think one of the piranhas broke off and I wanna go out and get it before it falls in the river." I said, "Well, just jump in and I'll drive you over there, we are slow." He gets in and we are up to load and we are going deadhead and nobody saw it and they load the boat. So Austin is sitting in the back of the boat and people are coming around, and you can't unload. I'm up front with one rogue skipper sitting in the back among the people. I do my whole thing and the backside of water and everybody is great, and he goes, "Hey, Skip, this is my stop." So I stop the boat and he just gets off and walks into the jungle. I just kept going and came around again and picked him up.

Brandon Kleyla, 2000s

Skippers were also known to go on safari to provide unsuspecting guests with a little extra entertainment.

Someone had a big, plastic, fake thermometer. He took the Honey I Shrunk the Kids lab coat from costuming and went out there and yelled, "I'm checking the rhino's temperature." You remember the rhino had a little hole on the side of it, so he's shoving the thermometer right up the rhino's ass, and the guests are like, "Oh!"

I've got pictures of Ritt and we went out to the lion's safari scene and we took a whole bunch of ketchup packets from the Inn Between and he smothered his mouth with it. We are going by and Ritt comes out and he's looking both ways at the lions and he's got all the ketchup on his face.

Jeremy Wayland, 2000s

CHAPTER SEVENTEEN

It's a Holiday in Cambodia

Working at Disneyland means having to work on holidays. Often, the other cast members become a surrogate family that makes working during a holiday not so bad.

At times after the park was closed, we would take a boat around the jungle with all the lights and animation turned off and it was really spooky. Sometimes I would tell ghost stories for Halloween. Sometimes we went caroling out in the jungle and sang to all the different animals.

Tiffany Davis, 2000s

At first I was really mad that they had me work holidays. But I found that working holidays at Disneyland was really nice, especially during Christmas; everybody there was so nice.

Javi Gonzalez, 2000s

April Fools Day.

I'm ride operator, Chapman is the lead. I had found this camera in the bushes, it was all rusty and obviously fished out of the river. So I got it and cleaned it up and thought this is April Fool's, I've got to be able to do something with this. I kept it in my pocket and was waiting for just the right group of guests on the boat. Fairly late in the day, there was this one family sitting up front laughing and having a great time. At the unload, I ask, "Can you help me with something?" "Yeah, what?" "See that guy standing over there? He's my lead, all I need you to do is walk around (this is when you could get to the lead's desk by load) and tell him you left your camera on my boat." And he's like, "What are you going to do?" And I tell him you'll see. So, I took the camera out of my pocket and put it on my seat. "Excuse me, sir, I think I left my camera on the boat." Chapman always had that hat pulled way down over his eyes. "Somebody leave a camera on your boat?" "What? Oh, yeah." I pick it up, and as I walk over to him to hand it to him, I drop it in the river. The guest now figures out what is going on so he starts yelling, "He dropped my camera in the river." Chapman has one foot on the bow of my boat just looking at me with that Chapman stare. Then I go, "April Fools!" and the guest starts laughing.

Larry Kaml, 1980s

Bat Day began in August 1999 and stayed on that month for ten years; it is now held in May. The August date was because it was the last day that the park stayed open late and the lowest annual pass was still able to enter the park. I There is nothing more fun than Bat Day because there were always all these Goth kids trying to act all sad and depressed at the Happiest Place on Earth.

The only Bat Day that I can remember is this one guy walking around who was 6'5" with a black leather top hat and the boots and the leather trench coat, the black this and the black that. I remember him walking around and him going, "God, it's hot today." He was wearing a black leather coat in summer and he was hot.

Brandon Kleyla, 2000s

I'd finish with a joke and would follow up with, "Aaaahhh, aaahhh, did you get it?" They wouldn't laugh.

Jeff Bautista, 2000s

Dapper Day is an unofficial Disneyland day when guests come dressed in their finest, usually vintage clothing.

Dapper days are always fun, too. We love it when people show up with the jungle or Tiki theme to their outfits.

Maureen McLandrich, 2010s

Gay Days is another unofficial Disneyland event, held the first weekend in October. Guests are encouraged to wear red shirts to demonstrate their support of the LGBTQ community. Skippers generally love working this weekend; many consider it the most fun weekend of the year.

Everybody wore red shirts and kids are asking why and the parents are saying because the Angel game just got over. We are all snickering. I loved Gay Days because you could be bitter and kind of mean. And they are all, "I love you, if I was straight I'd totally marry you."

Kat Thrailkill, 2000s

One of our leads had been an animator for *The Simpsons* and on one Gay Day in the lead log, instead of writing about the events of the day, he drew a picture of Smithers leading Mr. Burns around and Burns asking why he had to wear a red shirt. It was pretty funny.

David John Marley, 2000s

They were the nicest people in the entire world, and I loved working Gay Days because I used to get phone numbers all the time. I'd say, "I don't bat that side of the plate, but I really appreciate it." Cause they are the most discerning and I took it as an absolute compliment. I was all "OMG, someone finds me hot!"

The worst Gay Days were when the Angels were in the playoffs. The Angels all wore red shirts, so you got these huge guys wearing this and you got these gay guys wearing red shirts and people hitting on the wrong guy and fights broke out. You had parents going, "I don't want to sit in this thing on Jungle Cruise," and I would ask why, and they would say, "Well, I"m not sitting next to them," and it's makes you sad. It was one of those things that was really eye opening and I'm glad I worked those days, because you see an entirely different intolerance toward people, and I wonder if that's what someone looks like when they are that intolerant that they literally can't sit with someone, they would rather ruin the ride than sit next to a person like this. It is the saddest thing in the entire world and you just lose your faith in humanity and you just get depressed over it.

Jeremy Wayland, 2000s

Gay days were fun, I used to not like the joke where the rhino had the safari guys running up the pole. It was dirty but not dirty and we'd just cruise up to it, stop the boat, and then just say, no comment, then move on. That was my regular thing, red day, gay day. They loved it, and not in an offensive way at all. They thought I made that joke up for them, but I didn't, it was my regular line.

Ritt Mesee, 2000s

Halloween

I have worked Mickey's Halloween time, where guests will come dressed up. And there are always little kids that come dressed up as skippers. One year a group of people came as the attacking natives. They were wearing khaki clothes, had hula skirts on, and painted their faces. It's really nice when people appreciate your attraction and they want to dress up like it.

Maureen McLandrich, 2010s

When I worked at the park guests were not allowed to dress up for Halloween, so it was kind of like a normal day for us. Little kids were dressed up, but then again the little kids were often dressed up.

David John Marley, 2000s

I also liked the Halloween parties, especially because of the Jungle Cruise families. This one family came and the stroller was the boat and the baby was dressed like a skipper and the dad was the trapped safari. One family came with the stroller as Schweitzer Falls. Everyone is happy and they're getting candy.

J'Amy Pacheco, 2010s

Thanksgiving

I remember working Thanksgiving because it would just suck. You'd have a shift at night and you'd just eaten this huge meal and you just wanted to sleep.

Andrea Freeman, 2000s

One year on Thanksgiving after the park closed I took everyone on safari. We went out to the native village where the dancing natives are and we communed with them to celebrate Thanksgiving.

Tiffany Davis, 2000s

Christmas and the two weeks surrounding it and New Years are the often the busiest times of the year. This makes it nearly impossible to get a day off since Disneyland overstaffs positions knowing that people will call in sick since they couldn't get the day off.

Working on Christmas was usually kind of quiet. What could be better, it was pretty, and people were in good moods up to and including Christmas. Between Christmas and New Year's, it would get really busy and we could get the Santa Ana winds, it could be 90 degrees. I always enjoyed the Christmas season. You would bring in the Rose Bowl teams, everything just seemed real special. It was fun.

Ken Snow, 1970s

The only thing I remember about working holidays is that for the four years that I was there I worked every Christmas Day. I remember my family would get up with me at 5am for Christmas so I could be to work by 8:30am.

John Verdone, 1970s

Christmas on Jungle was sad, because everybody who couldn't get the day off and families, a lot of divorced men, would take their kids to Disneyland on Christmas. For some reason they got the kids, they are living in some condo or apartment, and want to show they're the good dad. I didn't get that until later in life. Especially in the mornings it was divorced dads, and they bring their girlfriends and their kids and you'd hear this awkward conversation, "Well, this is not how Mommy does it," or "This is not how Daddy does it." That's how Christmas stuck out for me.

Jeremy Wayland, 2000s

I used to wonder who are the guests that come in on Christmas? At least in the 1970s It was mostly people from out of state who came to California for the week.

John Verdone, 1970s

The Jingle Cruise is the Christmas overlay at the Jungle Cruise. It began in 2013 and ended in 2016, although it is still ongoing at Walt Disney World.

Skippers love or hate Jingle, there is no in between. We were the same closing crew, we were all working 6 days a week, 8 to 10 hours a day, and it was just Jingle, Jingle, Jingle. And that is when we bonded as a crew because we all worked together.

The guests prefer Jingle because it is something different, the spiels are different. With Jingle we have no freedom in our spiel because it is holiday themed, which can be controversial. Jingle is also always changing, so it's cool to see what they add, what they take out. Last year's Jingle Cruise (2015) was the best I'd ever seen. I saw it two years as a guest, but last year was the best. They put in crates that said "Ship to Arendale" (from *Frozen*) and it was covered in snowflakes and we told them, "No," and imagineering came in to fix it. Why does everything have to be *Frozen*?

Anonymous, 2010s

During the Jingle Cruise, there were lots of added props and elements added to both the jungle and the water during the overlay. It was taught that if something should come lose, we should avoid it and react appropriately. If it was something small, like a present or a fruitcake, we could bump it and report it when we get back to the dock. If it was something larger, like a crate, we were to 3 shot and wait for instructions.

Eddie Agin, 2010s

I love the Jingle Cruise. I love it. That is my niche of humor. I love exuberant, over-the-top jokes, and that is Jingle. It is cool and new and it brings more people to the Jungle Cruise that are excited to be there. People are happier during that time of the year, even though the park is crowded. I know some skippers don't care for Jingle, but I love it. It smells good and it's pretty.

J'amy Pacheco, 2010s

We would have almost all of our queue open. When we tied off at the dock and only ran six or seven boats, we would have a 45-minute wait. Jingle is fun, you either love it or hate it, but you just have to roll with it. The spiel is a little bit challenging because there are no transitions. Each scene is specifically themed. Normally at Jungle, the show scenes all play into the jungle theme, but not with Jingle. In the elephant pool they all have wreaths around their heads, then at the gorilla camp they are baking cookies, so it is all very jarring. I found the transitions challenging. Some skippers will make it their own and do a rhyming spiel. They do a "twas the night before Christmas" spiel. I know one skipper named Christine who did that. I think that is a cool approach to Jingle. There are a lot of "watch your biscuits" because there was a joke at the gorilla camp that was about how the mom is holding her baby and dunking him into a bag of flour and the joke was "watch your biscuits." It became a phrase between the skippers.

The only thing I didn't like about Jingle was when it was January 15 and it was still there. They extended holiday time by two weeks and it was awkward. We'd tell guests, "We're getting ready for next year." I think what we were supposed to do was act like it was the day before the holiday, but it had been over for three weeks, so it was hard to maintain and most skippers had gone back to their normal spiel. Disneyland holidays are always way before and way after. You learn to fluctuate with it.

Maureen McLandrich, 2010s

New Year's Day

I remember working New Year's Day and being super hung-over, the most hung-over I'd ever been. I was really messed up. I was throwing up and everything. It was a bad day. I didn't throw up in front of anybody, I'm a lady. I threw up backstage.

Andrea Freeman, 2000s

Normally, I hate working New Years because of the noise makers that they hand out. When I worked classics (routes in Fantasyland) it drove me crazy because they were so loud. At Jungle this year the best day I've ever had was on New Years. We quickly closed down so we could celebrate. They pulled my boat to the catwalk and I was standing there, waiting for a boat to show up so I could cross, holding my set up and the gun. Right before midnight a boat pulled up and I ran across. A bunch of people from Indy came over and we stood on the catwalk so that we could watch the fireworks. One skipper named Eddie tried to make it back to the dock, but was stuck out there with guests. But it was New Years and I had this great moment. I felt like I'd really made it. Last year I was annoyed at Fantasyland and today I'm standing on a bridge with a bunch of people that I know and love. It was an incredible night.

J'Amy Pacheco, 2010s

So in our story the year is 1938 and the only time that changes is on New Year's Eve. The park is open two hours after midnight into New Year's Day so that's considered 1939 and then the next day we reopen, it's back to 1938. The other thing that happens is that after the midnight fireworks, everybody leaves. They get their one or two "first rides of the year" in and then leave. I was at unload, only about three people in the queue. One brave skipper moves up from unload and began to spiel to the guests. "Happy New Year, everybody! 1939! What a great year! Nothing can go wrong this year, I'm going to go visit my family in Poland!" I was on the dock laughing my head off.

Eddie Agin, 2010s

In addition to regular holidays, there were mix-ins and after-hours parties where groups could rent out the park in the evenings.

For a private party, a company with more than 10,000 employees would rent out the park. At that time, lots of Friday nights were private parties. But if you only had around 5,000 employees, they would do a mix-in and announce the park was only open 10 to 6, but the park would stay open until 1am and at 6pm they would let the other 5,000 people in. Working on the day shift, you would say, "Oh, by the way, we are open until 1am," and that would make the guests' day because they were getting ready to go home at 6pm, and it was actually a mix-in and they could stay. Guests would not get kicked out because we were still open, and Disney wanted to get the numbers in for food and beverage sales. So we had private parties and mix-ins.

Gordon Lemke, 1980s

CHAPTER EIGHTEEN

Grad Nites

Grad Nites were a senior-year highlight for high schoolers from California, Arizona, and Nevada. They were also a special level of hell for the cast members who worked them. Usually, the park would close at 8pm and then be transformed into Grad Nite. Disneyland would then reopen at 10pm and run until 6am.

Grad Nite was especially tough for skippers because they had to be alone with crazy and sometimes half-drunk high school kids all night long. It was also the time when they were the most at risk of being assaulted or harassed, especially the female skippers.

During a Grad Nite, not all of the attractions were open, and for those that were open, we could loosen the rules just a bit. One of the most famous secrets about the Jungle Cruise and Grad Nite is the existence of an adult version of the spiel, the infamous Grad Nite Spiel.

In the past decade, Disneyland has killed Grad Nite, first by moving it over to California Adventure, then making it a "mix-in," meaning grads would spend the day at Disneyland with regular guests, then move over to DCA for the evening. Recent skippers have been spared the horror of Grad Nite.

It is interesting to go back now as an educator and see the changes. We had to dress up. I remember going through the jungle at 3am with people who just wanted to rest fo 12 minutes. Being up all night was no fun.

Vince Fragasso, 1980s

We called Grad Nites, Grab Nites, because all these kids were just trying to grab each other. Everybody had a Grad Nite spiel, but they wouldn't let us have the guns. I think they thought that the kids would get all boozed up and crazy and try to grab the gun and shoot it. It must have happened at some point because it was SOP to not have guns on Grad Nite. Nobody questioned it. The guns were still on the lanyards, so they weren't going to get stolen, but it was part of the SOP.

Some of the Grad Nite jokes were the worst. One guy did a joke about the dragon's blood trees that only turns red once every 28 days. At some point there must have been a chaperone who looked like a high school kid, and a skipper didn't notice and they got ratted out for their spiel.

Dave Lewis, 1970s

I worked lots of Grad Nites. I remember kids vomiting a lot. Jungle Cruise was an X rated cruise, with skippers saying anything and everything. I worked Jungle, Big Thunder, Pirates, and Splash Mountain on Grad Nites. Pirates were the best stories. For Jungle Cruise, you could mostly just say whatever you wanted, and that's why a lot of skippers liked to work it. I had a kid throw up on my boat. Most of them with the exception of this one kid had enough common sense to stick their head over the side of the boat. This kid is just sitting there in the back of the boat barfing, it took like 6 bags of barf dust. The barf dust would come in little bags and we used to joke about the amount of vomit by how many bags we had to use to clean it up. That one was a 6-bagger.

Jerry Whitfield, 1980s

I worked a Grad Nite on one of my Jungle shits. I went to four different Grad Nites as a guest. I was working a day shift and was dating a Hungarian girl who lived in Pasadena. I drove out there, attended her graduation, got on the bus, rode all the way back went to Disneyland, stayed all night long, rode the bus back to Pasadena, took her out to breakfast, and drove back. That was the longest thing. In my junior year, I went to Grad Nite, then senior high, I was dating a girl. So then when I was working a Grad Nite some years later, some kids got on the boat, they were very disdainful of me, thinking I'm a loser for working at Disneyland. They just kind of ticked me off, so when we got to the elephants, I didn't slow down and I let the boat tilt just a little bit and soaked them. It was at night, and I thought I was going to get into trouble on that one, but they were laughing and having a good time, so when we docked they just got off and went into the night.

David Schwab, 1970s

I hated working Tiki on Grad Nites because you had four nerds and a chaperone. It'd be 3am in this big theater with four people. Jungle was pretty good, I just stayed on the same script, it never got racy. Some of my college roommates were on board with their wives and they were heckling me, and finally this one guy said, "This ride is boring," and I said, "I know, I just saw your wife." Good thing he was my friend.

Gordon Lemke, 1980s

I had my Grad Night spiel, but I think I only told it twice during Grad Nite. Most of the time I would find a very funny boat where most of the people had been drinking and they come in the boat and I'd do the Grad Nite spiel. "Hey, ladies, Trader Sam's the guy you wanna see if you want to give your boyfriend a little head, hey, over here is the anaconda snake, the second largest snake in the jungle. If you want to see the first largest, well, I'm off at 8 o'clock tonight." I would always tell those jokes on Grad Nites, but I would always measure it, make sure I knew the boat. Most of the time I let them make out on the boat. I'm sure one or two children were conceived on my boats out there. I'd just turn my back and turn the lights down. As we were leaving the dock, I would say, "You guys are a bunch of couples, right? You like the girl next to you? Go at it, I'm turning my back, have fun." Every once in a while I would look back to make sure they didn't jump off, and most of the time they were making out. They didn't have cell phones back then, they're not texting, they were talking and having their own thing. Once in a while I would let somebody get up there and have their own spiel. Here's the microphone, go nuts. And he'd try to mimic all the jokes and I'd go, "Yeah, that sucks dude. Not so easy, is it."

We entertained ourselves as much as possible, and by 3am they are dropping like flies. But we go to the office, they had a bunch of pixie sticks in the damn shipping office, and they go okay, we've got pixie sticks, who's doing the pixie sticks challenge. This was before the stupid cinnamon challenge. You would snort them up your nose. My eyes were bleeding by the time I had done that, because I never, ever back down on a challenge like that. And I'd go on the boat and my eyes are all watery and I'm thinking this is just sad, this is my life.

Jeremy Wayland, 2000s

They were the easiest to please. For what I do and for my style, I could please crowds easily. I wasn't afraid to open up certain spiels, and not appropriate spiels, say all kinds of stuff. I would say the procreation habits of jungle animals. It was always about "could you pick out the chaperone on the boat" and I was not very good at doing that, and so I think I was lucky enough that even if I would be vulgar for Disney, I was personable enough. Chaperones would say, "Look I know none of that was right, and I know none of that you should have done, but I appreciate this night."

I think they were having such a hard night with the kids that I was able to appeal to that part of them where they have a laugh for a moment. Some people were able to have a crazy night with no chaperones, and I'm wondering why do I always get the freaking chaperones? But I never got busted.

Procreation spiels were always fun. I would just make up mating habits of the different animals. I didn't have a set spiel, I would do improv.

Jeff Bautista, 2000s

I remember pulling away from the dock and asking the guests if they want me to spiel or just shut off the lights and be quiet, and that is usually what they wanted. There were dirty jokes and if you felt like it was a crew that was into it, you could do those.

Andrew Green, 1980s

I never did the dirty Grad Nite spiel. I told people they could ride other boats if they wanted that, although on Grad Nites I would be much more topical with my spiel. I was only 21, so I wasn't that much older than they were.

Brian Vestal, 2000s

Our spiels were pretty racy. It was kind of fun to work for a while, then it gets a little tiring. I was never one to want to stay up all night and watch the sun come up. Some people can do that, but I need a little sleep in between. So, I did it for a while, but I was happy to get more seniority so I didn't have to do it. We had some guys that liked to do it, we had some real comics that just really did some great things. We had a blue spiel, more racy. Half the time most of the people were so tired, they would just sleep. Who knows where they got the alcohol.

Ken Snow, 1970s

Sometimes even the skippers at Grad Nite are having too good of a time.

I remember I did a whole double shift and I end up going to Chili's and I left my car in the K lot and I got plastered. I get a call and I still had my flip phone, and they say we need you to work Grad Nite, and I said I've been drinking a lot, I don't know, and they said, "I didn't hear that, can you come in?" Sure, why not. So I got a ride back to Disneyland, I can't see anything, I got my buttons half wrong, and I get on Jungle and I get two guest compliments out of the damn thing. This is Grad Nite and they went to City Hall. I worked it and I was so plastered and to this day, I have no idea what I said, I have no idea who the hell was on my boat. I still have the two compliments stuffed in a shoe box.

Anonymous, 1990s

Most hecklers were on Grad Nites. One time they were so mad because we couldn't unload them, we didn't have enough people, someone had walked off for a break, that they decided to protest and chant all the way around with a "we know better, we're in charge of ourselves" kind of attitude. They got a second trip and they were complaining and saying everything sucked.

Kat Thrailkill, 2000s

One Grad Nite the lead asked me to join him to check out the jungle. We walked down the Indy queue and noticed that one of the huge doors was slightly open. These doors, which are now padlocked, were used to get trucks to the back of the jungle at night. We opened the door more so that we can get through and walked along the path past the back of the Indian elephant bathing pool. Soon we came upon a group of four teen boys, clearly drunk out of their minds, stumbling in the dark as we approached with our flashlights. The boys explained that they were looking for Main Street, and we relieved them of their booze, which we threw away, and walked them back out of the jungle.

David John Marley, 2000s

I did confiscate a lot of pot and never gave it back. I didn't smoke it, but I gave it to skippers who did.

Andrea Freeman, 2000s

We called them fornication checks in the Treehouse. In Tiki Room you take your flashlight to make sure there wasn't any monkey business going on. People would think things like that at Grad Nite. But I would do trips cause the kids would be from Nevada, New Mexico. People don't get that they've been in a bus for 8 or 9 hours all day. They are exhausted, and now they have to stay up all night at Disneyland. I had one boat and I'm pulling up and they all load in, a bit noisy, and I do the safety spiel and turn the lights off. I turn around and the entire boat is asleep, on each other, asleep, so I just kind of thought, okay, I put my mic down, and I just drove through the jungle and we got to the hippo pool, I shot my two shots and scared the crap out of all of them. But I did it where they never even knew I had it. Then we got to Trader Sam, and I said, "Okay, it's time to get up now, hope you've enjoyed your trip, as we come to the dock, keep your hands and arms..." and I pull up to the dock and turn the lights on, huge applause, they all went nuts and I don't know why, but they went crazy. Now the leads are really concerned. "What did you say?" "Literally, my safety spiel." I just let them sleep for 8 minutes and they loved it. Other than that, we would always say with Grad Nite shifts, you haven't earned your stripes until you've watched the sun come up on the dock. We would go to IHOP or Denny's, those were our regulars at 7am, then go to sleep and come back and do it again. I think I've slept in every hotel in the Anaheim area during Grad Nite.

Brandon Kleyla, 2000s

I remember Grad Nite, let's talk about Leo. He was a veteran and working my first grad night. Leo was always talking about the girls. He would tell us some gnarly jokes, like, "There's a large anaconda, and I get off at six and I hope you will be saying that too." Then he would say, "I'm going to take a dead head with this girl," just the two of them. I remember hearing stories that were crazy - we did the walk through over at the Treehouse, and someone would say, oh yeah, I caught someone having sex over there. Or a group of them having sex over there, and the same thing with Aladdin Oasis. You hear moaning from Aladdin Oasis and you think "what the hell is going on over there?" Grad nights were kind of crazy, I remember around 4 in the morning you'd be so tired of talking you were basically hung over from being up so long. You just tell everyone "hey, you want the jokes or just want to lay down and take a quiet stroll through the cruise?" Everyone wanted to lay down. OK, cool. Instead of 8-minute trips we would make it 15.

Tameem Sabry, 2000s

I caught a couple having sex at the exit of the Tiki Room. It was at the exit doors. There was a show going on and there were only two or three people in there, and I think they left during the show. So before the next show began I walked around the room, cleaned up to make sure everything is nice and ready for the next set of guests, and I noticed that the exit doors are closed. The exit doors open automatically and stay open until you start the next show, so that was weird. I push the button to open the door and nothing happens, so I push the button again, still nothing. I go over there and I give the door good push and I hear this noise and then these two teenagers running away.

Javi Gonzalez, 2000s

I found Grad Nites were really tedious and working one at the Jungle Cruise was really hard because you had such a difficult audience. There was nothing worse than going to check out your schedule and you see nothing but Grad Nites and then a Sunday shift that starts at noon. You'd be so tired.

John Verdone, 1970s

Being a woman at the Jungle Cruise could be challenging, but during Grad Nites it could actually be dangerous.

I thought I was going to get raped and murdered on my boat. There was one night where Grad Nite was all from bad neighborhoods. I had this boat, and it was predominately male. There were only one or two other women on the boat. These guys were saying really lewd and terrible things to me. Things like, "Yeah, you're all alone in the jungle and we're gonna do things to you." And there was one nice guy who kept telling the other guys to knock it off. Finally, it got to be too much and I turned around and said, "Fuck you all, if you try to do anything to me, I will fucking tell. I have a radio here and the cops will be waiting, so everybody better shut their mouths for the rest of the trip." I was really scared. They were saying terrible and gross things. When we got back to the dock, I was shaking and horrified and this one little guy came up to me and apologized for how the other guys behaved. I was in tears and terrified. We didn't have guns then, so I couldn't use that to threaten them. All that radio could do was call the shipping office, not security, so I would have been in trouble. Most Grad Nites were super fun, that was the only one that worried me.

Andrea Freeman, 2000s

A not-so-great Jungle Cruise moment that I had at Grad Nite was when only some inner-city schools were there. They loaded the boat and I was the only girl on the boat. All of the guys seemed to be these giant football players. They were so loud that I couldn't even do my spiel. When I got to the Cambodian shrine, I was having a hard time getting them to listen. I asked them whether they could hear me and a voice in the back yelled, "Yeah, we can hear you, but we want you to take it off." So I just go back to doing the trip, but by the elephant pool they were yelling "Take it off!" I said something silly to diffuse the situation. But starting at the gorilla camp all the way for the rest of the trip, they all just kept chanting, "Take it off!" That was the first and probably the only time I just hit that throttle full speed and raced back to the dock for security reasons. I even radioed the lead.

I'm pretty sassy and sarcastic, so I was good at keeping these kids and their space, but that was tough. Some people got into those dirty Grad Nite spiels, but I never did. I was also pretty good at dealing with hecklers. I was good getting their friends to laugh at them. Sometimes you could tell who was going to heckle you at the dock. That was a good time to let them know it wasn't going to work. Jungle Cruise is the only attraction that has that back and forth between cast members and guests.

Tiffany Davis, 2000s

For a few years, Disneyland changed Grad Nites to all-day events. High school-ers were allowed to mix into Disneyland during the day before being moved over to DCA in the evening for the private event. Having large groups of high school seniors in the park led to problems.

Grad Nite was interesting. I liked it better when we closed down the whole park. I still disagree letting those kids run wild all day, that's non-sense. The last day-time trip, one of the high school kids stole a stuffed animal off a stroller and threw it in the river, so the family got off the boat and found out their kid's favorite doll was missing and the next boat comes up and the kids were laughing so we knew damn well what had happened. It's in the river and even if we get it out, it is ruined. I was just horrified, and I asked is this really what we want to do, let these kids go wild and completely nuts around families on their vacations? This is ridiculous.

Siobhan Armstrong, 2000s

Thankfully for current skippers, Grad Nites as they existed for 50 years are gone. I have yet to meet a skipper who laments their move to California Adventure.

Grad Nites are at DCA now, so they mostly come over to Disneyland during the day. I've never had a bad interaction with them. They will be loud on a boat, but they laugh and have fun. They are 18 and on top of the world.

Maureen McLandrich, 2010s

CHAPTER NINETEEN

Changes Over Time

People assume that the Jungle Cruise hasn't changed much since the park opened in 1955, but the opposite is true. The animals are different and more technologically sophisticated. The boats are new, the spiel is regularly updated, and of course each generation of skippers have their own take on comedy. Even the ethnicity and gender of skippers have changed over the decades. Let's see what skippers had to say about the physical changes of the Jungle Cruise.

We didn't have that whole safari set. You had the rain forest, you had the Asian temple with Old Smiley the crocodile and the circling crocodiles, and then you came around into the elephant pool with the big bull elephant talking to his mate on the other side and then you came to Schweitzer Falls and then into the hippo pool and then the natives and then the backside of water and then you came down through the rapids and then Trader Sam was there trying to get ahead and then back to the dock. It was a 9½ minute trip, then after they added the safari it went 10 or 11 minutes.

Tom Nabbe, 1960s

My first summer was the summer of 1962 and it was the first time the jungle had been expanded significantly. I remember that the Indian elephant bathing pool was there. I thought it was great. Those elephants were so cute. The elephant in the shower was there. To my recollection, the African veldt was there.

I remember that Ganesha was there and that the treehouse was under construction. The trapped safari was definitely in operation while I was a skipper and I was a skipper until spring break of 1964. That's the last time I drove the boats and the trapped safari was there. I even remember doing jokes about the guy at the bottom getting the rhino's point across. Some people have told me that it wasn't operating until the summer of 1964, but I was at the New York World's Fair in 1964 and

I remember working with it and it wasn't there. The trapped safari was running before the summer of 1964 when the animals were added to the veldt. They come and change things, the animal positions. The animals were less violent, they took the meat away from the lions because it was kind of gory.

I thought the Indian elephant bathing pool was fantastic. The African veldt was always too cramped and it wasn't too effective. You couldn't show the Serengeti plain. The trapped safari gag was pretty cute. It was a pure Marc Davis gag and it always got a laugh.

Alan Coats, 1960s

In the 1970s even more of Marc Davis' ideas were integrated into the jungle.

That's when they put in the safari encampment (gorilla camp). The gorilla and crocodile scene and the tiger in the shrine. All of that was new in 1977. The first summer that I was there in 1976 they told us that they were closing it and they gave us hand-outs about the new animation and we were all very excited. I thought the gorilla camp was pretty cool. I don't know if you remember what used to be there, but it was a rhino and two babies would run away. The safari camp was good. The gorilla and croc didn't turn out like the pictures we had seen. The gorilla was supposed to be hitting the croc on the head, but he didn't and it was just dumb. So as we came around the corner we'd say, "Hey, look folks, it's Cal Worthington and his dog, Spot," and you're not allowed to do stuff like that. Once I had these people from Alaska on my boat and they laughed really hard at that joke and I asked them how did they know who Cal Worthington was and he had a car showroom up in Alaska.

Jeff Rhoads, 1970s

In the early 1990s a section of the Jungle Cruise was removed to make room for the queue for Indiana Jones and the Temple of the Forbidden Eye. Sections were either taken out or moved to other parts of the jungle.

I didn't notice a lot of difference. We dropped the hornbill jokes, that was the only part of the attraction that was affected by it. Everything from the shrine to the end was the same; we did add a spiel about Indiana Jones.

Larry Kaml, 1980s

They ruined it when they put in Indiana Jones. I used to love that when you left the dock you were in the jungle. Now you get in the jungle and you go around the corner and there's this huge mass of people, it completely destroys that illusion, getting rid of the padded seats on the bench, it seems so unfinished now, you just sit down on the raw wood and it seems cheap. The last time I was on it was about two years ago, there was black mold on the hippos, they needed to be cleaned, it was like it wasn't being maintained. You have that much valuable real estate in the middle of the park, you need to respect it, but seeing the Indy Jones line and all this other stuff, it just felt neglected.

Gordon Lemke, 1980s

The boats were even different in the early years of the Jungle Cruise.

And the boats were different. In the 60s they had gas-powered boats. We only had two gas-powered boats, you had a tiller, your pedal was down on the floor. The other ones were natural gas, so you had everything up front. The gas-powered boats had a tiller, a transmission forward and reverse, and the gas pedal on the floor, so if you were talking to the guests and you turned to face them, you had to use the accelerator with your heel. By 1971 they had converted the other two boats, but I got the chance to operate the gas-powered boats too.

Ken Snow, 1970s

Sometime around 2002 or 2003, Imagineering came to the Jungle Cruise and took a boat for a couple of hours. They were to test if the attraction could be automated, a recorded spiel with no skipper on board. None of us were happy that they were there, and our lead just glared at them and grumbled to himself. They'd cruise by the dock and wave, and he'd just nod. We were happy when they left.

David John Marley, 2000s

One of the biggest changes, from a skipper's perspective, was the removal of the guns from the boats in 1999.

I was working the last two weeks we had the guns. But I ended up working the very last shift where we had the guns. Being there when they brought them back was also really cool.

Matt Nerrie

One of the elements you might assume would change was the culture of the Jungle Cruise and Disneyland in general.

It's amazing to me the amount of freedom I had in 2002 vs. 2007. Gerry was still there. The people you worked with were different, and nothing against them, it wasn't their shtick to be slapstick. It didn't feel like they supported each other in that creative front. I don't think they looked at it in 2002 as the way we looked at it. This is a big stage for all of us. 2007 was just, "No, what are you doing?" People were telling on each other, so it got to a point with all the jokes that I loved to tell I couldn't tell. Even the personas I loved to do I couldn't do. It soured the second time around, but from what I could gather it was from how riotous the previous years were that management had to make a change, people were getting too liberal with what they were saying, throwing out stuff here and there. The previous generation could get away with murder, but the next generation had the clamps on, so it seems like that dynamic was playing out there. It felt like it to me, because we had a lot of fun. In 2002-03 we had a lot going on. Those were great years. You talk to camp counselors and they have their favorite summers. It was that. It was fun.

Jeff Bautista, 2000s

Socially, outside of Disneyland it has changed and people are less creative because they've been helped along so much. They fit into that little box now, because that's how they've been brought up. They can't think for themselves in a unique way. That's not the only reason, but it's part of the reason. And that starts taking away from people's individuality and their creativity. It mutes everything. I've been there a dozen years, so I've seen the change; it was very gradual, but it has changed dramatically. It's still fun for me because I'm still the same, I haven't changed. I do the things I do because they are entertaining to me. I try to get current skippers to relive it, but the task is too great and turnover is too high. It's not as bad as it used to be, but it's still really high. Two years is now a long time, it's rare to see anybody with more time than that. You see it more at Big Thunder Mountain, because that takes people with more experience and by the time to get there they start dropping out.

Kipp Hart, 2000s

One significant change to the Jungle Cruise has come about due to changes in Disneyland. Until the early 2010s, Disneyland still had an off-season. You could visit the park when it wasn't summer or Christmas and not see crowds. Those days are now gone and it has impacted skippers, too.

When I talk to people from my era, one of the things we always say is do you remember how quiet it used to be? Opening up Jungle first thing in the morning and it was just silent out. It's not like today where they have the big rope drop and there is already a few thousand people on Main Street getting ready to run to their favorite rides. Those quiet times at the Jungle Cruise were just wonderful. You would be sitting in your boat waiting for people to come on the ride.

John Verdone, 1970s

It was a much more casual pace and you ran less boats, you could do longer trips and spend more time with the guests, spend more time talking to the guy on the dock, cause there's longer time between boats. There was more camaraderie. Now there's no off season and it never really slows down. Every evening after fireworks, we went down to rear load and just had one line. With tickets you were limited, and you didn't have passports for unlimited rides, you had to use a ticket, and it was night time.

Gordon Lemke, 1980s

I remember that in 2005 with the 50th anniversary of Disneyland the park was really busy. There was a lull In 2006 and 2007 when the park still had off seasons, and it could still close early. It seems to hit when they did their Year of a Million Dreams promotion, and things got bigger and bigger with Disney buying Marvel and the Pirates movies kept coming out and the park got more crowded. As a result, there was more of a microscope on the people that work at the park. People that I worked with during my last years at Jungle Cruise were amazed that we used to be able to go off the script; that concept was completely foreign to them. And that is one of the reasons why I left, it just wasn't fun anymore.

Javi Gonzalez, 2000s

Bad management decisions also had an impact on the Jungle Cruise.

It changed when Paul Pressler was there, the budgets were cut and facilities never fixed anything. Animatronics often wouldn't work. I remember the gorilla stopped working for three weeks. We hung a sign around his neck that said "Out of Order." Then we put a sign that said, "No shooting, please, they didn't restock the ammo." We just pretend to be shooting and say, "Bang, bang," or they give us 10 pieces of ammo for a four-hour shift. They were rationing ammo. Those signs were up for three or four weeks before a manager even noticed it.

Jeremy Wayland, 2000s

Anaheim was chosen as the site for Disneyland in large part because it was predicted to be the center of suburbanization from Los Angeles in post-war America. The majority of people moving to the suburbs then were white, hence most Disneyland cast members were as well. As Orange County began to become more ethnically diverse, so did Disneyland. Even in 2018 the black population of Orange County is just below 2%, while the Asian and Hispanic populations have moved into the high double digits. So while people who are hostile to Disneyland like to accuse it of racism, the facts don't line up when you study the employment pool available to the park. So what was it like when more non-white cast members began to work at the Jungle Cruise? Jerry Whitfield remembers being one of the few blacks who worked in attractions at Disneyland in the late 1970s and early 1980s.

When I hired in, I don't think we had any Asians at all. I remember they really changed a lot over the years and I got to the point where after about 5 years I stopped counting how many black people were at the park. But looking around in the beginning, I don't think that was ever more than one or two at a time. I was the only one in Adventureland a that time. Actually, there were five of us in the park total and we all knew each other, and I think two guys were gay which was even worse for them at the time, but it was myself and a guy named Alden. Right out of the navy he came and got a job at Disneyland. He and I were best buddies for a lot of reasons and we had lots of laughs about the things we heard and saw at Jungle Cruise.

Jerry Whitfield, 1980s

So what was it like being black and working with mostly white people on an attraction about the jungles of the world? First Jerry had to deal with other skippers.

They used to have this unload joke and at the time I decided to go the Jackie Robinson route and just not say anything about stuff that was done. But there was this unload joke they used to use and it was, "Hey, there's unloaders Jerry and so and so." They would say the old cookie jar joke, "Well, you know these skippers, their moms used to tell them if they steal from the cookie jar she would beat them black and blue." That was the joke they used to tell. Some of the skippers figured out very quickly that was not a happening joke.

Jerry Whitfield, 1980s

And then Jerry had to deal with guests from around the United States and the world.

A lot of the guests would make comments or say things and some of them didn't quite understand. With certain skippers their brain is pre-programmed with "this is what I'm going to hear, this is what I'm going to expect." With me, they would expect someone who didn't speak in any ethnic fashion that they expected. And I had guests say at the end of the ride, "How did you lip sync all that for the entire ride." What I learned is a lot of pre-conceived ideas and notions are programmed through their life experiences.

Sometimes people would say things they didn't honestly realize what it was they were saying or how it was going to come across. It's the same when a guy says to me, "My best friend is a black guy." Why do you feel the need to say that? It's because it's their way of saying, "Hey I'm OK with you," but they don't understand that the way you said it makes it look like you're trying to justify that in your own mind. But anyway, a lot of skippers I work with and a lot of guests had to get past that, so my normal response was to just blow it off. But I got a lot of that, and then at the end of the day when the microphone was down and I would talk to them and you can see the light come on and then they change the subject, "Oh, that was the best spiel I ever heard." That happens more often than not, but over the years I was there that kind of thing happened. I was hired in right on the edge of when all the traditional people hired by Walt Disney people were still there. So a lot of that was still trying to get out of that John Birch Society mentality.

One of the lines at the Jungle Cruise that I exploited later was the fact that I had a unique capacity to communicate with the headhunters and the guests had no problem with that. They made that assumption, part of the thing I would say was, "Oh, that's my last crew," they'd laugh, and I'd say, "Well, folks, you're in luck, because I know these guys, and I think I can talk about our way outta here." So I go up and I'd say something back which sounded like Nigerian or an African dialect. I'd say, "What's that?" By this time the boat is gently parked because I didn't want to hit the sensors. "They won't attack the boat if we agree to give them this person or that person, but you gotta make up your mind fast, so who's it gonna be." I always pick some person who was not paying attention. Then I'd say, "Oh, you took too long," then the guys would attack. And as I got the boat around the corner, I'd say, "It's a good thing I speak their language or we'd all be dinner now."

The kids would be terrified because they'd think it's real and they would be on the bottom of the boat. The moms would be into it which is funny because they bought into the whole stereotype thing, too. After one ride, a kid came up to me and gave me a hug.

As far as the spiel, it was pretty involved in those days, it was basically old-school spiel, but of course we all had our own ad libs. I quickly found out that there are certain things I could get away with that didn't necessarily work for the other skippers. I could say things in the head hunter village, I could speak to them in Swahili or Nigerian or whatever else.

Jerry Whitfield, 1980s

I remember at Jungle Cruise it was like they'd only let one black guy work there at a time. If one quit, they would hire another. It was weird, we had every ethnicity under the sun, but always only one black guy.

Anonymous, 2000s

Tameem Sabry's parents came here from Egypt. He was born and raised in Huntington Beach and attended the most prestigious Catholic high school in Orange County. He claimed his speaking level of Arabic is kindergarten, but that didn't stop him from coming up with a great bit for his boats.

I remember one time all the managers piled on my boat. And they said, we want to hear your Arabic spiel. So, we are going on, and I give them my spiel with the accent, I would slay the jokes on purpose because they are funnier that way, especially to the annual passholders. I see people getting on my boat and they expected a certain punchline, and I would deliver something different. I think what I liked about watching other people is they would do something edgy and you wouldn't expect it, and it would make me laugh. "Wow, look at all those rocks there," pointing out the most arbitrary things there. "Hi, my name is Tameem, and I'm here on an exchange program to learn the English the best I can, I live with a friend, he is pharmacist, he work in pharmacy." I would start driving. "Oh, here we have Bengal tigers, don't get too close they can jump 50 feet and they might jump on you." I would drive off, and if they weren't responding to the joke, I would do the punch line in the script. Sometimes I would do the joke so bad it was funny. At the end I would say, "If you want to contact me, that's my email address right there on the wall," and the people would laugh.

Tameem Sabry, 2000s

Jeff Bautista is ethnically Filipino and also from Orange County. Because he grew up in the predominantly Vietnamese city of Westminster, he developed an amazing spiel using a Vietnamese accent that became very popular.

I didn't have a lot of material to draw from, but I definitely wasn't afraid to put stuff out there. I don't even know how the Vietnamese even came about. In high school I had always done these funny videos with my friends; now that I look back, it was quite insensitive. Back then you didn't give a shit, you are 23 years old. I had grown up in Huntington Beach and around Vietnamese culture, so I have a lot of love and fondness for them, but at the same time I picked up the phonetics of their accent and I over-sensationalized the accent, but it was funny in that sense because it was characterized. One day it just made sense to do it, someone had said, "Yeah, we had a skipper here before who was

Japanese and did the rice hat thing," and he played on the fact he was Asian. There was even a white skipper who did a trip pretending to be a Japanese scientist. He rode my boat to check mine out.

So, I tried mine, and I think he was on that boat, and it came across to him as border-line authentic, but you can tell it was a joke. I think it played well with everyone. They knew it was a joke. At the same time, they were buying into it. I didn't add the hat until the end or whenever it was around. I would adapt and if people started to feel uncomfortable, wanted to laugh, but were holding it back, I might just ad lib in regular English, so they never knew what my real cultural background was, but at least they knew I was putting on a show and it was okay to laugh.

I do this stupid leprechaun Scottish accent and I was able to combine the two—Vietnamese doing a Scottish accent. I don't know how I pulled that off.

On my last day I don't remember how many requests I got for the Asian spiel. People in the boat were just coming up and saying it. I think skippers were saying, "Hey, ask for the Asian spiel." I was not asked by other Asians, and I didn't want to offend them, so I never did it.

Jeff Bautista, 2000s

So what was the Vietnamese spiel like?

A lot of it was I wasn't just using the accent, I'd do some social commentary. One of the big jokes was, "Hey, kid, you want to go round the park today and find Mickey Mouse?" The kid would say yes. "Well, you tell Mickey Mouse I want my paycheck, he owes me money, I work overtime, I come to this country..." I would say stuff like that, I would allude to immigration, the American dream, so it wasn't just doing the accent with the jokes, I was interjecting stuff. People would respond and laugh, there was that sense of realism to the joke and those are always the best jokes. I always wondered whether they knew I was faking it. At times I thought they knew, they are looking at this character and not taking me seriously. What privilege does this play into?

Jeff Bautista, 2000s

I remember the first time I saw Jeff do the Vietnamese spiel. I talked to him after a trip and said, "How can you get away with that? You don't look remotely like you're Vietnamese." And he said, "Most white people can't tell the difference." As a white person I was a bit offended, but I watched his next boatload of guests talk as they walked away and he was 100% right.

David John Marley, 2000s

How do skippers deal with a guest that is openly racist?

When I would tell my Arabic spiel and it was right after 9/11, I had this guy in the front, I did the whole spiel: "Hey, I come from Egypt and I'm here in America to learn English the best I can." And the guy goes, "Hey, look Billy, a terrorist." The kid was about 7 years old. I was like, "Look, man, you know, there's two things here, first you don't need to be telling that to your kid, and second, you don't need to be riding in my boat." I just kicked them off the boat. That trip ended quick. I backed it up to front unload, and I said, "Get off the boat." I was just not going to have that. As a skipper you are supposed to be this upbeat person, telling jokes to enhance the attraction, and as you are going, your mood alters the guests experience, and it altered those guests' experience for a few hours. I tried my best to be professional, but I'm a person.

Tameem Sabry, 2000s

Being of a non-white ethnicity also meant you could get complaints from members of your own ethnicity who didn't think you fit in their idea of how their group should act.

I would get some of that flack, too. "Oh, I'm speaking to a Filipino American," but culturally Filipinos speak English. There were moments where Filipino people would ask, "You don't speak Tagalog?" and when I told them no and that I was born and raised here, they would attack my parents.

Jeff Bautista, 2000s

Another change at Disneyland was cultural. As the LGBTQ community began to gain more open acceptance in society, people had a chance to openly interact with them and have their perceptions altered in a positive way.

Up until I worked Disneyland, I knew one gay person in my entire life. I'm from Orange County, went to a Christian church, the whole nine yards. A skipper on Jungle Cruise was the first person I knew who was openly gay. He had flowers around his neck. I'd go, I like this guy, and it was kind of eye opening for me, and I think anybody who is anti-gay needs to work at Disneyland and meet people for the first time. It opens your eyes and you stop being such an asshole and realize all these people that are hard-liners, anti this and anti that, you need to wake up because you realize it is an entirely different world that you have not opened your eyes to. I never knew it. I grew up in an environment where "homosexuality is bad." Working with gay people at Disneyland you learn these are the greatest guys in the world to work with, and

I'm glad they are gay because I don't have to compete with them for the other girls. They were the nicest people in the entire world.

Jeremy Wayland, 2000s

The one thing that never changed through all these changes was the essential character of the Jungle Cruise. It is always going to be the odd man out.

Disney is one of those companies, like Google, Apple, button-down and perfect, so for something like that has gone on at Disney, all the CEOs at Disney that have come and gone, the Imagineers that have come and gone, but Jungle Cruise is still weird, bizarre, it's not an attraction per se, its not a movie or a show or a thing that happens, it really is just hit or miss which is the beauty.

Ritt Mesee, 2000s

CHAPTER TWENTY

Tales of Love and Occasionally Outright Sexual Harassment

Disneyland is a match-maker's dream come true. So many young people spending hours and hours together means that sparks of love are inevitably going to fly. Up until the mid 1990s when women were allowed to work at the Jungle Cruise, it was difficult for the male skippers to find young ladies to talk to. That meant they were on the lookout for guests who, especially during the summer when the temperature gets hot, wore skimpy clothing.

Now that the attraction is all genders, skippers have even gotten married to each other. The dark side of all these hormones is the effect on the female skippers, most regularly when male guests can't understand a joke when they hear one.

Once this handsome young skipper got a guest compliment that said, "He wasn't very funny, but he was so dreamy." They showed us the printout. We never let him live that down.

David John Marley, 2000s

Tens of thousands of guests come through the queue all day long and some of the lovelier ladies will get noticed by the skippers. Since it's bad show to openly talk about them, a series of code words were developed to allow skippers to talk out in the open, even over the PA system.

We had a scoring system back then for pretty girls. Someone would see a girl, yell, "Scores!" and we'd all look in that direction, see the girl, and we'd yell back "Seven!" or "Three!" or whatever. It was pretty uncivilized, but we didn't care. We were there to screw around and meet girls.

A skipper named Joel made us use another system for loading his boats. He'd scan the line for a hottie. He'd then say, over the live mic,

"Number six, red," which meant the girl he wanted to have seated right next to him was sixth in line wearing red.

We had codes for things during my time there, too. A "914" started out as a dress code violation security used for radio transmissions. It usually meant some girl in a halter top had too much of her goods exposed. We also used "Herman" to signify the presence of a girl with big boobs. "Herman's here." or "There's a 914 in the next boat."

Dave Lewis, 1970s

We were always looking for the cute girls and yelling, "The 914 is coming." It was for a cute bra-less girl.

Ken Snow, 1970s

Prior to 1995, the girls who worked at Tropical Imports were often the only female cast members a skipper would see during his shift.

Tropical Imports was there, and Adventureland was there, and it was fun to go to see the girls, they knew they had the attention of the boys. And they would milk it.

Larry Kaml, 1980s

When I worked there, there was unload and load and in between those two positions was a hut that sold souvenirs and cute girls worked there. It might have been called Tropical Imports, but we'll called it the hut. You would banter with the girls, chat with them, and at the time a girl named Kathy worked there. Kathy Mangum is currently a senior vice president for Disney. She opened Cars Land. We used to chat with her all the time.

At Jungle Cruise some of the only girls we could talk to were the girls that worked at the Sunkist juice bar. And the girls that work there worked for Sunkist, they were not Disneyland employees. So you'd make friends with them and go by early in the morning and they would slip you an orange juice and sometimes one of those weird donut things they sold. You had to have friends in key places at Disneyland

The best thing was to have a tour guide on your boat. They were always the best-looking women. *Mark Twain* was the best for that. The guide would bring them on the boat and then let them stroll around and the guide would come up to the wheelhouse to hang out with you. Jungle Cruise had a special type of person, and the guides were a special type of person. The tour guides told me that they always loved the west side, it was always the most fun.

John Verdone, 1970s

In the 1990s, the tour guides were always the hottest girls, and by the early 2000s they were all middle-aged women and gay men. I don't know what happened.

Anonymous, 2000s

People love to get engaged at Disneyland and the Jungle Cruise at night is one of the few places where a private quiet moment can be arranged.

A guy proposed to his wife on the cruise. I was the skipper, I was told to take him out on a private boat, I was to pull a bottle out of the water and open it up, and I was like if I can plant the bottle in the water, I can stage fake it and pop down and got it, so I did that. We were in the hippo pool and I reached down to grab the bottle and I almost fell into the water. I slipped. I locked my foot against the pole. I almost fell in and that would suck because I wouldn't know how to explain that. But I was able to get it and the guy even reached over to help me. I come up, open the bottle, and say what is this, why are people dumping stuff in the river? Oh, wait, there's a note inside, and I picked it up, and I said, I don't understand this odd language, so I said can you read this note to me? And I hand it to the guy, and he read it, and it was the proposal to his wife.

Jeff Bautista, 2000s

One skipper proposed to his skipper girlfriend in the hippo pool, with the help of lots of other skippers along the way.

Rita was the lead at the time. I had told her it was under the guise of our parents meeting for the very first time. So what happened, we signed each other's parents into the park and we are going over there and I said, "Hey, they've never heard your spiel, so why don't you give them a ride and I'm going to go get your Christmas present." She loads them all up and it's just her family and my family, and we were both off duty and Rita let us do it. So I run around to the Indy exit queue and I had a boat waiting up there so I jumped onto the boat, landed on the middle box, nearly dislocated my shoulder, it really hurt. Next thing I know I see her boat and I yell, "Gun it!". By the time she got out to the trapped safari, I was on the back of the boat, I had two of the glowing red roses from Main Street and I had a radio with the music playing "Can You Feel the Love Tonight" over the entire PA on Jungle. I don't know what everyone else on the ride thought. Here she comes right up behind me and I say, "Will you marry me?" and I take her over to the lead boat and I had the skipper put a "Just Engaged" sign on the back of the boat. The marriage turned out to be absolute crap, but the engagement was very cool.

Jeremy Wayland, 2000s

Jeremy was going to propose. He had trained me, so we set up a jungle police and I was the front boat. You box a boat in, so I stopped my boat, which was a deadhead. Then her boat got stopped at the hippo pool and Jeremy jumped out into her boat and proposed, and then it was like "Yeah!" so I drove my boat back alone, which is the opposite to being proposed.

Ritt Mesee, 2000s

I think most male skippers were not as popular with the ladies as they thought, but there was certainly never a shortage of available women.

I didn't experience anything outrageous in that sense. The guys worked over at Jungle Cruise and the girls all worked at Storybook. There was a sense of brotherhood. Because it was all guys, girls would tend to come over. A buddy would say, "A girl was on my boat today and she's got some friends and she wants me to get some of the skippers and meet up at Videopolis." So we'd go.

Vince Fragasso, 1980

If there was a young couple on the boat, I'd try to flirt with the woman. I'd say things like, "May I ask you a personal question? Is this relation- ship solid? Do I have a shot at all?" and usually everyone would laugh and the girl would shake her head no. So then I'd say, "What if some tragic accident happened, like he was mysteriously thrown overboard while on a trip through the jungle and eaten by crocodiles, would you mind if I gave you a call?" Nine times out of ten the girls would say yes and everyone would laugh, and I'd say, "OK then, there's hope! Let's go find some crocodiles," and roar away from the dock.

David John Marley, 2000s

Sometimes a skipper would play matchmaker with less-than-stellar results.

It was my first spring at the park and I was trying to figure out what these Grad Nites were. It was all a bit confusing because I didn't even know when Grad Nite ended. So I'm in the boat and Skipper David is at load, and he loads the boat with one guy and then yells "Hit it!" I told the man, "Well, I guess you're going to get your own special VIP tour of the jungle tonight." I don't use the microphone, I'm just talking to him. and we're chatting and I'm pointing out animals and I'm doing puns and I felt just a little awkward because it was just the two of us. So I asked him whether he wanted to do something fun. I explained to him what dead skipper was and asked if he wanted to do that. So we get behind Schweitzer Falls and I have the inside lights on and we're just talking and waiting for another boat to come up so we can pretend to be dead. We were waiting and no boats are coming and we keep waiting and I don't know how long we were there, but somebody told me it was 20 minutes. It was the longest trip I've ever taken. So I say we better go back to the dock, I don't know what's happening. As we pulled up to the dock, I see the other two boats are tied off and all the lights are off. When they see me coming out of the jungle with just this one guy everybody starts clapping and hollering. They were all acting like I had just scored in the jungle. I got on the dock and they unloaded the guy. David didn't tell me that I was the last boat. He was trying to be a matchmaker, but it was the most awkward jungle trip I'd ever had.

Tiffany Davis, 2000s

The girls at the Tahitian Terrace were beautiful and I always wanted to get the nerve to go talk to them but never did. They did their own thing.

Vince Fragasso, 1980

In Skipper Stories *you heard of couples falling in love and getting married. It turns out to be much more common than anyone knew. One skipper realized that Disneyland was playing matchmaker for generations of young people in Orange County.*

I married a girl from the park, many of us did. Disneyland was a great place to date because all of the women who worked there were great. They were beautiful, smart, and had great personalities. I realized that casting was creating a population of beautiful people who were all very similar. It was like before Tinder, they were swiping right, they were selecting the best people. When my son got a job there at Canoes I told him, "Your job is to have fun and find a spouse."

John Verdone, 1970s

We met backstage when we were both working Jungle. He was mostly days and I was mostly nights. I didn't know very much about him and at the time I had hit the "I've been single for a year" market and I was sniffing around. When I hired on at Disney I was six months off of a break up and I'm thinking this is going to be a meat market. I realized that most of the guys are into each other. So, it became like a call of the wild thing, to get to know somebody a little bit someone would say, "How old are you?" That was usually my first question and they would say, "I'm 19," and I'd say, "Nice talking to you." So I'm backstage with this guy, and he's got really good charisma and he's nice to talk to, he hasn't cut me off and said he's gay, which was almost like the first three sentences when I started talking to somebody, and I asked, "How old are you?" He says, "23," and I'm all,

"Me too!" Sold, he seemed pretty neat, but we really never really crossed paths, and then I started sniffing around, and I found out he was not the most likable guy and I couldn't understand why. He was one of those guys where people would go, "Meh, I don't want to work with him." I couldn't quite understand it until we worked together then worked apart, but at a point when we were not seeing each other and I would be put on as a boat partner, because we are both awkward or whatever, then I started to understand, he is kind of an asshole at work. He is this different guy, he is there to work, not to make friends, and he's sort of obnoxious, and a know-it-all, and one of those guys you tolerate, and you want to hate him, but he'll do the job, just not easy to work with. It took a long time before we started seeing each other, and it was after he left Disneyland that we started seeing each other again, and it was super, super casual. He joined the army and he went to Korea. A long time later he calls me and says, "I'm coming back to California and I want to talk to you." And I tell him I'm now engaged, and he says, "That's fine. I'll be your friend," and I said, "Even if I want to talk about wedding plans," and he says, "Yes, that's fine." So, when he comes back, he says, "Well, if you were still single I was going to marry you." I said it's really easy to walk into a clean room and say, "Hey, I was going to clean that." It was never a question, ever. My exes are exes for a reason, and this is the coldest thing I've ever done in my life. On the heels of telling off my fiance, I call this guy, and within five days he comes back from Korea and we were in Vegas and we were married. It was that fast. We've been married over 12 years. I look at my ex and it was a bullet side step, but man did I stomp on him hard. I felt like an asshole. But it has lasted and lasted, and you do that thing, where if we make it through this, we will live through everything.

Kat Thrailkill, 2000s

We all became such close friends because we saw each other at work and socially because we always have week days off at the time. We used to do trades with other places like a Mountain High, Bear Mountain, Snow Valley, they used to trade lift passes for our comp passes, so we would ski for free, a lot of places did that, Magic Mountain did that. So that's how we ended up together and making friends and being close and some people met their wives, like I did. It was amazing how people met their wives and significant others there.

Jerry Whitfield, 1980s

It wasn't just Grad Nites that were dangerous for female skippers. Men constantly make advances to skippers, and just about every other Disneyland cast member that they encountered.

It's another thing that happens to female skippers. It's this weird thing where we are sort of hyper-sexualized by middle-aged married men or just guys in general. I have a couple of instances on my boat, because I have some jokes in my trip about not having a boyfriend and being lonely, it fits my spiel. And people would yell things from the back. One time I did the joke at Trader Sam where I talk about having dinner there with my boyfriend and Sam's wife makes an incredible stew. Then I said, "Just kidding, I don't have a boyfriend," and then this guy yells, "Not yet you don't!" in this oddly threatening tone. There are ways to say that that are not so creepy.

The other day I was loading my gun and I heard this guy in line making comments to his friends about me having a gun. He said it really loudly, so I had to comment on it. He gets on the boat and ends up right in front next to me. I did the joke I always do, "Come sit as far forward as you can because you get a better view...of me." I do that joke every time. And so he says, "OK, great!" and I thought, *Oh god, this is going to be a fun trip.* On the trip I would do a joke and I could hear him trying to be funny, next to me, but I'm not going to talk to him, I have to entertain the entire boat. This went on the entire trip. It was like he kept trying to be funnier than me as a way to try and impress me. We pulled up to the dock and the entire boat empties and he stays behind and hands me his business card and says, "Call me sometime, maybe we can swap skipper jokes," and he threw it on the captain's crate. It was weird. It's that little thing consistently. Guys making weird comments to girl skippers. People will shout out things from the back of the boat. It's almost always middle-aged dads which is weird. It's not fun. They think they are funny. One guy tried to boo me, but he was laughing at the same time so I told him, "Sir, you got on this boat, you don't get to boo me. You walked into this," and he laughed even harder. I do this bit after the attacking natives where I'm hiding and I do this voice into the mic saying, "Thanks, Skipper J'Amy, you saved our lives, and you're so pretty, too." And people will wolf whistle from the back. It's little things like that and it's almost always from the back of the boat.

One time these guys got on the boat and sat right in front of me and one loudly says to the other, "Wow, she's really pretty," and I said, "Wow, thanks, but now is not the time."

One of my friends was at load and helped this older man into the boat and he turned to her and said, "You should come sit on my lap," and she just said, "I'm good."

There is this weird culture at the Jungle Cruise where people think it's okay to say that women are not funny, but still hyper-sexualize us. I haven't met a girl skipper yet who hasn't had an experience like that.

J'Amy Pacheco, 2010s

It got to the point where we got real protective of the female skippers. I remember it was the first summer that women worked jungle. One obnoxious guest was hitting on her in the boat, and at unload we could tell she was uncomfortable with this guy, so all the Jungle Cruise skippers just walked over to the boat and stared the guy down and made sure he was off the boat and not coming back. We let him know he was messing with one of our sisters.

Larry Kaml, 1980s

I remember going in, the girls on the rides really did get harassed then, it was the 90s, it was a little different then. They used to say you have to go out with every girl from the rides and they had this little checklist and I forget who was doing it, it was one of the older skippers that organized it. You had to try to check off each of the lands in the park. Just going out on a date, only that.

Jeremy Wayland, 2000s

By this point in the book it should be obvious that you should never mess with a skipper. One skipper's ex-boyfriend had to learn this, painfully, first-hand.

I had a boyfriend in college and we dated for about two-and-a-half years. He worked at Innoventions and he cheated on me with a girl from there. It was really awkward. I thought it would be OK since we worked at different ends of the park. I might run into him at Harbor Point, but that was about it. He ended up teaching at Disney University and he would always bring his tour to the Jungle Cruise and always request my boat. And I would think, *Why does he do that?* He did this about a week after we broke up. I was only 20, and when you're 20 and you get dumped it's just the end of your life. And so he comes on my boat with all of his new kids, the new hires, they fill up an entire boat. And I'm giving him dirty looks and then I decide to make the entire cruise about him and what a jerk he was. I said things like, "There is Ganesh, the symbol of love, not my love, he broke my heart. His name is Greg, he's sitting in the back, everyone look at him. " It was one after another. I made the entire trip jokes about our breakup. The boat figured out that it was real, not just a joke. When we got back to the dock I said, "Thanks for riding the Jungle Cruise, if you had a good time my name is Andrea. If you didn't, then my name is Greg and I work at Innoventions and Disney University and I like other girls more than Andrea." It was so brutal. So as they get out of the boat he came over and chastised me and said he was gonna get me written up, he was gonna tell my lead, he couldn't believe that I wouldn't honor the show and the magic. He was so pissed. Andy was the lead, and he was the total hero. He knew that I was really upset about it.

The Mousecars were happening on my 21st birthday and Andy came to the dock and got on one knee and asked me to go to Mousecars with him. Which was the sweetest thing. He had a girlfriend at the time and he got her permission to take me. She couldn't go because she didn't work at the park. I was so excited and it was my 21st birthday, so we went to TGI Friday's, and I was always a good girl, I never drank before, and everyone was buying me shots and they taste like candy. So I got drunk! And we go to the Mousecars, and Andy and I were all dressed up like old Hollywood. Andy and others were holding me up because I was so drunk. And we won attraction of the year, and so I decided to walk up to the stage and I fell over and rolled down the stairs. Right at that moment, my ex-boyfriend walks up with the girl he's been screwing. And it's only been a couple of weeks since he dumped me. And he said, "I just wanted to wish you a happy birthday and congratulations on winning attraction of the year," and I just yelled, "Fuck you!" Andy stepped in front of me and said, "Don't mess with her." Andy and I both knew how to swing dance and there was a swing band playing so we danced and danced. It was the best night, and Andy had to take me home because I was so drunk. It was the best night except for falling down the stairs at the Mousecars in front of everyone. Andy was so great because I was the worst possible date, I was drunk and yelling at my ex-boyfriend and falling down stairs.

Andrea Freeman, 2000s

I had just passed Trader Sam and I'm waiting for my turn to approach unload and I'm vamping and trying to buy myself some time, so I asked if we had any birthdays on board, any anniversaries, that one old bit. Any newlyweds. I wasn't getting anything. So I asked about divorces and one guy raised his hand. The whole boat moans and I said, "I don't have anything to add, nobody has ever raised their hand, but I figured I'd ask. Well, good luck with that." I just turned around and started driving again.

Brandon Kleyla, 2000s

CHAPTER TWENTY-ONE

Skippers After Hours

Years ago I was walking around a college campus with one of my young daughters and I got to chatting with another professor. As we walked away my daughter said, "Is he a skipper, too?" It made sense to her because most of my close friends are Jungle Cruise skippers. That place created a bond that I've never found any other place I've ever been.

Working at Disneyland, and especially the Jungle Cruise, means gong to parties after hours. I didn't really drink until I started working at Jungle. Then I made up for lost time. That seems to be a re-occurring theme with many skippers.

I had just finished training, I hired in during May and before summer started, Benny has this "Weekend at Benny's party," and I got invited. Casey, the only person I really knew, wasn't there, and I was feeling everyone out. As a social butterfly you have a drink with as many people as you can. So, I had one too many drinks. I guess I had dodged that point where I was sloppy and passing out, and Matt, Andy, and Jeff were like, "Man, we will take care of you," but they don't know what to do with me. So, they bring me in from the outside backyard area into the kitchen area, right across from where you enter Benny's home. They wonder where to put me, and finally stick me at the dinner table, right by the door. I started throwing up. There were a bunch of empty pizza boxes there, so they just grabbed a pizza box and put my head in it, so that it would collect my vomit as it spewed out. Jungle parties went for quite awhile, because cast members get off at midnight, so people are still coming in after midnight and they would come through the front door and ask who I was. "I don't know, he's the pizza boy." People believed it and said, "That's rad, the pizza boy came in and partied with you." The next time on the dock, people are like, "Hey, aren't you the pizza boy?" And that's how the legend was born. You are young and back then the crew was really close. I guess I made my way into the group and it stuck.

Jeff Bautista, 2000s

Working at Jungle Cruise is where I really got my drinking game on. So many parties. I remember we'd head over to the Lost Bar (a now closed bar at the Disneyland Hotel) and drink. I drank a lot of beer because of a skipper named Brian. We'd also go over to the TGI Friday's at the Block in Orange. Sometimes we drank so much that we'd have to call in. There was this guy who also worked scheduling and he was drinking with us. I was so drunk I called the scheduling line and was leaving a message that I was going to be sick the next day, so I couldn't work. And when I finish the call he was standing there watching me. "Are you calling in for tomorrow? I heard you telling people to shut up while you were on the phone. I'll go in early and erase your message so you don't get fired." So I really appreciate what Aaron did for me that time.

Javi Gonzalez, 2000s

In Skipper Stories *I told tales of the infamous Banana Ball, the annual, end-of-summer party held by skippers. This drunken festival was the highlight of many cast members' times at Disneyland.*

So 1976 was the Banana Ball at the Orange County Fairgrounds in that big airplane hangar. I remember dancing with a girl that I was attracted to and having a good time. When she had to leave I walked her to her car and as I was walking back to the party there was a guy sitting on a planter out front projectile vomiting what must have been cheap red wine. It looked like a fountain. I couldn't believe what I was seeing. He was just sitting by himself on the edge of the planter and his vomit was like a rainbow. Otherwise, I remember the music and beer flowed and everyone was having a good time. There was a big build-up to it. You'd see flyers all over the place and they'd sell tickets. One guy, Chris, we called him Cola Nuts because of the 7-Up commercial with the guy with the deep voice. He was a really good artist. He designed the t-shirts for the Banana Ball. Everybody went. All over the park, people went and everybody wanted to go. It was hot, sweaty, and we didn't care.

Dave Lewis, 1970s

John Verdone was there for one of these most notorious events.

What people will tell you about the history of the Banana Ball was that it started out as a Jungle Cruise banquet. I honestly don't know if it's a true story or not, because I haven't met anyone who went to it. I'd love to know. So the Banana Ball hadn't been done for a few years. The big year I did it was run by myself and a guy named Jim, and we decided to do it at the OC Fairgrounds. We looked at lots of places, but we rented a large exhibition hall. We found a company to bring in a beer truck with lots of taps, we had t-shirts made. We sold tickets, $8 and $7 if you buy them early. We got people selling tickets all across the park, east side, west side, foods, stores. We tell them that if they sell 20 tickets then they get in free. We promoted it in *Jungle Drums*, the skipper newsletter. One of the ticket sellers was from Fantasyland and she came to me while I was at the *Mark Twain* dock and we're talking as the ship is leaving the dock. So she hands me the ticket stubs and the cash as I pull away from the dock. I'm looking through this stuff and she's $8 short. I thought she was really cute, so I talk to her and tell her that she shorted me $8. We had this back and forth thing going on, and that is how I met my wife. Since she shorted me I decided to punish her in the worst way possible, so I married her.

It was pretty sophisticated to get this entire thing set up. So many things to do. We sell all the tickets. Jim and I are worried and we hope that we break even. We realize that as the money comes in, like the day before we realized that we covered our costs with the pre-sale tickets. And we need people to work the party, so we sign up people to work an hour shift serving beer or taking tickets. We had a spreadsheet for all the positions. We had to find people we could really trust to handle the money.

On the day we are setting up, someone comes up to us and says, "Have you looked outside?" There were probably 80 people waiting in line to buy tickets, and then we realize we are going to make a fortune. Tickets that night were more money. George Trullinger is playing and the place is getting crowded. Loud music, concrete floor that has beer spilled all over it. Like the movie *Animal House*. Guys started taking off their shirts and running and sliding across the floor on their chests. So eventually we are just problem solving. People were getting shocked at the beer station. The servers are standing in beer and they are grabbing the spigot on the truck, so every time they touch it, they got a shock. People were sliding across the floor. There are various levels of disrobing going on because it's dark. Then we hear there had been an accident. We go over to this girl and clearly her arm is broken. As we look at her we realize that she is young and realize that we haven't been checking people's ages as they enter. Probably a third of the people there were underage and we're serving them beer. Then we realize that we are in serious trouble. So for whatever reason it is decided that I'm going to take her to Hoag Hospital. We go to the emergency room and it was empty and they take her back and they have me sign her in. They ask me her name and I tell them I don't know. They are looking at me suspiciously and they ask about her insurance and I tell them that I'll be paying cash, and I pull out this huge stack of beer-soaked $1 and $5 bills, that's what people were paying with. So I pay the bill, she comes out in a cast, and I ask if she wants me to drive her home, but she wants to go back to the party. The entire thing took maybe an hour.

I was back at the party solving more problems. Somebody comes up and drags me to the door and says, "There is a camera crew from NBC channel 4 here. Tricia Toyota is here and they want in." I grab Jim and say, "Hey, there is a camera crew here!" and he said "Oh yeah, I invited them, I told them about this huge end of the year Disneyland party. I didn't think they'd actually show up." I remember that we talked to her and were doing the interview, but we are not going to let them go inside. They cannot see the debauchery that is going on. We try to make it seem like a wholesome party of hard-working people. They interviewed a few people, took a few shots. I remember seeing it on air.

Finally it's all over. It's only Jim and me there and they turn the lights on and the place is a battlefield. There is beer and cups, shirts, trash everywhere. The OC Fair people tell us that they have to lock up the place at 2am and then it will be unlocked at 5am when the cleaning crew arrives. But there was still stuff that Jim and I needed to do. So they lock us in the building for three hours. This was my favorite part of the night, Jim and I are finally able to count the money. By the time we get done, I'm trying to remember the exact amount, I think we each made $1,300 profit, and that was more than I made that summer at the Jungle Cruise. I was making $2.65 that summer. Jim and I went to Hawaii for vacation, and for years we didn't tell anybody that we made any money. We told them we barely broke even. When we did that skipper show I finally told people that we made lots of money at the Banana Ball. In later years, other people took it over and it began to have problems, like lots of non-Disney people heard about the party and wanted to go and then one year a bunch of bikers showed up.

John Verdone, 1970s

Skippers did more than just have drunken parties. Sometimes their activities were actually healthy. One popular annual event is the Disneyland canoe races, and the Jungle Cruise teams did about as well as you might expect.

We weren't very good and we went to Denny's a lot. It was a lot of fun and that's why we did it. Other reasons I wanted to do it in were that my dad had worked in the park before and after he was in the Air Force and in Vietnam and one of the things I remember him telling me as a little kid was about doing the canoe races. I grew up in Orange County, we had annual passes and went all the time. When you're a little kid you want to go on the canoes because it's fun. As an adult, you don't like going on the canoes because it's work. It was always a fun thing my dad would talk about. So when I finally got into attractions, and I had some friends that wanted to do it, I was able to make that happen. It turned out to be a whole lot of fun. We never had the expectation that we were going to do well or anything. It was about getting out and having a good time. It was about experiencing something different. I mean, you get to paddle around the Rivers of America the wrong way at 5 o'clock in the morning. That's not something that a lot of people get to do. Bringing people into that experience was really cool thing for me. I remember people vomiting in the river because they were hung over, people were missing and you would call before 5 o'clock in the morning to see if they were coming. Some people closed the Jungle Cruise every night, so you knew they may not make it. Certain people were never going to show up. You are always crossing your fingers that you had enough people just to go out and practice. You wanted ten, but you had to have eight, and you always had hope that the fourth girl would show up. But it was a whole lot of fun.

I saw a picture on Facebook where I had everyone sitting on a docked Jungle Cruise boat practicing their switches over the box. I don't remember that, but the picture jarred my memory a little bit. But in my defense I was consuming large amounts of alcohol at that time plus I was working a lot. The fact that I don't recall those little details isn't super surprising, but it sounds like something I would've tried to have us do. I think I did that our second year when I saw some kind of glimmer of hope that we might be able to do something. Practice makes perfect, you know.

The first year was before I got trained on Canoes. I had been trained to steer the boat since I had a little experience with canoes growing up. But to steer you have to know what you were doing. I crashed us into a Fantasmic float on the front side of the river stage, not very far into the race. The rule is if you hit stuff during the races you're disqualified automatically for that year. So that happened and they told us we were done.

The third year we actually made the sprint final. A skipper named Sherry had been a front steerer and I was in the rear. We made the sprint final, and in the sprint final the rear steerer is not allowed to paddle. They are only allowed to steer. It was 100-yard sprint sitting side by side. I really wanted win, I was going to have Sherry steer in the back and I was going to be at the front so I can paddle. I over-thought it. I put two people opposite me to compensate for my massive power. And we ran into the lane line and got disqualified.

We knew we were not going to win, we were just there to have fun. We didn't go out and rent canoes to practice. We were just out there to have a good time and we accomplished that more often than not.

Matt Nerrie 2000s

I did it one summer and it was a lot of fun. We always got beat by the canoe guys, it seemed a little unfair. I didn't like having to get up so early.

Vince Fragasso, 1980s

Disneyland used to hold parties for its cast members during the Christmas holiday and at the end of summer.

My favorite moment on Jungle Cruise was when the Disney company finally worked out a contract with the owners of the Pan Pacific Hotel (renamed the Paradise Pier Hotel). This was when they were making their way toward building California Adventure. Pan Pacific was right next door to the Disneyland Hotel. So they had negotiated to buy that property, made the contract, and as a thank-you celebration, they invited the big wigs. The parent company was Japanese, but the administrators were from America. They have this special reception for them at Club 33, full bar and everything. They go on the Indy ride, then go back to Club 33 for dinner. They wanted somebody to take them from Club 33 to Indy and back again. They wanted it to be a kind of immersive experience, and they knew about us doing the characters on Jungle Cruise. So they said, we want your six best to be there and interact with people in character, and small groups walking over to Indy, and back again. So I did Spike, my favorite character. The park was closed and we had the Indy queue door to ourselves. I was going to be part of the character on Indy. I had my revolver out. "Stay back everybody, this is the most dangerous part." And when we got to the ride itself, we were told to just get them there, get them on the ride, wait for them to come back, and walk them back again. They'd hop in the Jeep and ask, "Aren't you coming with us?" "Darn right, I'm going to drive this Jeep for you." Of course the backstory of Indy is don't look into the eyes of Maura. Spike has the eye patch. So I just stayed in character walking them back to the club.

Larry Kaml, 1980s

Disneyland is filled with college students who are budding film makers and the Jungle Cruise is a great place to shoot a film. Whether it was for official or unofficial purposes, the end result was usually funny.

Jerry Whitfield used to do videos all through Adventureland and Frontierland and we would do it at the end of summer, a party the management would host at the Disneyland Hotel to celebrate making it through the season, with food and dancing. We'd show these videos and I made three. "Destination Unknown," a music video with Sue Barnaby as the singer. "Adventureland the Movie," with short skits, and one was the rookies take the skiff out on a joy ride and they get lost. Each sketch we would come back to them they would be in a different place, like the skiff on top of Schweitzer Falls, which was a bitch. Over in the pond at Big Thunder Mountain Railroad. Then they are over in the little river by Swiss Family Treehouse. So we had them all over the place.

The gag was that they kept getting lost and ending up in these weird places. We wanted to go into Storybookland canal then ended up in It's a Small World, but we couldn't get permission for that. "Jungle Cruise Christmas Carol" was the last one we did, with the main character Scrooge Muldoon, a direct rip-off of Don Chapman. Hat pulled down and calling everybody "guy." At the end he has a metamorphosis into a really nice lead. I played the Jacob Marley character, that was fun. We got permission to bring on a lead that quit years earlier to come back to be Ghost of Jungle Leads Past, one of the present ones, then we picked another guy as the Ghost of Jungle Leads Future. Shows that things had gotten so bad that even this guy could become a lead. The entire scene he had his scarf covered up so you couldn't see who he was until the very end. Usually the very end when there's a reveal that it's a skeleton and its death, and you pull it back and it was the guy that was the biggest asshole. Instead of dying alone, Scrooge was going to end up on Subs. "NO anything but that, I promise I'll change!"

Then there is the unofficial video. In 1991, I read in the *LA Times* that Hostess, the maker of Twinkies and Ding Dongs and other fine confections, was having a video contest to celebrate the 65th anniversary of the Twinkie. The original Twinkies were probably going bad just about that time. So I asked permission from supervision to do a video with the Jungle Cruise background and they said no. It wasn't for any Disney event, but we did it anyway. Paul, Noel, and I, the three of us would sneak into the park. Paul was in a management training program, so he could bring his car for doing this. In his truck was the video equipment. We would show up at Jungle Cruise at 5 in the morning, while the park was closed and the maintenance is out there and everything, We shot this video, Paul and I, we are hacking our way through the jungle and we get attacked by natives and we get across the river, because we are looking for the gold. And we come out to this clearing and Paul goes, look, we whip around and it's a convenience store like 7-11. We go running over there and we get the Twinkies. "At last we found the gold, the golden sponge cake with creamy filling, how I've longed to hold this gold in my hands." We get up to the counter and are told, "OK, it will be $1.50" or whatever it was. (Slaps his pockets for wallet.) "My wallet, the camp!" We go back to the camp and get our wallets. So we shot it and submitted it and I edited it and gave it to Paul to mail, and there used to be a post office in the back of Disneyland off of Ball Road. He goes to mail this video, gets an envelope and addresses it to "Twinkie Video Contest." The folks say, "We want to see it," so they take him back to the break room to a TV and VCR and made him show them the video. "Oh, that's great, now you're going to win for sure, where did you shoot the jungle sequence?" Paul says, "Costa Rica." The lady said, "Why didn't you just shoot it at

Disneyland, they have a jungle there." And he said, "Oh, we didn't think about that." We came in second place, nationwide. 600 entries.

Larry Kaml, 1980s

There is a tradition of skippers making movies about big events at the jungle, so when the new script update of 2004 was ready to be announced, two other skippers and myself decided to film a movie to introduce it to the rest of the skippers. Mike, Kaz, and I were on the update team, so we created a movie, which Kaz decided I need to star in. The vast majority of the five-minute movie was shot in the hours before the park opened. We'd get there at 6am and shoot scenes for a couple of days, then Mike, who wrote the basic screenplay, edited it all together. Kaz, with her theatre training, was the director. Poor thing, she had to work with me, the world's worst actor.

The basic idea of the film was me hunting around looking for a mysterious object, which turns out to be the new script. It was an Indiana Jones-style adventure with me running around things at Jungle, but mostly at Indy. Eventually, I walk into the Indiana Jones break room and find the script in a vending machine. The shots of me running back to the dock were filmed literally seconds after the park opened and in one of the final shots, where I'm looking at the merchandise at Tropical Imports, you can see the first guests running by on their way to Indy. We even got a manager to help out. We borrowed a huge pile of jewels from Tropical Imports and she carried them in on a tray as our reward for finding the script. It was all shot in black and white and was presented as an old-time newsreel.

My favorite part of the film was the only bit I added to the movie. As I'm walking down the tunnel of the Indy queue, I open an exit door and walk through. The next shot was in full color as the door I open has magically transported me to Mickey's Toontown. I walked out all confused, I see lots of kids, strollers, and crowds, and run screaming back to the door and the safety of the black-and-white world of Adventureland. That was also the weirdest part to film because it was shot during the day and a large crowd of guests stood around Mike and the camera, waiting to see what was going to happen. So when I burst through the door my first thought was, *Holy crap, there are like 50 people watching this unauthorized filming and I'm wearing a Jungle Cruise costume in Toontown.*

David John Marley, 2000s

CHAPTER TWENTY-TWO

Once a Skipper, Always a Skipper

Working at the Jungle Cruise is like being in the Mafia or the Illuminati: once you are in, you are in. Being a skipper means you are expected to be entertaining at parties and are expected to have wild stories to tell. So how do former cast members feel about their time driving around the rivers of adventure?

I'd still work there if they paid better. I loved working there and if I got a decent wage I'd still be there.

Andrea Freeman, 2000s

I bet other people have told you this, but the spiel is something you just never forget. It's like a party trick. I have been to parties where people asked me to recite the entire spiel.

Vince Fragasso, 1980s

I love Jungle so much. Anytime my friends see anything with a Jungle Cruise theme they bring it to me because they know I'll go crazy. My friends make fun of me for it. I joke that one day I'll be the 80-year-old lady who still drives boats because I can't imagine leaving. Jungle Cruise has ruined all of my future plans because I don't wanna leave. I want to travel and write and I wanted to do study abroad, but I don't want to leave Jungle Cruise and Disneyland won't give me the time off. I fought so hard to get here that I don't want to leave it. It's nice to have something that you love so much you don't want to leave it.

J'Amy Pacheco, 2010s

I still do this ride. For example, I fly to Wilmington, Delaware, and I have this group for two days, 25 physicians. I start out with a quick round of introductions and ask them a question like, "What was the first concert you went to?" I get to know people and I get to know the room, who can I banter with, who can I play off of. Who I expect problems from. This is going to sound arrogant, but I pride myself on being one of the best when it comes to this, people love me because I'm funny while I'm doing this. In fact, I have a hard time controlling the funny. I'm a straw-hat guy! So how did the Jungle Cruise allow me to get here? I think there are inherent characteristics of straw-hat Jungle Cruise people. They are quick thinkers, they are able to articulate back and banter, they tend to be funny. But, with that being said, if you take stand-up comedy as a parallel, comics tell you that it takes 10 years to become good. You have to put in the time every night to become good. What the Jungle Cruise allowed me to do is to take that raw thing that I had and thanks to repetition, it allowed me to hone my craft. It allowed me to get on stage and work out my routine that I use at work. It allows me to face different things, different people. Every boat is different, but I already know who they are. I just don't know which person is going to play which role on this boat. So I do that with my classes. You can quickly figure out who is who. Who gets a chance to have that opportunity at a young age?

John Verdone, 1970s

When I applied to work at Adventures by Disney, the form asked what trips you've been on and do you have experience being a tour guide. So I put down on my résumé that I have been leading tours through major rivers of the world for many years. I never clarified that it was only at the Jungle Cruise. They must have figured that out. Working at the Jungle Cruise helps tremendously. You have to speak in front of a crowd of people. It taught me how to watch for visual cues to see if people are enjoying what you're saying. It showed me how to have a sense of humor. The Jungle Cruise opens doors to just about anywhere. Working for Disney as a company is great, but the Jungle Cruise is a whole 'nother level. I will never take that off my résumé.

Tiffany Davis, 2000s

I remember when applying for jobs, "Oh, you used to work at Disneyland, what did you do?" and I'd say, "Oh, I was a Jungle Cruise skipper." "Oh, you were the guy on the boat." Then they want you to tell them a joke. I feel like the movie *The Wedding Crashers.*

Tameem Sabry, 2000s

Skipper Keith Hart helps run the popular Tiki Convention Tiki Kon in Portland, Oregon, and uses his Jungle Cruise skills to run tours.

I still use my training on the Jungle Cruise here on the Tiki bar tour in town. We put 150 people on 3 buses and they have a guide who goes with them to help wrangle around and make sure they are packed up and ready to go out on the next stop on schedule. I've been a skipper now for a number of years and I get to bring out some of my old Jungle Cruise jokes. We have so much fun with that and people request my bus year after year. The jokes are the same every year, but they love it. I wasn't a skipper this year, because my house was on the tour. But two years ago the whole bus started chanting, "We're #2! We're #2! because we happened to be bus number 2.

Keith Hart, 1990s

When I interviewed for my job with the government, I had been working at Disneyland for almost a year. I was ready to talk about my academic achievements and brought in my portfolio, and talk about cryptography, and code cracking, which is my specialty. All they wanted to hear about was the Disneyland Jungle Cruise, and that's all we talked about. I felt like that's why I got hired. They asked me to do jokes and I made it interactive where I walked around the conference table as I was walking around the room. And I always tell people that I would have never gotten my first job if I hadn't shown that I have the ability to be personable, to not take myself too seriously, in a very serious environment, and I let my portfolio speak for itself, but I had to use the Jungle Cruise, or they allowed me to use Jungle Cruise, to express myself as a person and they loved it. After the interview I could still hear them laughing when I walked out. I felt bad for the guy after me, I killed that room. I was hired to do analysis and testing on missile targeting systems. But I got it on the merits of being able to tell Jungle Cruise jokes. I was sent to Washington DC a lot to do presentations and basically deliver bad news to people that invested a lot of money into these things, generals and admirals that oversaw these programs. People would ask, "How do you calm people down so well?" They needed that type of person to speak confidently and calmly, and it's funny because we were all just a bunch of cut-ups at Jungle Cruise. The ability to adapt that I honed at Jungle played well with my career. We were trained to come up with a solution, let's not complain about things, let's fix it.

I don't think I could have done any of the things I have done now without drawing from that time at the Jungle Cruise. How impactful that year and a half of my life was. It has given me so much to draw from, strength and energy, and it's just from one season on this ride. It is always going to hold that special place.

Jeff Bautista, 2000s

People ask me about Jungle Cruise all the time and it has opened a lot of doors for me, especially at job interviews. I got my first design job because they asked me about working at Disneyland and working at Jungle Cruise makes you a celebrity. It's been a long time since I worked there and people at my work still bring it up. I get introduced to people by saying, "Do you know that Andrea used to, be a Jungle Cruise skipper?" It's like being a mini-celebrity. Some people, when they find out, just say, "Well of course you were," like they could tell.

Andrea Freeman, 2000s

One former skipper even brought an old copy of the Jungle Cruise script to his work.

I have my Jungle Cruise script in the back because it gives me street cred with my cooks. We have all these interns coming in and they expect me to be some arrogant asshole because I'm the chef so I drop some Jungle Cruise jokes and show them the script and they think I'm cool. It gives me immediate status.

Mark Mendoza, 2000s

I've joked with my wife that when I retire I'd love to go back and be a skipper for 20 hours a week. That would be a fun retirement.

Andrew Green, 1980s

It helped me be comfortable on a microphone and be comfortable in front of a diverse audience. It prepared me to do improv better. Whether it was somebody yelling from Indy or heckling, you were ready.

Brian Vestal, 2000s

What is it like to visit the Jungle Cruise as a guest after spending so much time working there?

It makes me sad to this day when I go there and ride a boat and the skipper isn't into it. I just want to grab the microphone and do it myself. I want to say, "Sit down and let me do this." Things were looser back then, now when I go to Disneyland and ride the Jungle Cruise it isn't the same. We used to have so much fun and these current skippers don't seem like they are having any fun.

Andrea Freeman, 2000s

Can you go back? My answer is yes; however, it is different each time. The balance between Disney's four keys has changed for the skipper. There is more focus on safety and efficient operations than ever. Part of that is due to emerging ride law. Part is driven by an effort to reduce wait times. Regardless of the differences, the draw to work on the Jungle Cruise can be very strong and is worthy of serious study. Just ask a skipper who has been there. Seriously, I don't know what it is about that place that attracts both skippers and guests alike. Some of my most powerful memories have come from that artificial jungle. But it is definitely real when you see three or four generations in a family sharing an experience offered for 60 years. I have often told people I was born to be a skipper. I was a skipper three times, trainer, lead, general lead, and manager, and it still calls for me to this day. It is part of who I am, so powerful I have to reject it from me like an addiction to drugs, alcohol, or sex to focus on a healthy life balance for me and my family. Is it a sickness? Maybe. But if so, I don't want to be healed. I want to forever be remembered as a skipper.

David Schoenwetter, 2000s

A special treat for a former skipper is the chance to take a boat and spiel again. This occasionally happens.

Trevor showed up one day at Jungle. This was several years ago. I asked him, "Would you like to spiel?" His face lit up and he said, "Really?!" And I said, "Yeah. Just come back and get in my boat." When he got in and we were on our way, I said, "Hi folks, this is a very special boat. Have you heard of Make a Wish? Well, we have a special guest here. His name is Trevor and he is going to spiel for you." Everyone looked confused. I hand Trevor the mic. By this time we were in the shrine. Trevor's first joke, "See those cobras? They're drunk."

Kipp Hart, 2000s

Back in those days they had a Christmas party they no longer call the Christmas party, and it was for employees only. Employees were encouraged to come to the park, go on rides. You could buy food and snacks at a discount and managers were the ones running the rides and serving the food. When I was working at the Disney Store my category was management, so I got to be one of the people that could go to the park and work it for the Christmas party. I signed up to work the Jungle Cruise. They gave me this questionnaire that asked about my experience at a theme park and I wrote that I was a trainer at the Jungle Cruise. They gave me a copy of the new spiel and it came time to get some training and there is a young kid on the boat who was going to train me. He wanted to know how much I remembered of the spiel. "You want to see what we used to do in the 70s?" He said sure. Because of liability issues he still had to drive a boat, but I was allowed to spiel to the guests. So my next trip I started doing jokes that had been approved in 1974 and 1975, but were a big no-no for 1993. The skipper was cracking up. I was just repeating what we all used to say, and this young skipper was howling, and he said there is no way we could get away with some of the stuff you guys were saying back then. Evidently the lawyers and insurance company said you can't have these rides being operated by people that are not doing it full-time, so it all got shut down. Then they said we can only be busboys or work crowd control. So the other Christmas parties I just went and worked at the magic shop.

Dave Lewis, 1970s

I don't go back to the park very often, but a couple of times when I did the skippers let me guest spiel. They find out I'm a former skipper and they hand me the mic. It's happened three times over the years. but not recently. It was great to do it again. One time my son was on the boat with me and he was very young so that was fantastic. I wish they could do some kind of alumni thing were former skippers come back and run the Jungle Cruise boats for a night.

Andrew Green, 1980s

A couple years after I left, I would go back with the kids and see who was working Jungle and watch people unload. They'd be like, "Are you Larry Kamal? I've heard stories about you." One time I was there with my family, and they needed to bring a boat out from storage, and they asked me if I wanted to throw the switch. So I did, this was when switches went to the electric ones. Before I first hired in, it was manual, you had to pull a pin out, swing the arm around, put the pin back in again, bring the boat, and then do the reserve. They let me touch the buttons.

Larry Kaml, 1980s

Probably the most common shared experience for skippers is dreaming of working at the Jungle Cruise. I don't think I've talked to a skipper who hasn't had the occasional dream where they are back in the boat.

I have a great job now, but when I used to have a really stressful job and I couldn't sleep, I wouldn't count sheep, I would do the Jungle Cruise spiel in my head. I would close my eyes and picture the jungle and I'd usually be asleep by the time I got to the elephant pool. Nowadays I start farther along in the jungle because I kept forgetting parts of the script.

Fred Martin, 1980s

I still have dreams that it is 1977 and I've left the park because then I have long hair, and I'm a guest at the park and somebody comes running up to me and they say we're short at the Jungle Cruise, we need you on the ride. I ask him do I have to get a haircut, they say no, just go to wardrobe and get a costume quick. So I come back and I'm getting the boat in the jungle, but then suddenly it's some weird new area I've never seen before. It is turned into some kind of dark ride like Pirates. Then we come out of the tunnel and suddenly we're in the parking lot and now the boat has wheels. There're times when I used to wake up saying the spiel. I used to be able to go all the way through it and last night I tried to see how much I could remember and I couldn't get much past Old Smiley in the Cambodian shrine.

Dave Lewis, 1970s

I've had so many dreams about working at the Jungle Cruise again. One time I had a dream that I went to Walt Disney World and as I entered the park these people ran up and begged me to fix their Jungle Cruise. It was a big lake and all 10 boats drove around nose to nose. I stood on the dock and yelled, "Show spacing! Keep your show spacing!" At the time I'd never even been to Walt Disney World.

David John Marley, 2000s

I started dreaming in spiel. Every once in a while, you see a post on Facebook about a dream someone had; mine now are different. My Target job and my Jungle Cruise job, and it's both the same way, I show up and nobody is there in charge, so I go to do something for myself and everybody gets in line, or gets on the boat, and I'm saying, "I'm not working, I'm not working." They have changed the ride on Jungle Cruise; it opens to a lagoon in Africa and it's dry and there's bugs. Like being on a boat out on the bayou.

Kat Thrailkill, 2000s

The Skipper Show remains a popular Jungle Cruise-themed stand-up comedy show even 12 years after its premiere.

After you left I told some other skippers, "David Marley gave me his card, is that cool?" and they were all saying, "Ah, man, you've made it." I'd heard of you and the crew of legendary skippers that you were a part of.

Javi Gonzalez, 2010s

I had been doing some media interviews for the Skipper Show and one reporter from the *OC Register* asked me if Disneyland was concerned about the show. It had never occurred to me. The next day I got an email from a buddy of mine who works for the State Department and was spending a year in Iraq. He asked if I would be willing to bring the skippers to Iraq to perform. I thought to myself, *Oh God, how powerful is Disney? They're trying to kill us all.*

David John Marley, 2000s

The Jungle Cruise is so important to people that they literally take it to their grave. The skippers that remain behind leave mementos of their fallen friends all around Adventureland and beyond.

Don Warner was hilarious and the nicest, sweetest guy ever. He had this gorgeous big skipper hat and it had features and looked rugged and was so cool. I wanted to hang it in Trader Sam's so we can always see it and toast Don. My friend, the great skipper Andrew Peterson (who sadly passed away in the summer of 2018) said, "Yeah, you can't do that, Don was buried with it." That's how much working at Jungle means to everybody, the guy was buried with his skipper hat, which is beautiful. So there is a picture of Don in there. There are at least four or five references to Andrew in Trader Sam's and one in Jungle, but that one I'm still not over yet.

Brandon Kleyla, 2000s

CHAPTER TWENTY-THREE

No Wonder They Got Fired

Everybody stops working at Disneyland at some point, and most leave on their own. However, there are times when the pressure is too much, the pay is too low, and people snap. That is when management steps in, escorts you from the dock, and walks you out the cast member gate. Here are tales of skippers getting fired or quitting. Let's start with people getting fired.

One skipper was a professional baker and he was really into the girls who worked Jungle and he liked to buy them gifts. One day a guest enters the queue wearing a Janet Jackson shirt where she was topless with a man holding her breasts. This skipper lost it and says, over the PA, that he wants to kill her. And he started yelling at her. That was new behavior to him. He was really pissed about that shirt. He was escorted off property by security and the police and fired, obviously.

Benny LeMaster, 1990s/2000s

The following story is rated PG for adult content.

At Jungle once there was an ROP college program kid who was slow and annoying and we didn't like him, but he got a ton of hours because he was in the college program. One night he was working Tiki and a skipper named Jeff kept crank calling over there and saying disgusting things to him about sodomy and what not. Eventually, he stopped answering the phone. When Jeff called again, a manager named Mark answered the phone. After a bit, Jeff realized that this wasn't the kid and he asked who it is and when the manager gave his name, Jeff thought it was a joke and said, "Would you still be my manager if I put my penis in your butt?" It was quiet for a while and he hangs up. Jeff told everybody not to say anything. I was on a boat when Mark showed up. Nobody would talk, but there was a trainer there and they threatened to take away her trainer status unless she talked. So she did. They walked Jeff out that day.

Andy McGuire, 2000s

I had to leave for about six months because my attendance sucked, and they are very covert about it, they keep you backstage and say, "Don't talk to anyone that's coming on." But people asked, "What's going on? You're standing there with two managers." "I'm being fired." "Shhh, don't say that." "But it's true, what do you want me to say?"

Kat Thrailkill, 2000s

The saddest day was when security walked out two skippers, Mandy and Andy. He had one of those fake swords from the bazaar and he does this Indiana Jones sword move, and Mandy pulls out a gun and shoots him right by the Indy queue and he falls back over the side of the thing, but the problem with Indy FastPass was that it was full and everybody hit the ground because they heard a gunshot. Sure enough, when they got back security was waiting for them and walked them both out of the park. It was sad, but it was a great way to go.

Jeremy Wayland, 2000s

I was in college and it was hard to get to Disneyland after class sometimes. I don't think it's any different now. They were not helpful to people that had multiple jobs. They didn't care. I was a waitress and worked at a bookstore and Disneyland wasn't nice about that. I was 21 and irresponsible, but they didn't make it easy.

Andrea Freeman, 2000s

Years later a friend worked in management at Disneyland and I asked him to check out my personnel file and see what's in there. He does and he tells me that I have a no re-hire status and the reason given was "John's attitude was not conducive to the Disney philosophy." I'm more proud of that one sentence than anything.

John Verdone, 1970s

We've already talked about pranks, but what about pranks that went to far? Some pranks were planned for a skipper's last day, while others ended up being the reason it was their last day. Either way, it made for a great story to tell.

I decided to go all out as a skinny Asian dark-skinned male. I was a natural fit to play Mowgli, so I stripped down to my boxers and was just showing up on scenes in the jungle as Mowgli. There was one part with the dancing natives and I went inside the hut to rest, then Skipper Andrea was coming around, and she had just stopped there to do the hokey-pokey joke, and I come out just as I was waking up and doing these stretches in my underwear, and I think some little girls goes, "There's a little boy out there," and I look up and she looks over and she's just shocked. And I look down and cover my nipples and run. I think I hurt my leg on that one because there are all these pipes for irrigation and I knew there was one there and Adam was out on safari and cut his leg on one. I think it was the same one that got me. Matt and Adam and me were always working together and so one of them was holding my clothes. I also went to the middle peninsula, just showing up, trying to find a way to get on top of it, but I couldn't get there, but I think I made too much noise, too many people were saying stuff, but the plan was to go out to the monkeys while they were on the rocks and go pick leaves off them, then everyone rides the rhino, and that's the one thing I regret, I never got to ride the rhino.

I did get out to the scene with the African veldt and I was just standing next to the animals. All of it in the buff, or as close as I could be. I think people were laughing, that's all I remember, because I was wearing boxers. It was obvious I was not an actor. That was a blast that whole last day.

Jeff Bautista, 2000s

For decades it was tradition to throw a skipper in the river on their last day.

I also got thrown in the river on my last day; that was a long-time tradition. It was on my very last day and I was expecting it to happen so I was on guard, but they still managed to sneak up on me and toss me in the river.

Andrew Green, 1980s

I wound up in the water on my last day. I either got in or I got pushed in. I saw that they were coming to push me in, so I jumped in. I was afraid I would hit my head on something if I got pushed in. As I finally climb out of the water, another skipper walks up with a 5-gallon bucket of kitty litter barf dust and dumps it on me. So I'm soaking wet, but I can feel the kitty litter sucking the water off of me. Thankfully, it was time for me to clock out.

Dave Lewis, 1970s

This is the legendary story of the legendary Larry Kaml's legendary last day.

My last day got a lot bigger because of my wife. It was July 17, 1996, that Shirley got a job as a teacher for the school district. We were wanting to get out of Orange County, we had two small kids. The idea was for me to continue to work at Disneyland, because she wasn't going to get her first paycheck until October. I called up HR and asked if I were to cash in all my sick pay and vacation hours, how much would that be?

$3,200. This is my 2-week notice. After I turned in my two-week notice, my opinion of management's style became a little bit more vocal, so one manager named Bruce wanted to make sure I wasn't coming back. So when I jumped in the river, it ended up there was a supervisor walking by as I went swimming past the Indy queue. He ran over to the lead who knew I was in the water and knew what was going on, but the supervisor came over and said shut the ride down you've got somebody in the water. He shut the ride down. When Bruce found out it was me, he made sure that I wasn't coming back again, and made a pretty big deal about it. It backfired because Disneyland got a lot of negative publicity around that incident.

My original intent was to swim the entire river. The river gets a current and it's going in the opposite direction from what you're swimming. The prop wash makes the water go clockwise so you are trying to swim counter-clockwise. The pumps are in boat storage, so the load area is getting sucked back into boat storage. You swim against that. I made it as far as the Indy queue and knew I'm not going to make it. My other idea was to get to Trader Sam and kill the engine and say that my boat is stuck, reach around and grab a tow rope, put it around the boat, jump in the water, and pull the boat to shore like in *The African Queen*. But I decided to go big or go home. The lead, Gerry, knew it was my last rotation and he gave me guest control.

I had my camera to take pictures of my last day, so they confiscated it when they arrested me. Bruce made sure I wasn't coming back again, and so they had me arrested for trespassing. We went back the next day as a family. I used my free passes, totally being the tourist, but the first stop was to go to security and get my camera back, because they just wanted to take the film and develop it to see if there was any evidence on there. There wasn't. I had people take pictures with their cameras. So, once they found out I was in the park, they sent a fox unit, undercover security, to follow me for the remainder of the day. Within 15 minutes of being there, we had a fox unit. We weren't there to cause trouble or anything. I did go to Jungle Cruise to say good-bye to people that I hadn't had a chance to say good-bye to because I was being dragged off to security. Within three minutes, my supervisor on the dock said, "Oh hey, Larry, are you here at the park with your family?" Yeah, and I can't remember her full name, a woman who was on Bruce's side named Kim.

Larry's wife, a former cast member herself, adds to the story:

Even so, Larry's over in Disney Jail, and we are all waiting at the Acapulco restaurant to celebrate his last day because we are moving in three days. I'm over there with the kids, and Jeff Wheeler comes in and said, "You know Larry's been arrested." I think it's a joke, and Jeff was serious. So we are waiting for him, and I get a page in the restaurant, and it's Bruce on the phone, he asks me if I knew Larry was planning to do this on his last day. And I said, "Bruce, everybody ends up in the water on their last day, whether they want to or not. This is nothing new."

Larry continues:

Bruce didn't want me coming back. I was pretty defiant with him when he was coming in, and he made sure my last two weeks were RO shifts. I didn't have a lead shift after I gave my notice. He would come down and say, "You better make 8 minutes and 22 seconds on this next cruise." "OK, Bruce." I would take my time out there, what are they going to do, fire me? Then I can collect unemployment. But he wasn't going to fall for that. Bruce got interviewed by the *Orange County Register*, he was interviewed by a radio station in Los Angeles. *Hard Copy* wanted to do an interview about how Disneyland was very hard-handed with security and they wanted to interview me and I said no, because security has saved my ass so many times with drunk guests and belligerent guests when I was a lead.

Larry Kaml, 1980s

For a while in the early 2000s, there was a tradition of the last trip. Once the park closed, a skipper, on their last day, would take a final trip with friends and skippers and share memories. It was fun, and eventually got out of hand.

My favorite parts about Jungle are the farewell trips. Those were always like the best memory because we would all hang out together and go to Denny's afterwards and it would be like major camaraderie, but we are also saying goodbye to somebody and that part blows. It doesn't blow as hard when it's the second time you are saying goodbye, or the third. I've been on some of those, you just say, "Go! We will see you in 6 months, it's fine."

Kat Thrailkill, 2000s

I remember going on Jeff Bautista's last trip and it was the first one of those I'd ever been to and It was like the last day of summer camp. Everybody was reliving these old memories. It was sad, but you can feel the love. We all have a shared experience. So we all had an emotional connection to it and there's the sense of it being a rite of passage.

Tiffany Davis, 2000s

As time went by, the managers got stricter and stricter about people having last trips. Too many skippers abused the privilege. I was in a meeting with Adventureland managers where some skippers were really arguing their case about the importance of having a last trip and that it was part of our history. On the word "history" they looked at me and a manager said, "Well?" I guess they saw me as the resident historian and this time it burned them. I said, "Having a last trip is a new phenomenon. I worked here 8 years ago and nobody did them."

David John Marley, 2000s

On my last day I took everyone out to the African veldt and read the book *Where the Wild Things Are*. I knew that people did crazy things on their last shift, but I wanted to go out in a nice way. Disneyland is based on stories, so I wanted to tell a story. I told everyone to bring a flashlight and about 40 people came out with me. I sat on the rock next to the dead zebra. After everyone left, I hid something in the jungle. I had a small plush of the character Max from the book and I hid it out there. I felt that it represented me and my adventure at Disneyland. I knew it was going to be my favorite job and it still is the best job I've ever had.

Brian Vestal, 2000s

I was on a last trip with a guy a who turned it into a hateful rant about the leads and managers and he even jumped on the island by Trader Sam and started throwing stuff into the river. I was in the back of the boat, but a bunch of us were yelling at him to stop. We were trapped. Then a lead gets in a boat and reverses it toward us and this guy backs up, too. Finally, enough people yelled at him and he went back to the dock. Mangers were pissed at all of us and I'm sure they made notes of who was on that trip.

Anonymous, 2000s

Some people didn't get fired, they just quit. Sometimes for good reasons, sometimes not.

I worked at the park for a total of five summers, 1976 to 1980. And I had this sense that I had to get out, I had to leave. It was an internal thing. I knew that if I didn't leave, I would be happy working there for the next 30 years. So when I left, I just left, I didn't have another job to go to or anything.

John Verdone, 1970s

My first time working at the Jungle Cruise was in 1996. I worked nights all spring and most of the summer, but had a final coming up at Cal State Fullerton, so I put in a request for a Wednesday morning off, just to be safe. As Disneyland "fate" would have it, I got scheduled that exact morning, the only morning shift I ever was given in 1996. This morning shift was for training on some video game in Tomorrowland. I called in sick, since they wouldn't let me out of the shift, and I thought nothing more of it.

A month later I went to check my schedule and saw that for the next two weeks I was scheduled for nothing but that video game host job. I went to the main schedulers and told them that I only wanted Jungle. They didn't realize that I was never trained there, so the scheduler removed the two weeks, then gave me two weeks of Jungle. He then told me that after that, I was never going to see Jungle again, because I was going to be at the video game. (It was explained to me that as a host I would buckle the guest in, take their cash, and feed it into the machine. Worst job ever? Maybe.) I told him that I wasn't interested in working that, and he told me, "Tough luck, that's where you're going." I then told him that I would quit before I left Jungle. He then said, "Fine, quit." I was almost speechless, I had never encountered that kind of attitude before. He didn't care at all. I was just a cog that could be replaced. Since I was moving to Washington, D.C., for graduate school, I only needed to work for one more month, just through August, but he wouldn't budge, so I gave my notice.

The irony was that later that same day the managers of the narrations department came to the dock to present me with my first guest compliment, which they had made into quite a production. I was given a handwritten card, Mousecar moolah, and a copy of the guest compliment with the guest's name blacked out. As my manager thanked me, she asked me how things were going, and I told her that I had just given my two weeks' notice since I was being taken off Jungle Cruise forever. She just looked at me and said she was sorry, but that was it. Two weeks later I was gone and one month later I was living in Washington, D.C.

Disney called my apartment in the nation's capital that November to see if I'd be interested in coming back to work Jungle Cruise for Christmas. I was, but didn't have the money to pay for airfare to California. What I did have was a job at a Mexican restaurant in Arlington, Virginia, which is where I spent a very unhappy Christmas break from grad school.

David John Marley, 2000s

Sometimes your last boat is memorable.

The best one would probably be my final trip around the jungle. I was heading home in a few days. I had to go home and pack. It was literally my last day on the jungle late at night and I had pulled up to unload and right in front of me three of my buddies are getting off the boat in front of me. And I'm like, wait a minute, that's not cool, you're going on his boat, you have to go on my boat. So they run around and get in line and right in front of them comes a group and they might have been over at the hotel for a little while hitting the bar because they were loud and they were having a good time. So they load, my buddies load, and this group is super loud and I don't know how I'm gonna pull this off in any way because this group is not gonna listen and not gonna hear a thing. The next thing I hear is, "Hit it, skip!" and I go. I didn't say a word, didn't stop or do anything until the elephant bathing pool, I flip the exterior lights on to set up the punchline, flipped them off, and went again. I did this a couple of times and about the hippo pool I stop the boat again. I flip the exterior lights and this time I'm not standing in the boat, I'm out on the bow. I do the quick punchline, turn the lights off, and go again, and everyones is wondering what the heck is going on. Aftre a couple more of these, we finally get back to the dock. The loud, obnoxious group gets off and the four of us are laying on the mats laughing hysterically. My lead comes over and says, "I don't care what you said, if you get one complaint you're out of here." one of the other guys catches his breath just enough to say, "That's just it, he didn't say anything." So after that I was bumped to unload, bumped to break, and that was the end of my shift. I will always remember that they were just so loud.

Keith Hart, 1990s

Acknowledgments

There are a number of people I'd like to thank for their help during the course of this project. First of all, I appreciate the support from my fellow faculty at California State University Fullerton's History Department, especially Jessica Stern, Jasamin Rostam-Kolayi, Kristine Denehey, Nancy Fitch, Dimitri Papendraeu, and David Freeman. I will be forever in debt to two men who were mentors to me when I was a student at Fullerton, Ronald Rietveld and Lawrence deGraaf. The staff of the history department are also amazing and have to put up with all my diva behavior, so thank you Linda Rodgers, Rachael Amaro, and Art De Leon Tell.

Thanks to Trevor Kelly for his great artwork on the cover. The title *More Skipper Stories* was his idea and I must admit it is a much better idea than mine. Trevor also took the photo of me at the Skipper Canteen in Walt Disney World.

A special thanks to Bob McLain from Theme Park Press. He is a joy to work with.

Thank you, David Koenig, for your continued support and inspiration, and especially for introducing me to some original cast members from 1955. Thanks to my former student, a Ph.D. grad student in psychology, Christa Call, who explained to me why so many skippers dream about working at the Jungle Cruise even decades after they've left.

This book was made possible, in a very tangible way, by my loving sister Lin Fern who volunteered to transcribe many of my interviews. Not only did she transcribe, she'd tell me which stories she liked which also was a big help.

Thank you Greg and Barbara Gerovac, the owners of the Anaheim Brewery, for holding a book release party for the first *Skipper Stories*, and for making delicious beer which helped me get both volumes done.

My wonderful family was supportive during this project, especially Jeri South, Tony Fern, Chuck South, Terry Wolfsen, Erla Curtin, and my beautiful and brilliant wife, Deb Marley. My daughters, Olivia and Isabelle, heard most of these stories many times and even came with me to some of the interviews during their school vacations.

Tiki Oasis 2018 was a blast and a half! Hundreds of people showed up to hear me tell tales of Disneyland and the Jungle Cruise. Some of the stories in this book were shared there for the first time. I only put in the stories that got a laugh. I'm also grateful to the staff of micechat. com for inviting me to talk about the Jungle Cruise and meet some authentic legendary skippers.

All skippers past and present, especially those named and anonymous ones here in these pages who helped make this book possible. I'd also like to thank all my students in my spring 2018 classes at Cal State Fullerton who got to class early so they could hear me read some of these stories.

I'd like to thank Todd James Pierce, Greg Ehrbar, and all my friends at the Hyperion Historical Alliance. I also appreciate the kindness of the Walt Disney Company and their various media relations staff who helped make this book possible.

Finally, I'd like to thank a number of people who helped me in many ways during this project: Jessica Kelly, Tony Clifton, Daisy Rain Martin, Albert Falls, Kevin Lively, Monique Nguyen, Casey Gillins, Chris Ramirez, the entire Eames Family, and of course, Trader Sam.

About the Author

David John Marley, a former Disneyland Jungle Cruise skipper, has a Ph.D. in American History from George Washington University, and currently teaches in the history department at California State University Fullerton. Marley is the creator of the first class to specifically focus on the history of Disneyland. He is a member of the Hyperion Historical Alliance, a group of scholars who work with the Walt Disney Company. His last Theme Park Press book, *Skipper Stories, True Tales from Disneyland's Jungle Cruise*, was the first oral history of a Disneyland attraction. He has appeared on the History Channel, published articles in scholarly journals, and other professor type things. He is the creator and producer of the popular Jungle Cruise based stand-up comedy show, *The Skipper Show*.

Under the name Dr. Skipper, he creates Tiki- and Disney based art available online at etsy.com/shop/DrSkipper.

You can follow him on Instagram at dr.skipper.marley.

David "Dr. Skipper" Marley next to his barrel in the
Skipper Canteen at Walt Disney World.

About Theme Park Press

Theme Park Press publishes books primarily about the Disney company, its history, culture, films, animation, and theme parks, as well as theme parks in general.

Our authors include noted historians, animators, Imagineers, and experts in the theme park industry.

We also publish many books by first-time authors, with topics ranging from fiction to theme park guides.

And we're always looking for new talent. If you'd like to write for us, or if you're interested in the many other titles in our catalog, please visit:

www.ThemeParkPress.com

∙∙∙

Theme Park Press Newsletter

Subscribe to our free email newsletter and enjoy:

- ⬥ Free book downloads and giveaways
- ⬥ Access to excerpts from our many books
- ⬥ Announcements of forthcoming releases
- ⬥ Exclusive additional content and chapters
- ⬥ And more good stuff available nowhere else

To subscribe, visit www.ThemeParkPress.com, or send email to newsletter@themeparkpress.com.

Read more about these books
and our many other titles at:

www.ThemeParkPress.com